Hackish C++ Pranks & Tricks

HACKISH
C++
Pranks & Tricks

Michael Flenov

A-LIST, LLC
295 East Swedesford Rd.
PMB #285
Wayne, PA 19087
702-977-5377 (FAX)
mail@alistpublishing.com
http://www.alistpublishing.com

This book is printed on acid-free paper.

Hackish C++ Pranks & Tricks
By Michael Flenov

ISBN 1-931769-38-9

Printed in the United States of America

05 06 7 6 5 4 3 2

A-LIST, LLC, titles are available for site license or bulk purchase by institutions, user groups, corporations, etc.

Book Editor: Rizwati Freeman

Contents

Chapter 2: Writing Simple Pranks _____ 61

Acknowledgements

Thanks to:

My parents, who gave birth to me. If it were not for them, this book would not have come about, or, at least, it would have had another author.

My wife, who has supported me and my children who sometimes gave me time to work and sometimes didn't.

The editorial staffs of the magazines where my articles have been published. Thanks to this, I gained a lot of experience in writing articles which helped me to write this book. I'm not a writer, and I couldn't put two words together some time ago, to say nothing of setting forth my ideas in a readable form using a computer. Thanks to getting considerable practice in Hacker magazine, now I can.

To the staff at A-LIST publishing house who believed in me as an author and helped to publish my third book. I'm thankful to my editors who edited my word stream and corrected my numerous grammatical mistakes.

I could keep on thanking people for a long time. In brief, I thank: tutors at my kindergarten, teachers at my school, professors at my university, the whole staff at *Hacker* magazine, and all my friends who put up with me, love me
(I hope), and help me when they can. Most importantly, I'd like to thank all of my readers.

Special thanks to you for buying this book. I hope you won't be disappointed and won't regret the time you'll spend reading this and the money you've already spent on it.

Preface

This book looks at programming in C++ from a hacker's point of view. What do I mean by "a hacker?" I give the word a different meaning than that some people do. I think a hacker is a computer professional, rather than a vandal or information destroyer. A hacker is a computer expert who, using his or her knowledge, doesn't necessarily make problems for other people. In a word, this book looks at the subject from the point of view of a professional in network programming and writing interesting programs, rather than of a vandal. For details of what "hacker" means see *Introduction, Section "Who Is a Hacker? How You Can Become a Hacker."*

In this book, you'll find a lot of non-standard programming techniques and examples of use of non-documented functions and features of C++ programming language. Most important, you'll see a lot of interesting methods for work with a network in Windows.

This book will disclose a few hacker secrets and teach you how to create prankish and network programs.

You'll discover how to create small, funny programs, which you can use to play jokes on your friends. You'll learn to write your own programs, and your friends will appreciate them. With the joke programs presented in this book, you'll demonstrate your knowledge of the computer and programming and make other people smile.

I'll comprehensively describe how to optimize the size and performance of your programs. This will help you create compact and fast programs in the future. This topic is still relevant despite the speed of cutting-edge computers and the capacity of their hard disks. Not all people have high-speed access to the Internet, so the size of the program is important.

A majority of the book discusses network programming for the Internet and Intranet. You'll see how to create a quick port scanner and a "Trojan horse" that will astonish your friends.

In addition to joke and network programs, I'll describe algorithms that are used in hacker utilities, so you'll know their internals. This will help you understand the adversary and create an effective protection. You can beat a hacker only if you know his or her weak and strong points.

Finally, I'll describe a few techniques for work with computer hardware. This topic is often left out in books on programming, and programmers have to look for additional material. In this book, I have tried to improve the situation and demonstrate how to work with the most common and frequently used hardware.

The material is presented in a simple format so that anyone can understand it. You don't need extensive knowledge of programming and will be able to understand most of the given examples and run them on your computer. To understand some points, basic knowledge of C++ programming language is a plus, however, it is not necessary.

Introduction

I'm an inveterate programmer by nature, so I don't have a writer's talent. However, I'll try to share my knowledge with you, and I hope to tell you something you don't know and disclose hackers' secrets. Perhaps, you know some pranks or tricks described in this book, but many people don't understand the code they use. I'll try to describe the code comprehensively and show you some "secret" programming tricks.

I'll offer you a lot of examples written in C++ programming language. There are many joke programs and network applications among them. This book contains little theory, but as much practice as possible. You'll see everything with your eyes and "touch with your hands."

If you are looking for examples of viruses in this book, you'll be disappointed. We won't do anything destructive. I'm a creator. None of the joke programs in this book leads to sorrowful consequences. A joke is good when it doesn't cause pain, but brings smiles.

About This Book

To work with this book effectively, you'll need at least minimal knowledge of C++ and minimal skills in using a computer and a mouse. You should know how to create a simple application and use loops. It is an advantage if you know addressing and pointers. This would help you better understand the examples given in this book. As for network programming, I'll describe it quite comprehensively, beginning with the basics and up to complex examples. Therefore, knowledge of the basics is desirable, but not compulsory.

I have tried to present the material in a simple manner. Most of the code is described very thoroughly and includes many comments so that you will enjoy reading. The structure of this book differs from other books' structures. There are no prolonged and boring theoretical discussions; only examples and source code. You can consider it a practice book. Only with practice will you be able to understand theoretical knowledge.

Programmers have a lot in common with physicians. If a doctor knows the symptoms but cannot distinguish between poisoning and appendicitis in practice, he or she should be kept away from patients. Likewise, if a programmer knows a network protocol, but cannot use it, his or her network programs will never work correctly.

This comparison is based in reality. In 2002, I ended up in the hospital with a stomachache and a fever. The doctor suspected appendicitis. For three days they couldn't decide whether to operate, and nobody could explain why I was in so much pain with such a high temperature.

On the third day, I left because it was my mother's birthday. At the birthday party, an acquaintance who happened to be a doctor (and by the way, an obstetrician) examined me, prescribed me some medication, and recommended that I be discharged from the hospital. You won't believe, but the temperature dropped after the first pill, and I could dance like Michael Jackson after the second. In fact, those doctors confused poisoning with appendicitis and nearly excised my appendix. They could have done so by mistake, for curiosity's sake, or simply because I was already in the hospital.

This case confirmed my attitude toward practice. Nothing can give you such an understanding of a subject as practice does. When you can "touch" things, you remember the theoretical bases better.

I have another example of this from my life. In 2000, I attended some Microsoft courses on database server administering and programming. The courses went well, and a tutor tried to explain the material comprehensively. However, Microsoft designed those courses to be theoretical with a small amount of practice. As a result, we understood well *what* a server could do. When I encountered actual problems in my work later, I found that I didn't know *how* to do one or another thing. I had to read over a manual on the courses and a bulk of theoretical material with just a few examples to solve actual problems. I wished they had told me in the courses how to solve problems rather than what a programmer was capable of doing. In my opinion, such teaching was a waste of time.

I'm not against all theory and I am not implying that there is no need for it. It is necessary to tell students *how* a task can be implemented, and *why* particular actions are needed. After that, the students will know how to solve problems and achieve their desired results.

It is hard to find practical manuals and simply good books with varied examples in our book shops. I hope my work will change this at least a little and help you in your future work and in implementing your programming tasks.

In a word, this book contains several examples, and despite its title, it can be useful for many people because it describes various programming methods that are used in everyday practice.

All the examples given in this book are located in the demo folder on the accompanying CD-ROM. However, I recommend that you do everything on your own and refer to the files only when you encounter problems to compare my file with yours and detect an error. When you create something yourself, you gain good practical skills, and you remember information much better than after reading a hundred pages on theory. This is the second reason why there are so many examples with source code in this book.

Even if you decide to use a ready example, make sure you understand it well. Try to change some parameters and look at the result. Try to modify the example by adding a few features to it. This is the only way to understand the working principles of the functions and algorithms used in the example.

Who Is a Hacker?
How You Can Become a Hacker

Before you proceed, I'd like to "load" your head with some theoretical information. More precisely, before you start reading, you should know what I mean by "hacker." If you give the word one meaning and I give it another, we will never understand each other.

There are many questions, which most people can't answer correctly. What's more, people use a lot of words without having the vaguest idea of what these words mean. For example, many people are unaware of the meaning of the word "hacker." Everyone may consider his or her opinion the most correct. I won't assert that my opinion is the only correct one, but it is based on a correct notion.

Before I proceed with a discussion of this word, I should recall history and a time before the Internet came about.

The word "hacker" appeared when the first network, ARPAnet, began to spread. In those days, this word denoted a computer expert. Some people meant a hacker was a person "crazy" with computers. The word was associated with a person who aspired to explore everything that related to his favorite "toy." Because of this aspiration and a desire for free information exchange, the Internet started to develop rapidly. Hackers backed up its development and created FIDO. They also created UNIX-like open-source operating systems that currently work on many servers.

There were no viruses at that time or incidents of breaking into networks and individual computers. The image of hackers as destroyers arose a bit later. However, this is only a faulty impression image. True hackers have no involvement in breaking into systems, and if a hacker aims to destroy, his or her actions are strictly criticized by the community.

A true hacker is creative, not destructive. Since there are more creators than destroyers, hackers started to call the destroyers "crackers" or "vandals." Both hackers and crackers are experts in the virtual world. Both strive for free access to information. However, only crackers break into sites, databases, and other information sources for money or fame. These people are criminals.

A hacker is an expert in a particular area. In this book, I speak about computer experts who know their subject well, create something new and unique, and help other people. Anyone who accuses these people of vandalism is mistaken. True hackers never use their knowledge to do harm to other people, and I encourage constructive hacking in my book. I give only helpful and interesting information that you can use to widen your knowledge and improve the quality of your programming.

Now let's discuss how you can become a true hacker. This discussion will help you understand these people better.

❑ You should know your computer and be able to control it effectively. If you know its hardware, you will be at a great advantage. What do I mean by being able to control a computer effectively? I mean you should know all possible ways of performing each particular action and use the best of them in each situation. In particular, you should learn keyboard shortcuts and not use your mouse for trifles. Hitting keys is much quicker than moving the mouse. Make yourself use the keyboard, and you'll appreciate it. As for me, I use the mouse rarely and always try to use the keyboard.

A small example: My boss always uses toolbar buttons or a pop-up menu (that appears when you click with the right mouse button) to copy and paste data via the clipboard. If you also use these methods, you might know that not all applications have such buttons or pop-up menu items. In such cases, my boss types text manually. However, it is possible to use a shortcut such as <Ctrl>+<C>/<Ctrl>+<V> or <Ctrl>+<Ins>/<Shift>+<Ins> that are universal because they are implemented practically in all modern applications.

Copying and pasting data in standard Windows components (such as text boxes) is the responsibility of the operating system, and no additional code is needed to implement these operations. If the author of a program didn't provide an appropriate button, this doesn't mean these operations are impossible. They are available through shortcuts.

❐ You should know as much as possible about computers in the subject you're interested in. If you're interested in graphics, learn the best graphics packages, learn how to draw scenes with them, and how to create the most complicated worlds. If you're interested in networks, try to learn as much as possible about them. If you think you know everything, buy a voluminous book on the subject, and you'll see that you're wrong. Computer technology is an area, in which it is impossible to know everything.

Hackers are experts in particular areas. These areas don't need to relate to computers or programming languages. It is possible to become a hacker in any area, but I'll talk only about computer hackers.

❐ It is desirable that you know how to program. Each hacker should know at least one programming language. It would be even better if you knew more than one language. I recommend that you begin with Borland Delphi or C++. Borland Delphi is very simple, fast, and effective. Most important, it is very powerful. C++ is a standard adopted worldwide, but it is a little more difficult to learn. All this doesn't mean you should only know one language. You can use any language you like, even Basic (I don't advise you to use it, but it is useful to know it).

Though I don't like Visual Basic for its inconvenience, weakness, and other disadvantages, I have seen a few splendid applications written in this programming language. I'd like to call their author a hacker because this is a masterly and perfect work. Creating wonderful things out of nothing is a hacker's art.

A hacker is a person who creates something. In most cases, this refers to program code, but a hacker can create graphics or music. This is also a hacker's art. However, even if you create computer music, knowledge of programming will improve your skills. Nowadays, it isn't as difficult to create programs as it used to be in the past. Using languages such as Borland Delphi, you can quickly create simple utilities, and nothing will limit you. Don't be lazy; learn to write a program.

In this book, I'll tell you what a hacker programmer should know. In addition, I'll show you many interesting programming methods and examples in C++. If you don't know this language well, this book will help you to learn how to program in it.

❐ Don't try to hamper technological progress but don't go to extremes. Hackers have always struggled for freedom of information. If you want to be a hacker, you should help other people. Hackers should promote technological progress. Some of them write open-source programs, and some share their knowledge with other people.

Availability of information doesn't mean you cannot make money. Hackers cannot be faulted for making money. They have to earn money to live and support their families. However, money isn't the most important thing in their lives.

The most important thing is to create something new. This is another difference between hackers and crackers. Hackers create information while crackers, so to speak, destroy it. If you wrote a unique prankish program, you're a hacker. However, if you wrote a virus that erases information from a disk, you are a cracker (and I would say, a criminal).

When struggling for freedom of information, a hacker may break, but only non-destructively. You may break into a program to see how it works, but you shouldn't remove protection from it. You should respect other programmers' labor, and you mustn't infringe upon their copyrights. This is the way they earn money.

Imagine that somebody had stolen a TV set from a shop. As a theft, it should be punished legally. Many people understand that and don't steal because they don't want to be punished. Why do crackers break into programs without fear? This is also theft. As for me, I make no distinction between breaking into a program and stealing a TV set. I think that both actions are criminal.

I'm a programmer, and I sell my programs. However, I never install complicated protection systems because common users will encounter problems, and crackers will break through any protection system. Large corporations have invented many protection systems to protect their copyrights, but most of their applications were tampered with even before their official releases. Other methods should be used to struggle against unauthorized copying, and systems with activation and keys are useless.

In the civilized world, a program should have only an input field for a code that confirms the payment and nothing more. It shouldn't require activation and complicated registrations. The users should be honest because any work should be paid. If a good (such as a software product) can be accessed for free, this doesn't mean you should acquire it at no cost.

❑ Don't reinvent a wheel. This is a hacker's creative feature. Hackers never stay in place and always share their knowledge. For example, if you write some unique code, share it with other people to save them from creating the same. You don't have do disclose your secrets, but you should help others.

   If you have another programmer's code, feel free to use it (with the programmer's permission). Don't reinvent things already invented and approved. If everyone tries to invent a wheel, nobody will invent a carriage.

❑ Hackers are not disconnected people; this is a culture. This doesn't mean they wear the same clothes and look alike. Each hacker is an individual. Don't try to mimic another person. This won't make you a hacker. Only your individuality will make your name.

If you are well-known in some circles, this is an honor. Hackers are people who make their fame with knowledge and good deeds. Therefore, any hacker should be famous.

How can you know you're a hacker? It's easy. If people say you're a hacker, then you are one. Unfortunately, it is difficult to achieve this because most people confuse hackers with crackers. As a result, if a person cracks something, people will call him or her a hacker. However, this is wrong, and you should resist the temptation. Seek fame only with good deeds. This is very difficult, but it can't be helped. Nobody promised you this would be easy.

❐   What is the difference between a programmer, a user, and a hacker? When a programmer develops a program, he or she knows what it should be and implements his or her ideas. A user doesn't always know what a programmer designed and uses the program in accordance with his or her understanding.

A programmer cannot foresee the customer's actions, and programs aren't always well-tested. Users can enter parameters that make a program unstable.

Hackers deliberately look for loop-holes in a program to make it work in an incorrect or unusual manner. Imagination and unconventional wits are required for this. A hacker should feel code and see things hidden from others.

If you want to be a hacker, you should be able to make plain things interesting and funny. To do this, you should use your imagination. In this book, I'll repeatedly show you common and familiar things from an unusual point of view. This will help you write joke programs and create effective algorithms.

Finally, you should read "*How to Become a Hacker*" by Eric S. Raymond, a renowned hacker. I disagree with some of his ideas, but this article conveys the spirit of hacking.

You might be wondering why I attribute writing joke and network programs to hacker art. Well, first, hackers always demonstrate their knowledge by writing interesting and prankish programs. Viruses don't belong to this category because they are destructive though some of them are interesting. Jokes have been always appreciated in hacker circles. By joking, a hacker demonstrates his or her knowledge of an operating system and makes their friends smile. Many hackers have a good sense of humor, and it should be utilized. I recommend that you implement your jokes with inoffensive programs.

As for network programming, it has been inseparable from hackers since its inception. Hackers have become so numerous thanks to networks and an understanding of their functionality. Hackers have made a substantial contribution in the development of the Internet. This is why I'll discuss network programming in detail from a non-standard point of view.

One last thing: I already mentioned that a hacker should be able to write programs in a programming language. Some people think a hacker should know how to program in the assembly language. This is not the case. Knowledge of this language is desirable, but not mandatory. I like Borland Delphi. It allows me to do anything I wish. Most importantly, it allows me to do this quickly and at a high level of quality. Nevertheless, I also use C++ and the assembly language.

You should use programming languages in a wise manner. Despite my love of Borland Delphi, I admit it isn't convenient for writing computer games. This has always been a domain of C++, and it always will be. In network programming, sometimes C++ is more convenient than Borland Delphi, and sometimes vice versa. However, writing large applications in the assembly language is both ineffective and silly.

You should also understand the necessity of technologies. Even before graduating from my university I knew that the customer is always right. Strangely, this law is invalid in computer technologies.

A simple example: Now, many programmers implement support for XML in their applications, regardless of its necessity. In fact, not every user needs this format, and not every program should support it. Following Microsoft's recommendations isn't always reasonable because you write for your customer, not for Bill Gates. You should always do what your users need.

Microsoft regularly puts something new on the market, When a new technology appears, programmers rush to redo their software so that it conforms to the new standard. As a result, they spend huge resources on modifications. If your program uses DAO to access data, you can leave it as it is without redoing it for ADO. Your users don't care which technology is used to get data from a database; all they need is the data.

Another example is the interface. MS Office interface changes continually, and it is always declared that the latest interface is the most convenient for users. Programmers rush to change interfaces of their programs, but Internet Explorer and other Microsoft applications look like they did ten years ago. Nothing has changed in their appearance because Microsoft doesn't waste time on it. However, its competitors spend months rewriting a tremendous amount of code.

I agree that if you follow trends, your programs will have a certain appeal. However, you should keep your individuality.

Programmers and hackers impose their opinions on others in regard to which programming language is the best. Usually they manage to convince their customers because the latter don't understand programming. However, which language you use is irrelevant to your customers; their only concerns are the terms and quality. As for me, I can work against time and maintain good quality only when I use Borland

Delphi. With C++, any programmer (including me) can provide the same quality only within much longer terms.

In this book, all examples are written in Visual C++ because this language is the most widely used, and many people have adopted it as a programming standard.

When a customer demands a compact or high-speed program, I use the assembly language and C (don't confuse C and C++). However, this is seldom because up-to-date media are capacious enough, and up-to-date computers are a million times quicker than their predecessors. The size and speed of a program are no longer crucial, and the terms and quality of a programmer's work are more important for customers.

Well, that brings the introduction to a close. Now, we'll proceed on our merry way to look at practical exercises in "martial art" where the most important things are secrecy and succeeding with a minimum of expended energy.

Chapter 1: Making a Program Compact and Invisible

What is the most important thing when writing joke programs? Invisibility, of course. Programs created in this and subsequent chapters will hide in the system and execute certain actions when a certain event occurs. This means the program should appear neither on the taskbar nor in the program list in the window that appears after you hit <Ctrl>+<Alt>+<Del>. Therefore, you should know how to hide your program before you start writing it.

In addition, joke programs should be compact. Applications created in Visual C++ with cutting-edge technologies (such as MFC) are rather "heavy." Even a simple program displaying only one window will take up a substantial amount of space on the disk. If you decide to send such a joke via e-mail, sending and receiving a message with your program will be time-consuming. This is definitely undesirable, so this chapter demonstrates how to make programs created in Visual C++ as small as possible.

1.1. Compressing Executable Files

The simplest way to decrease the size of a program is to use a file compressing utility. As for me, I like ASPack very much. You can download it from **http://www.aspack.com** or copy it from the accompanying CD-ROM in the Programs folder (the installation file name is ASPack.exe). The program compresses EXE and DLL files very well.

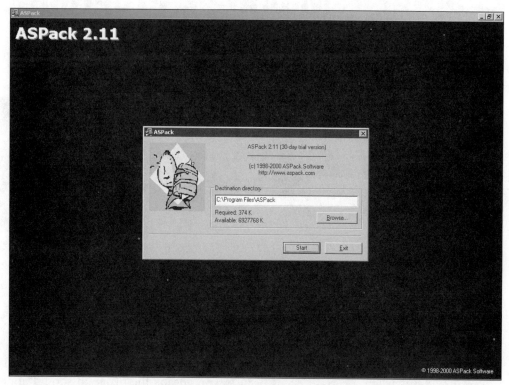

Fig. 1.1. ASPack installation window

Start ASPack.exe, and you will see an installation window. Just specify the path to copy the files to and click the **Next** button. In a few seconds, the program will be installed and starts.

Its main window (Fig. 1.2) contains the following tabs:

❏ Open File   ❏ Options   ❏ Help

❏ Compress   ❏ About

There is only one button, **Open**, on the **Open File** tab. Click it and select the file you want to compress. As soon as you select the file, the program will move to the **Compress** tab and start compression (Fig. 1.3).

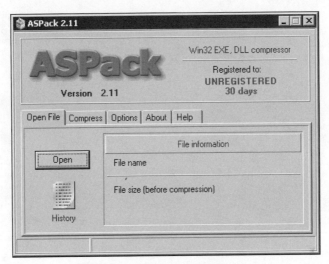

Fig. 1.2. ASPack main window

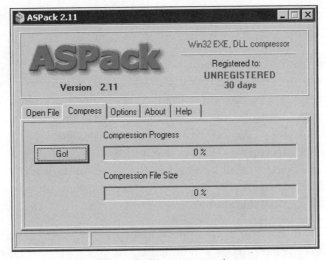

Fig. 1.3. File compression

The compressed file immediately overwrites the existing one, but the old, uncompressed version is saved with the BAK extension, just to be on the safe side. You can disable the creation of a backup copy, but it is inadvisable. A comprehensive description of this option will soon follow.

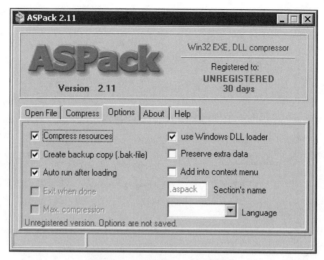

Fig. 1.4. ASPack settings

There are only a few ASPack settings, and they are all located on the **Options** tab. Let's discuss them.

❏ **Compress resources** — If you use Microsoft Foundation Classes (MFC) when writing your programs and create dialog boxes in resources or store bitmap images there, the executable file will contain a large resource section. As my experience shows, images take up most of the space because they aren't compressed. If you check this checkbox, ASPack will compress this section.

❏ **Create a backup copy** — ASPack will create a backup copy before compressing. The original contents will be saved in the same folder under the same name, but with the BAK extension. For example, if you compress a file named myprogram.exe, its copy will be myprogram.bak.

I recommend that you always check this checkbox because ASPack is sometimes unstable, and some parameters can damage your program. In that case, you'll be able to recover the original file from the backup copy by changing the BAK extension to EXE. If you don't want to check the checkbox, I advise you to make a backup copy on your own.

When you have the program's complete source code, you can recover the damaged file by compiling. However, when you compress another person's program, it is impossible to recover it without a backup copy. So try to avoid creating additional problems for yourself.

After ASPack compresses your program, test its operability. In most cases, if the program starts, there won't be any problems with it in the future. Errors in certain windows are seldom, but not unlikely. Test each feature of your product before you send your customer the final version. If you are creating a commercial project, you'll want to avoid any error messages, which no one likes.

❒ **Auto run after loading** — If this checkbox is checked, ASPack will automatically start compressing as soon as you open a file on the **Open file** tab.

❒ **Exit when done** — self-explanatory.

❒ **Max compression** — When you use this option, the probability of failures increases, but the compressed file will be as small as possible. Test your program with the maximum compression and uncheck the checkbox if any problems arise.

❒ **Use a Windows DLL loader** — There are two DLL loaders: the Windows standard loader and a loader optimized for earlier Borland C++ compilers. We'll use MS Visual C++ to write programs; therefore, you should check this checkbox.

❒ **Preserve extra data** — Some programs contain extra data at the end of the executable file. If ASPack tries to compress it, the data can become unavailable. An example of such a file is an installer file. It contains the executable code of a program followed by additional data that should be copied to the computer. Sometimes, these data shouldn't be compressed.

Now, let's look at how the compression works. First, all program code is compressed by the packer. If you think this packer is something "fancy," you're wrong. A common packer optimized for compressing binary code is used. Second, the code of an unpacker is appended to the end of the packed code. The unpacker will unpack the program at the time of execution. Finally, ASPack changes the header of the executable file so that the unpacker runs first.

ASPack's compressing algorithm is very good, and the unpacker is quite small (less than 1 KB). This is why the original file is compressed considerably, and only 1 KB is added to it. As a result, a file of 1.5 MB can be compressed to a size of 300 KB to 400 KB.

When you start your compressed program, the unpacker will start first. It will unpack the binary code to the computer memory. When it completes unpacking, it will pass control to your program.

Some people think compressed application will work slowly because of unpacking overheads. In fact, you won't be able to tell the difference. Even if does work slowly, it will be unnoticeable (at least, on cutting-edge computers). This is because the packing algorithm is well-optimized for a binary code. Actually, unpacking is executed once and doesn't affect the running program. Therefore, the slowdown caused by compression is imperceptible.

In any case, a program is loaded into the memory before execution. If its code is packed, it is unpacked during loading. There are two issues involved here: time is spent on unpacking, but the program takes up less disk space and is read faster. A hard disk is one of the slowest components in a computer. Therefore, the less you have to load, the sooner the program starts. This is why the resulting slowdown is insignificant.

With common programming, i.e., when using advanced features such as visual and object programming, you obtain a large amount of code. However, it can be compressed by 60% to 70% with a special packer. At the same time, it is much quicker and easier to write such code.

Another "pro" when using compression is that it is difficult to break compressed code. Few disassemblers can read packed commands. Therefore, you obtain protection against code-breakers in addition to decreasing the size of your file. To tell the truth, a professional will be able to break your program because there are many utilities on the Internet that make it possible to detect the packer and to unpack the file. Nevertheless, a second-rate code breaker won't take pains to disassemble a packed binary code and will leave your program alone.

NOTE

On the accompanying CD-ROM, the \Demo\Chapter1\Screens1 folder contains the files with the figures in color.

1.2. Neither Windows, Nor Doors...

Another method for decreasing the program size is hidden in the answer to the question, "Why are Visual C++ programs so large?" This is because C++ is an object-oriented language. In this language, each program component is an object with its own properties, methods, and events. Each object is self-sufficient and can do a lot without any of your instructions. This means you just need to associate it with your form, change its properties appropriately, and the application is ready! It will work without your detailing of its activity.

There are a few disadvantages in object programming. Objects implement many actions that a programmer or user can execute. However, in any actual program only two or three of these properties are used. The others are extraneous, and nobody needs them.

How can you create a compact code so that a program takes up as little space as possible on the hard disk and in the memory? There are two ways to do this.

❑ Don't use the MFC library (the VCL library in Borland Delphi) that simplifies programming. If you do, you'll have to type all your code manually and use only WinAPI. The program will be of a limited space and work quickly. The resulting code will take up less space than when you use MFC and the maximum compression. On the other hand, you'll miss the simplicity of visual programming and feel all the inconvenience of programming with "pure" WinAPI. For further decreasing the file size, you can use the assembly language. However, it is too complicated, and it would take much more time to write in it than in the pure C. This is why this topic isn't discussed in this book.

❑ Compress completed programs with packers. The object code will be compressed by several times, and an application created with MFC can turn from a 300 KB "monster" to a little "hamster" that takes up from just 30 KB to 50 KB on a disk. The main advantage of this approach is that you will enjoy object programming and not have to deal with the inconvenience of WinAPI.

We already discussed the second method, so let's look at the first one.

If you want to create a really small program, you should abandon any hopes of comfort. You won't be able to use visual forms and other helpful modules created by Microsoft to simplify a programmer's life. You won't be able to use classes or ActiveX components. You'll confine yourself to Windows API functions.

Now let's look at these things by way of example. Start Visual C++ and create a new project. To do this, select **File/New/Project**. A new project window will open (Fig. 1.5). The project type hierarchy is at the left. We are writing in C++, so select the **Visual C++ Projects** item. This item should be selected for all examples in this book. The **Templates** pane at the right will display icons for creating various projects with wizards. Select **MFC Application**.

There are two input boxes below the panes. In the first box, specify a name for the project being created. It will be the name of the executable file and of the file you'll edit. Let's have it be *TestMFC*.

In the Location box, you should specify the path to a folder, in which the development environment will create necessary files. I recommend you create a folder, say, *My C++ Projects*, in which you'll store your projects. Select this folder and click **OK**. When the wizard completes its work, your My C++ Projects folder will contain the TestMFC folder that will contain the files.

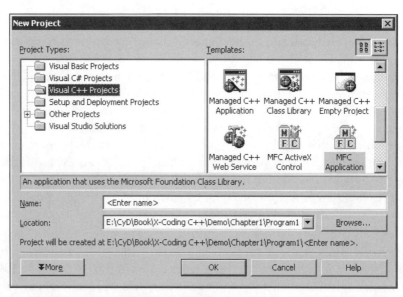

Fig. 1.5. Program settings

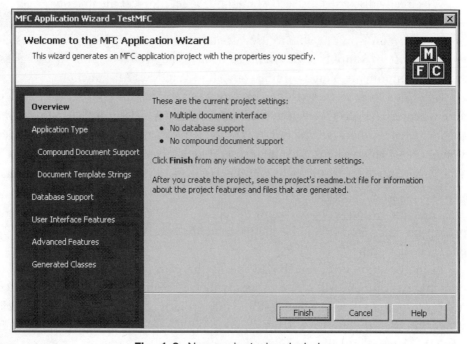

Fig. 1.6. New project wizard window

As soon as you click the **OK** button in the new project window, the MFC application wizard will open. You can click the Finish button to create an application with default parameters, or you can specify custom settings. Our current task is to create a small application, so let's try to optimize the application the wizard creates.

There are a few sections at the left. By selecting them, you'll get options for adjusting particular parameters. Let's select these sections in turn to delete unnecessary features and decide which settings will be used when creating applications for the subsequent examples.

☐ **Application Type**. This section defines the type of the application. Specify the following:
  - **Single Document**. One window will be enough. We won't write multi-document applications, and most of the examples using MFC will be based on this type of application or on dialogs (**Dialog based**).
  - **Project style**. We'll use the default style, the MFC standard, in all our applications.
  - **Document/View architecture support**. This setting doesn't concern us, therefore, leave the default.
☐ **Advanced Features**. In this section, only the **Windows socket** parameter will be required in the future. It will allow us to write examples that use the net.

In the other sections, leave the default settings because we won't use databases or documents. In most cases, we'll be satisfied with one window and a menu. In the first examples, we'll try to do without MFC.

Click the **Finish** button to finish the wizard. After this, you'll see a window like the one shown in Fig. 1.7. You'll use this window quite a lot, and I am going to describe it little by little. I would make a mistake if I told you everything about this window right now. You simply wouldn't be able to remember everything. However, you'll easily understand elements of the window as you work.

We are interested in the project parameters. We should disable everything that hampers us. When linking a Visual C++ project, two types of settings can be used by default: the debug and release settings. The first is necessary at the development stage. In this mode, Visual C++ creates an executable file that contains too much additional information. You'll need it later when debugging your program. In the second mode, this information isn't included, and the executable file will be smaller.

On the toolbar, there is a drop-down list that reads **Debug**. Change this setting to **Release**.

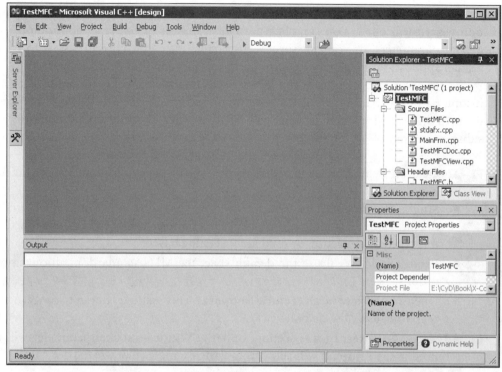

Fig. 1.7. MS Visual C++ development environment, main window

Visual C++ development environment can create executable files that use two types of MFC libraries: static and dynamic. The dynamic linking is used by default. The executable file will have a smaller size, but it won't work without dynamic libraries such as mfcXXX.dll where XXX is the version number of the development environment.

As a result, we'll have to send our customer the libraries in addition to the executable file so that he or she can run our program. This is both impolite and inconvenient. It is best to use static compiling. The executable file will be much larger, but it will contain everything that is necessary. In this case, no additional libraries will be needed.

To change the type of MFC use, select the name of your project in the **Solution Explorer** window and then select the **Project/Properties** menu. You'll see the property pages window looking like shown in Fig. 1.8.

There is a list of property categories in the left part of the window. We are interested in the **General** item. Select it, and you'll see a list of corresponding properties in the main pane. Find the **Use of MFC** property and change its value to **Use MFC in a Static Library**. Click **OK** to close the window and save the changes.

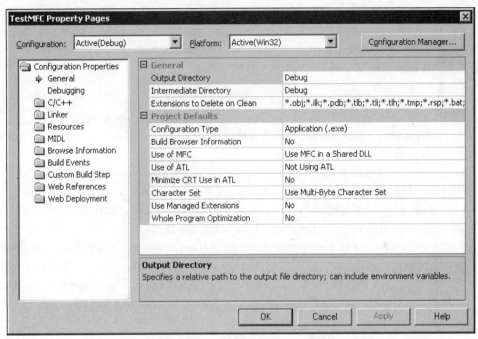

Fig. 1.8. Property pages window

Let's build our project to an executable file. To do this, select the **Build/Build solution** menu. At the bottom of the main window, the **Output** pane will display the progress of building. Wait until you see a message like this:

```
---------------------- Done ----------------------

Build: 1 succeeded, 0 failed, 0 skipped
```

Open the folder you allocated for your projects and find the TestMFC folder. It should contain source files of your project generated by the wizard. In addition, the Release folder contains intermediate files and the executable file created during compilation. Select the TestMFC.exe file and look at its properties (right-click the file and select Properties in the pop-up menu). The size of our empty project is 386 KB. This is quite large.

Try to compress it with ASPack. In my experiment, the compressed file was 187 KB. With a compression of almost 50%, this is a more or less reasonable size for a joke program.

An example of this program is located in the Demo/Chapter1/TestMFC folder on the accompanying CD-ROM. To open this example, select **File/Open solution**. You'll see the standard file-open window. Select the directory and open the file with the project name and **vcproj** extension.

To make the program even smaller, you have to abandon MFC and write in pure C. This is a little more difficult and rather inconvenient. However, this is acceptable for small projects.

To create a small program without MFC, select **File/New/Project** again and then select the **Win32 Project** type. Let's name it CTest and leave the path unchanged.

If your previous project is still open, there are two radio buttons below the location text box: **Add to solution** and **Close solution**. If you select the first one, the new project will be added to the opened project. If you choose to close the previous project, it will be closed, and a new work area will be created for you.

After you click the **OK** button, a wizard window will open. The first step is informative, so select the **Application Settings** section. You'll see a window like that shown in Fig. 1.9.

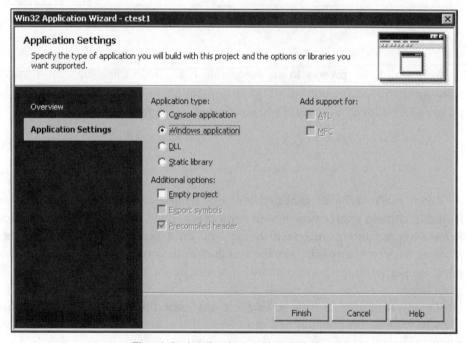

Fig. 1.9. Application settings window

We wish to create a simple Windows application, therefore, select the **Windows application** item in the **Application type** section. Don't check any checkboxes to keep the wizard from adding extra components. We just need a minimal application. Click the **Finish** button, and the new project will be created.

Here you should also change **Debug** to **Release** to obtain a project without additional information. You don't need to change anything in the project settings because the sample project created by the wizard neither uses MFC nor needs dynamic libraries. To check this, open the project properties and make sure that the **Use of MFC** property has the *Standard Windows Libraries* value. This means that there is no MFC, and the program doesn't need anything in addition to the standard Windows libraries.

Compile the project. To do this, select **Build/Build solution**. When the building process has completed, open the ctest/release folder in your project folder and look at the size of the resulting file. As for my file, it was 81 KB. When compressed, it will take up less than 70 KB. Such a program will pass via the net very quickly.

Of course, it can be optimized even further by removing a few components that aren't used but take up valuable space. However, we won't do this here.

1.3. The Program's Internals

In the first part of this book, we'll frequently use the sample created by Visual C++ when we select creation of a **Win32 Application**. This is why we should discuss a few points that will become urgent soon. A more comprehensive description can be found in specialized books on Visual C++, but now I'll give you only the necessary information.

I'll repeatedly describe the application generated by the wizard later in this book, and you'll gradually be able to understand everything. It would be a mistake to explain all the details at once because it might be difficult to remember a lot of information that you cannot use.

Open the CTest project and look at the **Solution Explorer** pane. It displays a hierarchy that contains all components of your project. The hierarchy of my project is shown in Fig. 1.10, and you'll see something like this.

The project consists of the following folders:

❑ **Source files** folder contains files with the source code. The main code is contained in the file with the name same as the project's and with the CPP extension. In our case, it is ctest.cpp.

❑ **Header files** folder contains files with various auxiliary information, included modules, and class definitions.

❑ **Resource files** folder currently contains icon files and the resource file ctest.rc.

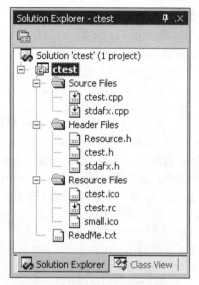

Fig. 1.10. Project hierarchy

1.3.1. Project Resources

Let's look at our resources. Double-click the ctest.rc file name, and the **Resource View** tab will appear in the same pane. It displays a hierarchy of the resources.

The **Accelerator** folder contains a list of hotkeys for the program. There can be several resources there, but at the moment the wizard has created only one resource named IDC_CTEST. We won't use hotkeys, and in most cases you can delete everything from this folder. To do this, right-click the resource and select the **Delete** item on the pop-up menu. On the one hand, the program shouldn't contain extra components, but on the other hand we won't gain much space.

The **Dialog** folder contains dialog boxes. If you intend to create an invisible program, it won't need any dialog boxes. By default, our sample contains the IDD_ABOUTBOX dialog box with information about the program. To delete the dialog box, right-click it and select the **Delete** item in the pop-up menu.

The **Icon** folder contains the program's icons. There can be several icons of various sizes and colors. They are often needed for joke programs, but they shouldn't be suspicious so that a user runs the program and sees what you "cooked." If you suggest to him or her to run the program, it won't be anything remarkable. However, if the user does so on his or her own, the surprise will make your joke sharp.

For the user to run the program, the icon should be familiar to him or her. For example, you can assign the icon of MS Word to your joke program. If the standard file extensions aren't displayed in the user's system (which is the default), he or she will take the file for a Word document. If, in addition, the file name is alluring, he or she will certainly run the file.

To change the icon and draw something effective and not suspicious, double-click the icon name, and a simple graphics editor will open in the main window (Fig. 1.11). There you can change the image. It is impossible to draw anything serious with this editor, so it is best to paste a ready picture (for example, via the clipboard). You can always find suitable pictures on the Internet.

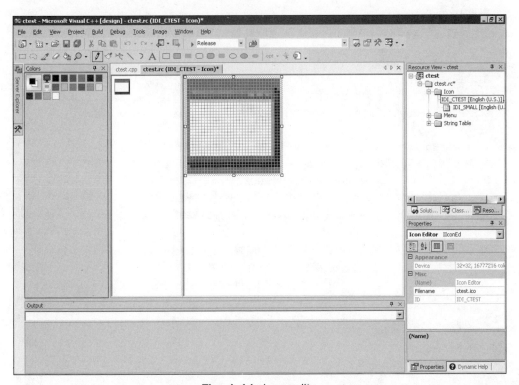

Fig. 1.11. Icon editor

In the **Menu** folder, you can store a menu for your program. We'll discuss it later, and I won't use menus frequently in subsequent examples.

The **String Table** folder allows you to store strings as constants. By default, it contains window captions. They don't take up much space, so leave them.

1.3.2. The Program Code

Let's look at the program code generated by the wizard. The code is contained in the ctest.cpp file, and it is shown in Listing 1.1. Of course, we won't discuss the code in its entirety. This book isn't a C++ tutorial, although necessary things are described here in detail. If you are already familiar with this programming language, you'll understand the code in the file. Otherwise, it would be enough to read the explanations below.

☺ **Listing 1.1. ctest.cpp source code**

```
#include "stdafx.h"
#include "ctest.h"
#define MAX_LOADSTRING 100

// Global Variables:
HINSTANCE hInst;                         // Current instance
TCHAR szTitle[MAX_LOADSTRING];           // The title bar text
TCHAR szWindowClass[MAX_LOADSTRING];     // The main window class name

// Forward declarations of functions included in this code module:
ATOM            MyRegisterClass(HINSTANCE hInstance);
BOOL            InitInstance(HINSTANCE, int);
LRESULT CALLBACK   WndProc(HWND, UINT, WPARAM, LPARAM);
LRESULT CALLBACK   About(HWND, UINT, WPARAM, LPARAM);

int APIENTRY _tWinMain(HINSTANCE hInstance,
                   HINSTANCE hPrevInstance,
                   LPTSTR    lpCmdLine,
                   int       nCmdShow)
{
    // TODO: Place code here.
    MSG msg;
    HACCEL hAccelTable;

    // Initialize global strings
    LoadString(hInstance, IDS_APP_TITLE, szTitle, MAX_LOADSTRING);
    LoadString(hInstance, IDC_CTEST, szWindowClass, MAX_LOADSTRING);
    MyRegisterClass(hInstance);

    // Perform application initialization:
```

```
    if (!InitInstance (hInstance, nCmdShow))
    {
        return FALSE;
    }

    hAccelTable = LoadAccelerators(hInstance, (LPCTSTR)IDC_CTEST);

    // Main message loop:
    while (GetMessage(&msg, NULL, 0, 0))
    {
        if (!TranslateAccelerator(msg.hwnd, hAccelTable, &msg))
        {
            TranslateMessage(&msg);
            DispatchMessage(&msg);
        }
    }

    return (int) msg.wParam;
}


// FUNCTION: MyRegisterClass()
// PURPOSE: Registers the window class.
// COMMENTS:
//    This function and its usage are only necessary if you want this code
//    to be compatible with Win32 systems prior to the 'RegisterClassEx'
//    function that was added to Windows 95. It is important to call this function
//    so that the application will get 'well formed' small icons associated
//    with it.
ATOM MyRegisterClass(HINSTANCE hInstance)
{
    WNDCLASSEX wcex;

    wcex.cbSize = sizeof(WNDCLASSEX);

    wcex.style          = CS_HREDRAW | CS_VREDRAW;
    wcex.lpfnWndProc    = (WNDPROC)WndProc;
    wcex.cbClsExtra     = 0;
    wcex.cbWndExtra     = 0;
    wcex.hInstance      = hInstance;
    wcex.hIcon          = LoadIcon(hInstance, (LPCTSTR)IDI_CTEST);
```

```
    wcex.hCursor        = LoadCursor(NULL, IDC_ARROW);
    wcex.hbrBackground  = (HBRUSH)(COLOR_WINDOW+1);
    wcex.lpszMenuName   = (LPCTSTR)IDC_CTEST;
    wcex.lpszClassName  = szWindowClass;
    wcex.hIconSm        = LoadIcon(wcex.hInstance, (LPCTSTR)IDI_SMALL);

    return RegisterClassEx(&wcex);
}


//   FUNCTION: InitInstance(HANDLE, int)
//   PURPOSE: Saves instance handle and creates main window
//   COMMENTS:
//   In this function, we save the instance handle in a global variable
//   and create and display the main program window.
BOOL InitInstance(HINSTANCE hInstance, int nCmdShow)
{
   HWND hWnd;

   hInst = hInstance; // Store instance handle in our global variable

   hWnd = CreateWindow(szWindowClass, szTitle, WS_OVERLAPPEDWINDOW,
      CW_USEDEFAULT, 0, CW_USEDEFAULT, 0, NULL, NULL, hInstance, NULL);

   if (!hWnd)
   {
      return FALSE;
   }

   ShowWindow(hWnd, nCmdShow);
   UpdateWindow(hWnd);

   return TRUE;
}

//   FUNCTION: WndProc(HWND, unsigned, WORD, LONG)
//   PURPOSE:  Processes messages for the main window
//   WM_COMMAND - Process the application menu
//   WM_PAINT   - Paint the main window
//   WM_DESTROY - Post a quit message and return
```

```
LRESULT CALLBACK WndProc(HWND hWnd, UINT message, WPARAM wParam, LPARAM lParam)
{
    int wmId, wmEvent;
    PAINTSTRUCT ps;
    HDC hdc;

    switch (message)
    {
    case WM_COMMAND:
        wmId    = LOWORD(wParam);
        wmEvent = HIWORD(wParam);
        // Parse the menu selections:
        switch (wmId)
        {
        case IDM_ABOUT:
            DialogBox(hInst, (LPCTSTR)IDD_ABOUTBOX, hWnd, (DLGPROC)About);
            break;
        case IDM_EXIT:
            DestroyWindow(hWnd);
            break;
        default:
            return DefWindowProc(hWnd, message, wParam, lParam);
        }
        break;
    case WM_PAINT:
        hdc = BeginPaint(hWnd, &ps);
        // TODO: Add any drawing code here...
        EndPaint(hWnd, &ps);
        break;
    case WM_DESTROY:
        PostQuitMessage(0);
        break;
    default:
        return DefWindowProc(hWnd, message, wParam, lParam);
    }
    return 0;
}

// Message handler for the About box.
// As we deleted the "About" window, we can delete the following code.
```

```
LRESULT CALLBACK About(HWND hDlg, UINT message, WPARAM wParam, LPARAM lParam)
{
    switch (message)
    {
    case WM_INITDIALOG:
        return TRUE;

    case WM_COMMAND:
        if (LOWORD(wParam) == IDOK || LOWORD(wParam) == IDCANCEL)
        {
            EndDialog(hDlg, LOWORD(wParam));
            return TRUE;
        }
        break;
    }
    return FALSE;
}
```

You already know that this program shouldn't have the "About" window, and we deleted it. However, the code still contains mentions of this window, and you cannot run the program. To run the project, delete everything that is below the line:

```
// As we deleted the "About" window, we can delete the following code.
```

This code displays the "About" window, and you can delete it completely.

Now, open the WndProc procedure and delete the call for the About procedure from it. To do this, locate and delete the following three lines:

```
case IDM_ABOUT:
    DialogBox(hInst, (LPCTSTR)IDD_ABOUTBOX, hWnd, (DLGPROC)About);
    break;
```

This is an event handler for the **Help/About** menu item of our program. All event handlers are located in the WndProc procedure and look like this:

```
case Identifier
    actions
    break;
```

Here, Identifier is a constant assigned to a control (such as a menu item). The case statement checks whether an event with this identifier has come from the control. If it has, the code up to the break statement is executed. We'll meet events in our practical work a bit later.

We deleted everything we don't need. We could delete a few more things (such as the menu or even the window when the program should be invisible), but they can appear useful in this book for illustration purposes. Therefore, let's decide in favor of this sample program. It is small enough, and there is little extra code.

When we create invisible programs, it will suffice to find and delete the following two lines:

```
ShowWindow(hWnd, nCmdShow);
UpdateWindow(hWnd);
```

These lines are located in the InitInstance procedure that is designed for creating and displaying a window on the desktop. You may leave the code that creates the window, but you shouldn't display it if you want your program to be invisible.

The first of these two lines shows the window created in the program, and the second one updates the contents of the window. Comment out these lines by putting two slashes (//) at the beginning of each. Now compile and run the program. When you press <Ctrl>+<Alt>+<Del>, nothing will be displayed on the screen or in the window. If you have Windows 2000/XP, you'll be able to find your program only on the **Processes** tab (Fig. 1.12).

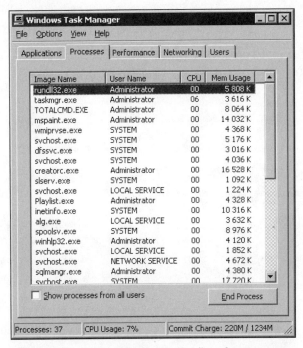

Fig. 1.12. Ctest program in the list of processes

If you are an inexperienced Visual C++ programmer, and you don't understand something, don't worry. Everything will become clear eventually. Later in this book, I'll explain much of the source code you're looking at.

Let's consider a few fragments of the code. The program starts execution at the _tWinMain function that looks like that shown in Listing 1.2.

☺ **Listing 1.2. The starting function**

```
int APIENTRY _tWinMain(HINSTANCE hInstance,
                       HINSTANCE hPrevInstance,
                       LPTSTR    lpCmdLine,
                       int       nCmdShow)
{
    // Declaration of two variables
    MSG msg;
    HACCEL hAccelTable;

    // Initialization of string variables
    LoadString(hInstance, IDS_APP_TITLE, szTitle, MAX_LOADSTRING);
    LoadString(hInstance, IDC_CTEST, szWindowClass, MAX_LOADSTRING);
    MyRegisterClass(hInstance);

    // Initialization of the application
    if (!InitInstance (hInstance, nCmdShow))
    {
        return FALSE;
    }

    hAccelTable = LoadAccelerators(hInstance, (LPCTSTR)IDC_CTEST);

    // The main loop for processing Windows messages
    while (GetMessage(&msg, NULL, 0, 0))
    {
        if (!TranslateAccelerator(msg.hwnd, hAccelTable, &msg))
        {
            TranslateMessage(&msg);
            DispatchMessage(&msg);
        }
    }

    return (int) msg.wParam;
}
```

I've used the word "function" several times, without providing a definition of it. If you have experience in C++ programming, you are familiar with it. There are things that are beyond the scope of this book, and I'll omit them. You should refer to specialized literature for more comprehensive information on C++. Nevertheless, I'll give you as much information as necessary to understand the examples.

In C++, all functions are declared as follows:

```
Type Name (Parameters)
{
}
```

- ❏ `Type` — the return type. In the function, `int` means an integer number.
- ❏ `Name` — can be any name you like, but the name of the main function is predefined.
- ❏ `Parameters` — variables and values passed to the function so that it can use them.

Our main function has the `APIENTRY` keyword after the return type. This points to the entry point of the program.

Now, look at Listing 1.1. I've included a few comments there so that you will understand the code better. As you know, comments begin with two slashes (//). The text that follows the slashes doesn't affect the program's execution and just explains the code.

Two variables are declared at the beginning of the procedure:

```
MSG msg;
HACCEL hAccelTable;
```

A declaration looks like this: `Type Name`. The type tells the program how much memory should be allocated to store the variable's value. You can access this memory with the name specified after the type. There are quite a lot of types in C++, and I'll explain them when discussing examples.

If a variable is of a simple type (such as a string, number, or structure), no additional actions are required. However, if it is an object or pointer, you should allocate memory for it. Objects are used when programming with MFC, and pointers are variables that point to certain areas in the memory. For a pointer to refer to a reasonable address, you should allocate memory for data.

What is the purpose of pointers? Many programmers fail to understand their power or are simply afraid to use them because of the absence of protection against going outside the allocated memory. Suppose you have a 1 MB picture loaded into the memory, and you want to give a function an opportunity to read the data of this picture. You can pass a megabyte of data to the function, but it will take a lot of time and extra memory. Instead, you can show the function the place where the picture is stored. In other words, you can pass the function a pointer to the memory with the picture data.

Another way involves the use of global variables, but this should be avoided. Global variables are seen in every function. As a rule, they are declared in a header file (with the H extension) or at the beginning of the program file, before function declarations.

Local variables are declared inside a function, and you can access them only within this function. Such variables are created automatically when the function starts. They are stored in a special memory area called a stack and are destroyed automatically when the function terminates. Automatically creating/destroying variables refers only to simple ones, not to pointers, which should be freed manually.

Variable declaration is followed by these two lines:

```
LoadString(hInstance, IDS_APP_TITLE, szTitle, MAX_LOADSTRING);
LoadString(hInstance, IDC_CTEST, szWindowClass, MAX_LOADSTRING);
```

These are two functions named LoadString. They load text from string resources. A function is a piece of code that has a name and can be called from other places in the program. In this case, the resource loading code will be executed. To tell the function which resource you need, and where it should be loaded, specify its parameters in parentheses. The parameters are comma-delimited, and in this case there are four parameters with the following values:

- ❏ hInstance — a pointer to the instance of this program because we need resources of our project.
- ❏ IDS_APP_TITLE — the name of the resource to load. If you now double-click the item with resources in the String Table section, you'll see a string table whose first column contains the string name, and the second column contains a text. This is the name you should specify in this parameter.
- ❏ SzTitle — a variable, into which the value should be loaded. We have two variables, szTitle and szWindowClass, declared at the beginning of the file:

```
TCHAR szTitle[MAX_LOADSTRING];          // The title bar text
TCHAR szWindowClass[MAX_LOADSTRING];    // The main window class name
```

As you already know, a variable declaration begins with a type. In this case, TCHAR is specified, which means a string. It is followed by the variable name and the string length (i.e., the maximum number of its characters) in square brackets, which is required in string declarations. In this code, MAX_LOADSTRING is specified. It is a constant equal to the maximum number of loaded characters. You could specify an actual number in square brackets, but it is best to use predefined constants where possible.

- ❏ MAX_LOADSTRING — the last parameter that denotes the maximum number of loaded characters. This is the same constant, which denoted the length of strings, to which the resource text was loaded. It turns out that the length of a loaded string is equal to the length of the string in the variable, and we'll never be able to load into the variable more resource information than the amount of allocated memory.

Then the `MyRegisterClass(hInstance)` function is called. It fills the `WNDCLASSEX` structure. What is a structure? It is a variable that stores a set of variables of any types. For example, a structure can store one string variable named `Name` and one numeric variable named `Age`. To read or update the values of these variables, you should write `Structure.Variable`. Here, `Structure` is the name of the structure, and `Variable` is the name of one of its variables.

The `WNDCLASSEX` structure is used when creating a new window class. To obtain a small application, you'll have to fill the following fields:

❑   `style` — the window style.
❑   `Lpfnwndproc` — a pointer to a procedure that should be called for all user events.
❑   `Hinstance` — the handler obtained when the `_tWinMain` procedure started.
❑   `HbrBackground` — the background color (generally, it is optional, but the window color is the default).
❑   `LpszClassName` — the name of the class being created.
❑   `Hcursor` — a cursor; the standard arrow cursor should be loaded here.

The structure is ready, and you can register the new class for a window. To do this, call a WinAPI function `RegisterClassEx(&wcex)`. Now, the system has a description of your future window. Why "future?" In fact, you haven't created the window yet. To do this, it is necessary to call the `CreateWindowEx` function. This is done in the `InitInstance` procedure which is called in `_tWinMain` after the call to `MyRegisterClass`. This procedure has quite a lot of parameters, and I'll describe them in more detail:

```
hWnd = CreateWindow(szWindowClass, szTitle, WS_OVERLAPPEDWINDOW,
    CW_USEDEFAULT, 0, CW_USEDEFAULT, 0, NULL, NULL, hInstance, NULL);
```

❑   The class name. We registered the class and stored its name in the `szWindowClass` variable. Therefore, we should specify this class here.
❑   The window name. This is just a caption that will be output. We already loaded it with the `LoadString` function and stored in the `szTitle` variable.
❑   The window style. We need the simplest `WS_OVERLAPPEDWINDOW` window.
❑   The next four parameters are the left and right positions and the width and height of the window. If you specify zeroes or `CW_USEDEFAULT`, the default values will be set.

❑ The main window for the window being created. Our window is the main itself, so specify NULL, which corresponds to zero.

I'll skip the other parameters for a while. After a window is created, it should be displayed. This is done by calling the ShowWindow procedure we spoke about earlier. It has two parameters:

❑ The created window.
❑ The window display parameters. Here, nCmdShow is specified. It is a value passed to the program depending on parameters specified in the properties of the icon that calls the program. The other parameter values can be found in the online help on WinAPI functions.

The last of preliminary functions is UpdateWindow. It simply draws the created window.

When you don't need a window and want your program to be invisible, delete or comment out the last two functions.

Now, let's look at the message processing cycle:

```
while (GetMessage(&msg, NULL, 0, 0))
{
    if (!TranslateAccelerator(msg.hwnd, hAccelTable, &msg))
    {
        TranslateMessage(&msg);
        DispatchMessage(&msg);
    }
}
```

The GetMessage function waits for a user or system message and returns TRUE as soon as a message comes. The message is appropriately converted with the TranslateMessage function and sent to a message handler with the DispatchMessage function.

Every program should have a message handler. Which one? We specified it when we were creating the window class, in the WindowClass.Lpfnwndproc property. In Visual C++, it is common to name it WndProc, which is the standard name used by default. As for the procedure, it should look like Listing 1.1.

The message handler should always contain a call to the defwindowproc function. This function looks for a default message handler for the received event. This is very important because it saves you from writing code already available in the operating system.

However, you should check the message first. If it is really necessary, handle it. There is no need to handle all messages; handle only those you need. The others will be handled in the default message handler. This is done by comparing the message parameter with standard messages. For example, if it is equal to wm_destroy, this means the program would like to be destroyed. Therefore, the handler can free the memory allocated for the program.

Well, now you understand the sample. If you start the created program right now, an empty window will appear. To close it, hit <Alt>+<F4> or click the close button.

If you want to make this window invisible, just delete the ShowWindow function from the code. This function displays the window, and your program will become invisible without it. Alternatively, you can change the second parameter of this procedure to SW_HIDE. This also results in invisibility. In appearance, specifying SW_HIDE is equivalent to the absence of a call to the procedure. As a rule, ShowWindow is used with the SW_HIDE parameter when it is necessary to hide the window without removing it from the computer memory.

We'll encounter the ShowWindow procedure many times later in this book.

To compile the project, select **Build/Build Solution**. This builds the project and creates an executable file. To start the program, select **Debug/Start**.

NOTE

The source code of this example is located in the \Demo\Chapter1\empt\ folder on the accompanying CD-ROM.

1.4. Program Optimization

A programmer's life is a continual struggle with slow-downs and lack of time. Everyday, he or she spends several hours on optimization. Each programmer tries to optimize everything that happens to be close at hand. Are you sure you do this properly? Perhaps, there is room for improvement.

I'm aware of the fact that people are lazy. As for me, I've become accustomed to having my computer do everything for me, and I don't remember what a ball-point pen looks like. I had to fill out an application on a sheet of paper not long ago. It turned out that I forgot how to write an English character, so I looked at the computer keyboard. Honestly! This is due to technical progress that allows me to do everything with my computer.

To write a two-line message, a person turns on his or her computer and starts MS Word or another text processor, thus wasting time. Why doesn't he or she write the message by hand? Because it would be imposing!

Programmers are especially shameless. Many of them don't care about the source code they write because nobody is going to see it. However, they are wrong. From this point of view, open-source applications have a great advantage because they are much cleaner and faster. Programmers are often too lazy to optimize the size and speed of the code they write. When I see such programs, I am driven to frustration. Unfortunately, this doesn't improve these programs. Hackers are even lazier.

This is a degradation provoked by MS. We grab our mouse and start clicking here and there, forgetting the keyboard and hotkeys. I'm convinced this should be stopped. I have been so lazy recently that I put away the keyboard, and now I start the on-screen keyboard and only use the mouse. The only other thing I need to do is to cover my body with fur and be put into a cage with monkeys.

Don't spend money on upgrading your computer! Upgrade yourself first. Optimize your work, and your computer will work faster.

This part of the book was originally intended as a description of how to optimize program code. However, I subsequently included one of my articles from my Internet site in this book. Everything should be optimized. I'll talk about the theory of optimization, whose laws are universal. You can use the same laws to optimize both your daily schedule to do everything on time and the operating system on your computer to make it work faster. However, the main discussion will relate to optimization of program code. Here, you'll find a little more information than in the article on my site.

As always, I'll try to give as many practical examples as possible so that you can use my recommendations and see that I'm not pulling the wool over your eyes.

I'll begin with the laws that are applicable not only to programming, but also to real life. In conclusion, I'll tell you things that can be useful when optimizing your code.

Law 1: Everything Can Be Optimized

Even if you think your work is done fast enough, it can be done faster.

This really is the case. This law is especially true for programming. There is no ideal code. Even a simple operation such as 2+2 can be optimized. To obtain the best result, you should act consistently and in the order described below.

Remember that each task can be fulfilled at least in two (or more) ways, and you should choose the best one that will provide the desired performance and universality.

Law 2: Search for the Weakest and Slowest Links

What is the point in optimizing the best links first? If you try to optimize them, you are likely to encounter unexpected conflicts. In addition, you will see few benefits.

I remember an example from my own life. Around 1996, I came up with the crazy idea of writing my own Doom-like computer game. I wasn't going to make a profit on it; this was just a mental challenge. After four months of hard work, I obtained a sort of an engine. I created one bare level, at which a gamer could move. Being very proud of myself, I started moving along corridors.

There were no monsters, doors, or scenes, but the program was very slow. I imagined what would happen if I added monsters, attributes, and AI, and I was humbled. Who needs an engine that is extremely slow without scenes at a resolution of 320 × 200 (that would have been cool...)? You're right, no one does.

My virtual world certainly needed some optimization. For a month, I struggled with my code and polished every statement of my engine. The result was the following: The world was drawn 10% faster, but it was still slow. Suddenly, I understood what the weakest link was: the display on the screen. My engine computed graphics fast enough, but displaying the image really caused a slow-down. AGP buses didn't exist at the time, and I used a simple S3 PCI video card with 1 MB of memory.

After a few hours of sorcery, I was able to get the most out of both my PCI and myself. I compiled the engine and entered my virtual world. I hit the "forward" key and immediately found myself at the opposite wall. There were no slow-downs, it operated at breakneck speed, displaying instantly.

As you see, my mistake was that I wrongly determined the weakest link in my engine at first. I spent a month on optimizing the mathematical portion of the code, with only an improvement of only 10%. However, when I actually found the weakest link, I could increase performance considerably.

This is why I tell you that you should start optimizing with the weakest links. If you speed up their work, it is likely that you won't need to speed up other parts of your code. You can spend many days or even months optimizing stronger links and gain a 10% improvement (which can be insufficient). On the other hand, you can spend a few hours optimizing the weakest link and see a ten-fold increase in performance!

The Weak Links of the Computer

I cannot understand people who update a processor and leave an old S3 video card, a 5400 rpm Winchester, and 32 MB of memory. Look inside the case of your computer and examine its contents. If you find that you have only 65 MB of memory, say loudly: "Dear DIMM, you're the weakest link, and you must leave my computer!" After that, buy 128 MB of memory, or 256 MB, or better still, 512 MB and enjoy acceleration of Visual C++, PhotoShop, and other "heavy" applications.

In such a case, increasing the processor clock rate by a hundred megahertz would provide a smaller increase in performance. When you use "heavy" applications and are short of memory, the processor spends too much time writing data to and reading it from the swap file. On the other hand, if there is enough memory in your computer, the processor only performs computation and avoids wasting time on swapping data.

The same is true for a video adapter. If your video card is weak, the processor will compute scenes faster than they are displayed. This will result in delays and little improvement in performance. In contrast, a good video card can display data fast and save the processor from some computation.

Law 3: Apply Optimization to Much Repeated Operations First

During the next step you should dissect all operations and locate those repeated many times.

I'll illustrate this law with a programming example. Suppose you have some code. (Below is just a logic, not an actual program.)

1.   A:=A*2
2.   B:=1
3.   X:=X+B
4.   B:=B+1
5.   If B<100 go to step 3

Every programmer will claim that the weakest link is the first line because it uses multiplication. This is true. Multiplication is a time-consuming operation, and you'll save a pair of clock ticks if you replace it with addition (A:=A+A) or, better still, with a shift. However, you won't gain anything, though unnoticeably so.

Now look at the code again. Do you see anything? I do. This code uses a loop: "While B<100 do X:=X+B". It implies 100 jumps from step 5 to step 3. These are quite a few. Can we optimize anything? It's easy. The loop includes lines 3 and 4. What if we duplicate them inside the loop?

1. B:=1

2. X:=X+B
3. B:=B+1

4. X:=X+B
5. B:=B+1

6. If B<100 go to step 3

Here a large loop is converted to a smaller one. The second and third operations are repeated twice. As a result, lines 3 and 4 are executed twice during one iteration, and only then a jump to line 3 is performed. This loop is repeated only 50 times (because two operations are done within one iteration). This means we have saved 50 jumps. Not bad. We saved several hundreds of clock ticks.

What if we write lines 2 and 3 ten times inside the loop? These lines will be executed ten times during one iteration, and the loop will require only ten iterations to perform 100 operations. This saves 90 jumps.

A disadvantage of this approach is that the code becomes larger. However, its speed increases significantly. This approach is good, but you shouldn't abuse it. On the one hand, the speed increases, but on the other hand, the size increases. Too much of an increase would be a disadvantage in any program. Therefore, you should look for the golden mean.

In every business, one of the most important things is reasonable sufficiency. The more you increase the size for the speed's sake, the less the resulting optimization.

There are a lot of examples in real life. Any cyclical operation can be optimized. Do you want an example? Here is one. Suppose your Internet provider has a few access telephones. You dial each of them trying to find, which line is free. A novice user would say that the provider should optimize their modem pools so that a user can dial only one number. However, an experienced user knows that not every user has a good connection to each telephone exchange. This is why providers have pools on different exchanges so that you can choose a pool with the best connection. Install a dialer (a lot of them are available on the Internet), and it will automatically dial the telephone numbers one after the other.

Another example: You have a one-hour prepaid card for access to an Internet provider. It would be pointless to enter the telephone number into your dial-up box because it is quite likely that you will never connect to this provider again. If you change the settings of your dial-up box and then reset them back, you'll spend more time than is required to call the provider with standard Windows tools. Conclusion: Carefully choose tools to implement your tasks.

Law 4: Think Twice Before You Optimize Infrequent Operations

(This law is an extension of the previous one.)

It is a waste of time to optimize operations that will only be performed once.

About a half a year ago, I read a story on the Internet called "The Notes of a Programmer's Wife." It is a cool realistic story. When I was reading, I felt like it had been written by my own wife. God bless my Little Red Riding Hood, she isn't that mean.

In the story, a pretty girl is getting married to a programmer, and they have to send out wedding invitations. Rather than typing them with a typewriter, the programmer declares himself an expert and writes a special program. He spends a day writing and another debugging.

His main mistake lay in failing to optimize his work properly. It would have been easier to create a template in any text processor and then change the names of the people invited to this poignant (according to my own experience) event. Even if a person doesn't have a text processor, it is really pointless to write a program. Doing so would be expensive, and the program would only be used once. In fact, it would be a better idea to use a typewriter.

Earlier, I criticized lazy people. However, laziness spurs you to create the most optimal environment. This is not an expert who works hard all day without a result, but rather who completes his job quickly and effectively. These things shouldn't be confused.

Law 5: Know Your Computer's Internals and Its Working Principles

The better you know how your computer executes your code, the better optimization you can achieve.

This law refers only to programming. It is difficult to give a complete set of ready solutions, but I'll try to describe a few techniques.

❑ Try to avoid floating-point computation. Any operation on integers is many times faster.

❑ Multiplication is a very slow operation; division is even slower. If you need to multiply a number by 3, it will be easier for the processor to add this number three times than to multiply it once. However, cutting-edge processors multiply quite fast, and there is a barely perceptible difference.

How can you perform the most effective division? You should know mathematics. A processor has shift operations. You should know that the processor "thinks" in the binary number system, and the numbers are stored in the computer with binary representation. For example, the number 198 looks like 11000110 for the processor. Now, let's look at the shift operations.

Right shift. If you shift the number 11000110 one position to the right, the last digit will disappear, and only 1100011 will remain. Now, enter this number into your calculator and convert it to the decimal number system. You'll obtain 99. As you see, this is half of 198.

Conclusion: When you shift a number one position to the right, you divide it by two.

Left shift. Let's take the same number 11000110. If you shift it one position to the left, the rightmost position point will become unoccupied, and then replaced with a zero. The result will be 110001100. Convert this number to the decimal number system, and you'll obtain 396. What is this digit? 198 multiplied by two.

Conclusion: When you shift the first position to the right, you divide it by two; when you shift it to the left, you multiply it by two.

Therefore, use the shift option whenever you can because it executes many times faster than multiplication or division, and even addition or subtraction.

❑ When creating a procedure, don't burden it with many parameters. Before the procedure is called, its parameters are pushed on the stack (this is a special memory area), and they are popped off the stack when the procedure starts. The greater the number of parameters, the higher the overheads on accessing the stack.

I'd like to mention that you should also be very careful with the parameters themselves. Mind you don't pass variables that can contain large amounts of data! It is best to pass the procedure the memory address where the data is stored and use this address inside the procedure. Imagine you need to pass a procedure a text whose size is equal to that of an issue of *The New York Times*. Before calling the procedure, the program will try to push this onto the stack. If stack overflow doesn't occur, you'll have to wait long enough.

❐ You can use the assembly language in the most crucial fragments of code (such as output to the screen). Even Delphi or C++ inline assemblers are much faster than the standard language functions. If the execution speed is very important in a fragment of code, you can separate the assembly code into an individual module, compile it with the TASM or MASM compiler, and link to your program.

The assembly language is quick and compact, but it is very difficult to write a large project with it. I recommend that you be circumspect and use it only where speed is crucial.

Law 6: Prepare Tables with Data Computed Beforehand and Use Them in Real-Time Mode

When the first version of Doom appeared, the gamer community was astonished by its speed and high-quality graphics. This actually was a masterpiece of programming because at the time, computers couldn't render 3-D graphics in real time. Nobody even thought about 3-D accelerators, and video cards only displayed data and didn't perform any additional computation.

How did Doom authors manage to create that 3-D world? Like everything else in our world, the secret was simple. The game didn't compute scenes. All complicated mathematical computation was done beforehand, and the results were recorded in a database that was loaded at the start of the program. Of course, it was impossible to fill the database with all conceivable data, so it stored only the main results. When a value missing from the pre-computed table was required, the nearest approximate value was taken. Thus, Doom performed at an optimal level and its 3-D images were of a good quality.

When Quake was released, the gamer community again was astonished by the quality of light and shadows in the virtual world of Quake. Computing light is an extremely complicated task, to say nothing of shadows. How could the authors have rendered such high-quality scenes and a game with such excellent performance? The answer is the same: by using tables with pre-computed values.

Some time later, the computer game industry was even more surprised. When Quake 3 was released with lighting computed in real time, its world turned out to be a bit unnatural. Even Half-Life that was released later on the engine of the old Quake looked much more natural. This was because computers weren't powerful enough to perform real-time computation, and rounding errors deteriorated the game environment.

Nevertheless, Quake has always been a legend because of its splendid world. If light and shadows were completely missing from its graphics, the game would remain wonderful. It is marvelous, and a real masterpiece created by real hackers.

Law 7: There Are No Unnecessary Checks

It is quite often the case that optimization results in unstable code because some programmers try to increase performance by removing checks they consider unnecessary. Remember: There are no unnecessary checks! If you think an unusual situation is unlikely, this doesn't mean your user will be immune from it. The user is very likely to hit a wrong key or enter wrong data.

Make sure you check the user's entry. Do this as soon as the data are entered and don't wait until you need it.

Don't make checks inside a loop. Extra `if` statements inside loops affect performance very much; therefore, make checks before or after a loop.

Loops are each program's weak link, and you should begin optimization with loops. Don't put checks inside loops. There shouldn't be extra operations inside a loop because they will be repeated many times.

Law 8: Don't Be Over-Zealous When Optimizing

An excessively diligent approach to increase performance can prove to be futile. Set yourself realistic goals and tasks. If you fail to optimize your code to a desired level, it is pointless to take the pains of relentless attempts. Quite likely, you will be able to find another solution to the problem.

It is often impossible to reach the ideal because optimizing the speed and the quality are opposite goals. This is especially noticeable when it comes to programming graphics. To speed up the rendering of a scene (for example, in a computer game), you can perform quick but approximate computation. As a result, the computer works quickly, but the image is lacking quality. To increase quality, a substantial amount of time is required, and you often have to choose between the two goals.

Developers of graphic editors sacrifice speed because real-time computing isn't required there. However, developers of computer games have to sacrifice quality. Otherwise, it would be impossible to play, and nobody would buy such a game.

Summary

If you read this section with due attention, you can consider yourself familiar with the basics of optimization. However, these are only the basics, and you still have to develop your skills. I could tell you more, but this would be pointless. Optimization is a creative process, and you can use various approaches in any particular situation. Nevertheless, the laws above are valid in 99.9% of cases.

If you want to get a deeper understanding of the optimization theory applied to programming, you should learn working principles of processors and operating systems. Most importantly, you know the laws, and the rest will come eventually.

1.5. Designing Windows Correctly

When you write your own program, which you intend to sell, it is very important to think over its interface. As is the case with people, the most lasting impressions on a program are the first. If its windows are disgusting, nobody will pay a dime for the program. How can you create something attractive so that a user spends more than five minutes on getting acquainted with your program? This isn't that difficult. Correct design is a sort of art.

Previously, I tried to find non-standard solutions in the main window to stand out against my competitors, but my programs sold badly. After three years of such a practice, I made a standard window with simple buttons and common menus, and sales increased three times. Users don't like to make heads or tails of complicated interfaces and strange controls. They like simple programs that can be used immediately after installation.

If you write a small utility with just a few features, its windows and buttons can be of any size, shape, and color. For example, a dialer can be round, oval, or look like an exotic animal (textured or smooth), and its interface can include three text boxes (the telephone number, login, and password) and a dial button. A user will quickly understand a simple interface regardless of how it looks. Therefore, you can use your imagination and attract new users with non-standard, but beautiful and convenient interfaces.

A good example of a small utility with simple features that conquered the world is WinAMP. The program is very simple, and the user will always understand how to play music, regardless of the appearance of the main window. In this case, the solution is atypical. However, a beautiful solution allows a program to win its market niche. If you add a feature that allows the program's appearance to be changed (supports skinning), you'll gain half of the victory. After that you can provide an original interface with serious features.

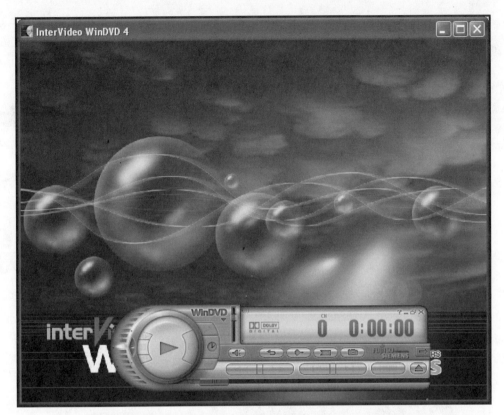

Fig. 1.13. Audio and video players can have any appearance

When you create a program with a lot of features and a complex structure, the main window should be rectangular and have standard Windows colors. Imagine Word's main window is round or oval. Perhaps, this would be beautiful and interesting, but I would uninstall such a program at once.

Make sure to stick to de facto software standards in the area you're working in. For example, PhotoShop interface became a standard for graphics editors. Previously, all software manufacturers tried to invent something special. However, they eventually reconciled themselves with the fact that Adobe introduces the fashion, and now they stick to its standards.

When Flash 5 was released, the developers at Macromedia tried to make its interface as close to PhotoShop's as possible. Despite one of these applications works with bitmap graphics and the other with vector graphics, they became alike. For example, the toolbar disappeared though it improves usability. As a result, Macromedia Flash 5 became extremely popular, especially with professional artists. In fact, graphics features didn't change much in version 5. The main innovations were advanced ActionScript and the new interface. Artists don't program, so they don't care about ActionScript. However, they liked the interface because it was familiar, and they didn't have to spend months learning and getting accustomed to it.

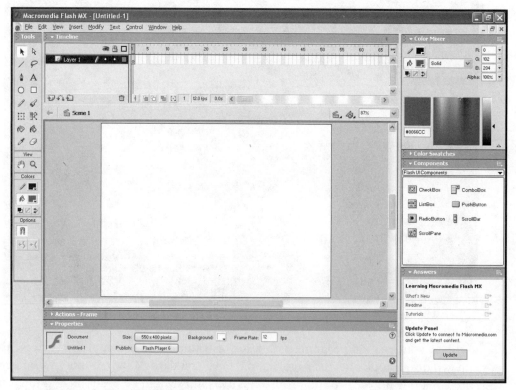

Fig. 1.14. Despite Flash MX changed its appearance, it resembles PhotoShop

When you start a new project, look at your competitors first. Pay special attention to those who control the market and has the maximum sales. You should stick to their standards. If the leaders use original solutions, you can try to make something similar. In such a case, movement in another direction, such as using classic solutions, will be mortal. Of course, you'll be able to find your customers, but they won't be numerous. Compete in quality, features, and convenience, not in bright toys. Otherwise, you'll lose.

If you are an innovator in grain, you can try your own way. Maybe it will be successful. You'll never know until you try. The risk of failure increases, but if you hit the nail on the head, you'll dictate the fashion and reap a rich harvest. If the programmers at NullSoft didn't risk and create something original, WinAMP never would have become so popular despite its performance level and myriad features.

I have seen a few players that could surpass WinAMP in many features, but it was a pioneer that conquered the hearts of many music lovers. The other programs are just followers, and now the player market is flooded with players with non-standard windows and support for skinning.

3D FTP is a negative example. Its developers liked WinAMP's success and provided skinning support in this FTP client. I've never seen such a terrible application. Can you imagine Adobe PhotoShop or Microsoft Word with skinning support? 3D FTP client was very powerful with plenty of features (that surpassed many competitors). However, it died. Its authors should have looked at Cute FTP or CyD FTP Client and made 3D FTP's windows look like the windows of these two applications. In addition, they should have deleted the skins and non-standard controls.

Windows operating systems conquered the market thanks to the standard interface and the unified appearance of all applications. Because of this, even an amateur would know where he or she should look for file open or print commands, edit commands, or anything else. Having started an application, it is easy to guess, which buttons to click to make it work.

Interface creation is a vast subject, and many books have been written on it. However, if you know at least its basics, you can achieve incredible success.

1.5.1. The Main Window Interface

What is designed first when creating any program? Of course, it is the main window interface. As you already know, the window should be rectangular and include the system menu. Never remove the borders of the main window unless it is necessary to do so.

There should be a menu and a toolbar with buttons for commands used most frequently at the top of the window. There shouldn't be any additional controls above the menu and toolbar.

There should be a status bar at the bottom of the window. It will display hints about selected commands. Don't think your users will be clever enough to guess anything without hints. Each command should have a brief but clear description that should be displayed in the status bar. The commands in the menu should be short, and a more detailed explanation of a command being executed should be displayed in the status bar.

When a toolbar with buttons is used in a program, sometimes it is difficult to guess the purpose of a button from the icon on it. Some programmers believe it is enough to put these icons next to the corresponding menu items to help the user. However, the user shouldn't have to open a menu to find the command associated with a particular button. He or she should be able to determine the purpose of a button with a pop-up hint or the status bar.

The status bar can also contain information on the current program's status or on the progress of an operation. Don't display this information on individual panes or additional windows. The status bar was designed for this purpose.

The names of menu items should be as informative as possible, but they shouldn't consist of more than three words. More comprehensive information can be displayed in the status bar. For standard items, use commonly-adopted names. For example, don't use **File/Create a new crack** instead of **File/New**. The first would be too long and senseless.

The toolbar also should be as standard as possible. The toolbar with the main commands (such as **New, Open, Print**, etc.) should be at the top of the window. Don't put it at the side or bottom. It is best to use standard icons that are used in MS Office applications or other Microsoft applications. Users have become accustomed to them; therefore, they will find your interface familiar.

If you cannot draw, find icons on the Internet, but don't create pictures, which nobody will be able to understand. On the other hand, if you have artistic skills, you can try to draw icons similar to those used by your competitors. Users who used other manufacturers' applications will be able to switch themselves to your product easily. This is very important, and you should give a considerable degree of attention to icons.

Icons should be explanatory and associated with the command. If a hippopotamus were drawn on a button that set a color palette, even Nostradamus would be unable to guess it.

It is recommended that you make the toolbar adjustable so that a user can remove unnecessary buttons and leave only those he or she actually needs. However, if there were just 10 buttons on a toolbar, such a feature would be excessive. In this case it would be best to allow the user to hide or show the entire toolbar.

The buttons on the toolbar should be grouped by purpose. When there are too many buttons, use several toolbars, but don't throw everything in one heap. When grouping the buttons, you can be guided by the arrangement of the commands on the main menu. If you provide more than two toolbars, you should allow the user to rearrange the toolbars and hide or show any of them. Thus, every user can decide how much of the working area he or she needs, and how it will be used.

1.5.2. Controls

All controls in all windows should be from the standard Windows set. Don't create irregular buttons just because you can. One time I made round buttons and plane textboxes. This didn't increase sales. In addition, it was difficult to create a consistent design.

Hundreds of professionals at Microsoft rack their brains making the user interface simpler. Don't consider yourself cleverer than they. You can create your own control only if the control you need to fulfill your task is missing from the standard set. However, you should try to achieve the simplest solution, not the most elaborate.

1.5.3. Dialog Boxes

Dialog boxes deserve special attention. They are used by users to enter data into the program and obtain the results. If something is inconvenient or annoying, the user will simply run uninstall.exe. You should design every control with special care.

Fig. 1.15. "About" window of The Bat!

The only window that can look as you wish is the About window. It is likely that the user will never see it. If he or she sees something unexpected, this won't be a problem. In the other cases, no decorations are permissible. However, even the About window should contain a **Close** or **OK** button because it would be difficult to guess that the window can be closed only by clicking a particular area within it.

What should a dialog box look like? Undoubtedly, it should be rectangular. In addition, it is desirable that its width be greater than its height. Such dialog boxes are perceived better because humans are used to perceiving everything in the horizontal plane. We watch wide-screen films, and the horizontal resolutions of monitors are greater than their vertical ones. This is why it is easier to make wide dialog boxes "appealing" and "pleasant."

Look at the backup dialog box of The Bat! (Fig. 1.16). Its height is greater than its width, and the dialog box is problematic. I understand its developers tried to provide as many options as possible in this dialog box. However, the box itself and uneven controls are a little annoying. In addition, the last checkbox is moved to the right. This is a mistake. All controls should be left-aligned, and such jumps to the right deteriorate the appearance of the dialog box. If a control depends on another, it is best to disable it (with the `Enable` property), rather than move the control.

The only successful arrangement in this window is that the controls are well-grouped. Checkboxes are in one group, and radio buttons are in the other.

Look at Fig. 1.17. I deleted a couple of unnecessary controls (they could be left, but the program's functionality won't suffer without them). In addition, I aligned controls and made the dialog box wider. Now it looks different and, believe me, in the application it looks even better and is much more convenient.

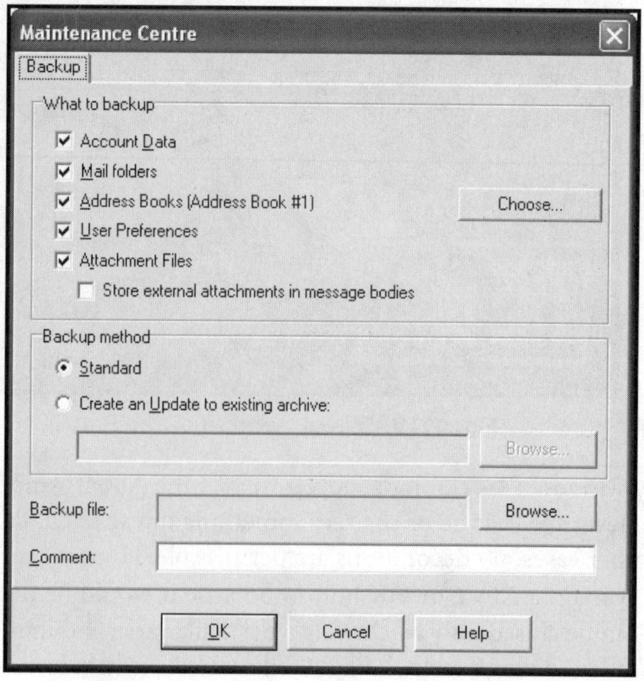

Fig. 1.16. The backup dialog box of The Bat!

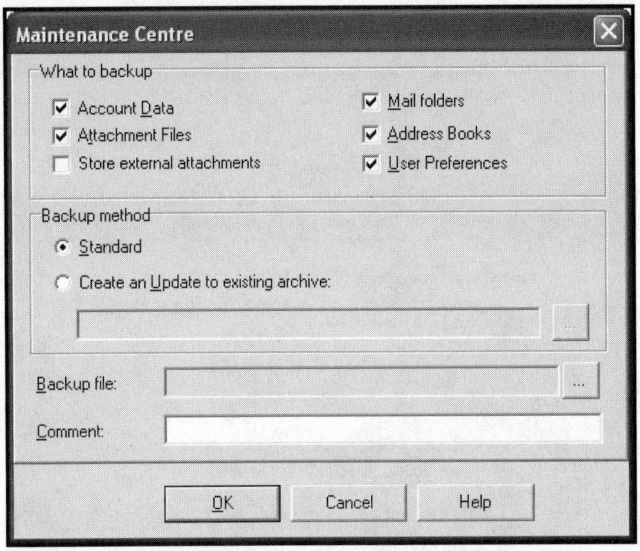

Fig. 1.17. The improved backup dialog box of The Bat!

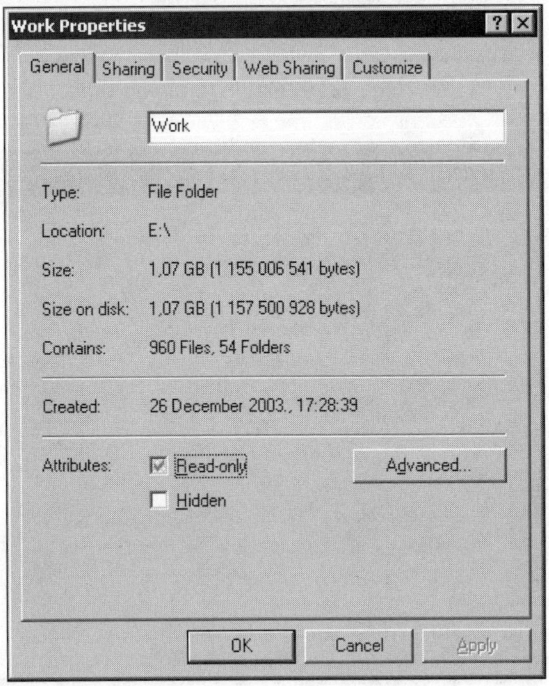

Fig. 1.18. Property dialog box

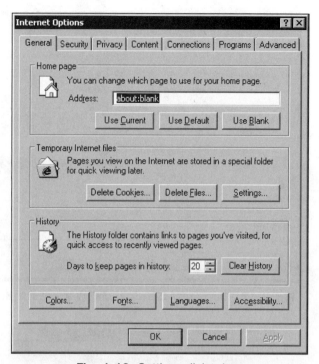

Fig. 1.19. Settings dialog box

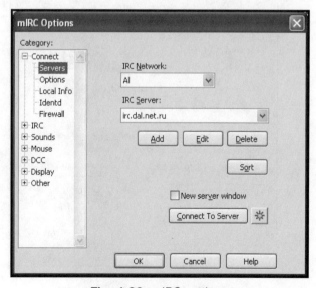

Fig. 1.20. mIRC settings

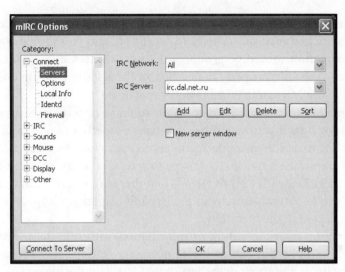

Fig. 1.21. Improved mIRC settings dialog box

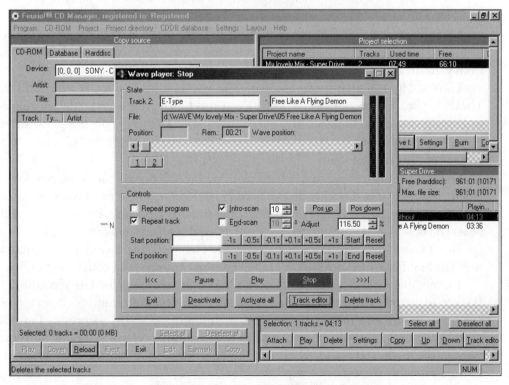

Fig. 1.22. Overloaded Feurio interface

If you need to display the properties of an object (document or file), the dialog box should be stretched vertically. This is an exception, and you should always stick to it.

All information should be grouped by topics using tabs. A good example of such an approach is the file property dialog box in the Explorer or the document property dialog box in the Microsoft Word (**File/Properties**).

No object has so many properties that it would be impossible to arrange them in four tabs of a dialog box. If your object has too many properties to fit in four tabs, you should optimize it. Try to decide what information is necessary for a user, and what can be deleted.

If your application has just a few parameters, you can create something in MS's style (Fig. 1.19), i.e., with a set of tabs. When there are many settings, stick to Netscape Navigator's style: Put a hierarchy at the left and display the appropriate settings when an item is selected in the hierarchy.

Don't try to associate a bulk of information with one item. Readability will decrease, and it will be difficult to locate necessary settings. Try to leave enough space between the items and use indentation so that to retain the dialog box integrity.

Look at Fig. 1.20 that shows mIRC settings dialog box. It is fraught with problems. The hierarchy is too narrow, and the dialog box itself isn't wide enough. Controls are haphazardly arranged and there are buttons that are completely unnecessary and can be moved to other dialog boxes. The **Sort** button is strangely separated and disappears from view. In addition, the drop-down lists have different widths.

Look at Fig. 1.21 that shows the same dialog box after I edited it with MS Paint. The dialog box has become wider, and its controls look better because they are aligned to left and have the same width. The button with a "Sun" icon has been deleted because it had no hint, and its purpose was vague since it simply moved a user to the settings of the **Connect** item.

Some unused space appeared in the dialog box, but this doesn't mean you can decrease its size. It is likely that the other dialogs need to be this size. In the main window, you can put as many controls as possible to make it as informative as possible. By contrast, in dialog boxes you don't have to use the space completely. Appearance is more important.

Don't waste time creating a convenient and elaborate interface. The best program with an abundance of features won't sell better than a simple and convenient utility.

I remember I described Feurio, a very powerful program for CD recording, for Hacker magazine. I spent a week learning its interface and concluded that it was a good program, and that each music-lover should have had it. However, I'm not a music lover, and I am wary of its inconvenience. I would prefer simple and convenient WinOnCD to the powerful, but unappealing Feurio. If I burned CDs every day, I would probably use a more complicated tool.

Remember, if you don't know what to do, look at your competitors!

Chapter 2: Writing Simple Pranks

Now, you can start writing simple joke programs in Windows. Since this operating system is the most popular, it is especially interesting to make jokes in it because it is very easy to find a victim. I know that every programmer will take pleasure in stealthily sending a joke program to a friend and shock the poor soul.

Since each of us has an innate desire for superiority and we all want to be the best, it's not surprising that programmers often demonstrate their superiority by writing something unique, interesting, or eccentric. This often results in joke programs.

Though programs in this book aren't harmful, they are intended to be sent to someone stealthily. Therefore, I'll call the person who is the object of a joke a victim.

Most of the jokes in this chapter are based on simple WinAPI functions. As I said earlier, some basic knowledge in programming is required. However, I'll try to explain all presented code most comprehensively. I'll emphasize the WinAPI functions used in the examples. Whereas you use some Visual C++ features every day, in all likelihood, you'll rarely use WinAPI functions. I don't expect you to know all of them.

I know excellent programmers who could write database programs "with closed eyes." However, they cannot write a program that moves the mouse pointer.

To understand what's going on, try to do everything described in this book on your own. You'll understand the material and remember everything. People remember practical lessons better than theoretical ones, so I'll give a lot of practical examples.

2.1. The Flying *Start* Button

I remember the first time I saw Windows 95. I liked the **Start** button with all the trimmings including the "Switch off the computer" radio button. Shortly afterward, computers in our institute were upgraded, and Windows 95 was installed on them. I wished to play a prank on other students and decided to write a program that would throw up the **Start** button. I wrote such a program and started it on all of the computers. Every time the **Start** button flew up, everyone flew up from their chairs. Sometime after that I found a similar joke on the Internet.

I'll repeat this old joke now and show you how to write such a program. Although that program was written in Delphi, I'll use Visual C++ in this book. Well, take your seat: The **Start** button will fly up to the height of 100 pixels!

In this example, I'll do a trick: I'll throw up a window with an image of the **Start** button, rather than the button itself. Later in this book, I'll show how you can access the system button, but now let's confine ourselves to this trick. In fact, this is more interesting.

Before you start programming, you should prepare a picture with the **Start** button. You can draw it manually with a graphics editor. However, if you are IBM-compatible, you can put the contents of the screen onto the clipboard using the <PrintScrn> key and paste the clipboard to any graphics editor. Then you can cut the image of the button and save it in a file.

I obtained a 50 × 20 picture, and you can find it on the accompanying CD-ROM in the Demo/Chapter2/Start Button/Start.bmp file. Feel free to use it.

Create a new project of the **Win32 Project** type in Visual C++ and name it *Start Button.* You should add the picture to this project. To do this, open the resources by double-clicking the Start Button.rc file. You'll see a window with the resource hierarchy (Fig. 2.1).

Right-click on this window, and select **Add resource** on the pop-up menu. You'll see a window that allows you to select the type of the resource being created (Fig. 2.2). Select **Bitmap** and click the **New** button.

In the absence of a **Bitmap** resource folder, one will be created. This folder will contain a resource to store the image. Below the **Resource view** window, you will see the **Properties** window (Fig. 2.3). The first thing you should do there is to change the Colors property by setting it to **256 Color** or **True Color**. Specify the **Width** and **Height** properties in accordance with your picture.

Open the image of the **Start** button in any resource editor (such as Paint) and copy it to the clipboard (most likely, you'll have to select the image and select **Edit/Copy**).

Return to Visual C++ editor and execute the **Edit/Paste** command. You'll see something akin to what is shown in Fig. 2.4.

Now let's proceed to programming. In this example, we'll look at techniques, which we'll use in the future quite frequently.

Fig. 2.1. Resource View window

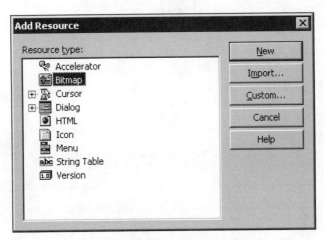

Fig. 2.2. Add resource window

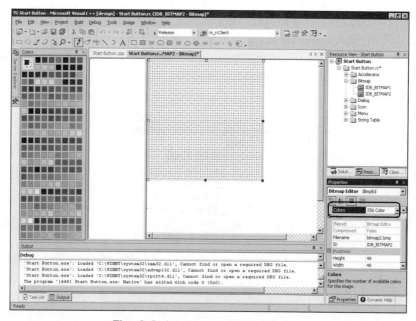

Fig. 2.3. Image properties window

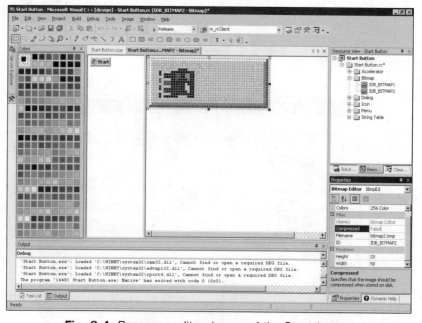

Fig. 2.4. Resource editor, image of the **Start** button

Open the Start Button.cpp file. To do this, locate it in the Source Files folder in the **Solution Explorer** window and double-click its name. Find the section with global variables at the beginning of the file. The section begins with the *"Global Variables:"* comment. Add two variables after this line:

```
// Global Variables:

HWND hWnd;

HBITMAP startBitmap;
```

The first variable has the HWND type. This type is used to store handles for windows. In this variable, we'll store a handle for the window created in this example to be able to access it at any time. The second variable has the HBITMAP type. This type is used to store pictures, and we'll store the image of the **Start** button in this variable.

Enter the _tWinMain function. Inside it, add the following lines of code after loading the window text and the class name from the resources:

```
startBitmap = (HBITMAP)::LoadImage(hInstance,
    MAKEINTRESOURCE(IDB_BITMAP1), IMAGE_BITMAP,
    0, 0, LR_DEFAULTCOLOR);
```

Here, we assign the startBitmap variable the picture loaded from the resources. To do this, we call the LoadImage function that takes the following parameters:

❏ An instance of the application. Here, we put the hInstance variable that was passed as the first parameter to the _tWinMain function. This variable contains the necessary value of the instance.

❏ The resource name. Our picture is saved under the name IDB_BITMAP1.

❏ The image type. In our case, this is a bitmap image: IMAGE_BITMAP.

❏ The size. The next two parameters are the dimensions of the picture. We specified zeroes to use the current size of the picture.

❏ The last parameter is a flag. We specified LR_DEFAULTCOLOR to use the default colors.

We won't change anything else in this function until we return to it later. Now enter the InitInstance function. Listing 2.1 displays the result.

☺ **Listing 2.1. The `InitInstance` function updated**

```
BOOL InitInstance(HINSTANCE hInstance, int nCmdShow)
{
    hInst = hInstance; // Store instance handle in our global variable

    hWnd = CreateWindow(szWindowClass, szTitle, WS_VISIBLE,
        CW_USEDEFAULT, 0, CW_USEDEFAULT, 0, NULL, NULL, hInstance, NULL);

    if (!hWnd)
    {
        return FALSE;
    }
    // The following lines are ours
    int Style;
    Style = GetWindowLong(hWnd, GWL_STYLE);
    Style=Style || WS_CAPTION;
    Style=Style || WS_SYSMENU;
    SetWindowLong(hWnd, GWL_STYLE, Style);

    return TRUE;
}
```

The code we added begins with a declaration of the `Style` variable that has the `int` type (integer). In the next line, this variable gets the result of execution of the `GetWindowLong` function that returns the window settings. It takes two parameters:

❑ The window whose settings we need. We specified the newly-created window.
❑ The types of the settings. We are interested only in the window style, so the `GWL_STYLE` constant is specified.

Why do we need the window style? By default, a window has a caption and the **Minimize** and **Maximize** buttons, and we don't want either one of them. We should delete all extra components and leave only the client rectangle. With this goal, the next two lines delete the window caption and the system menu with the buttons from the window style.

Then the `SetWindowLong` function, which writes the values back to the window settings, is called. If you then run the program, you'll only see the gray client rectangle without a caption, buttons, or borders.

Move to the `WndProc` function, which handles all messages. We are interested in painting, so add the following handler:

```
case WM_PAINT:
    hdc = BeginPaint(hWnd, &ps);
    // TODO: Add any drawing code here...
    Rectangle(hdc, 1, 1, 10, 10);
    hdcBits=::CreateCompatibleDC(hdc);
    SelectObject(hdcBits,startBitmap);
    BitBlt(hdc, 0, 0, 50, 20, hdcBits, 0, 0, SRCCOPY);
    DeleteDC(hdcBits);
    EndPaint(hWnd, &ps);
    break;
```

A complete version of the `WndProc` function is shown in Listing 2.2.

☺ **Listing 2.2. The `WndProc` function with a handler**

```
LRESULT CALLBACK WndProc(HWND hWnd, UINT message, WPARAM wParam, LPARAM
lParam)
{
    int wmId, wmEvent;
    PAINTSTRUCT ps;
    HDC hdc;
    HDC hdcBits;

    switch (message)
    {
    case WM_COMMAND:
        wmId    = LOWORD(wParam);
        wmEvent = HIWORD(wParam);
        // Parse the menu selections:
        switch (wmId)
        {
        case IDM_EXIT:
            DestroyWindow(hWnd);
            break;
        default:
            return DefWindowProc(hWnd, message, wParam, lParam);
        }
        break;
```

```
case WM_PAINT:
        hdc = BeginPaint(hWnd, &ps);
        // TODO: Add any drawing code here...
        Rectangle(hdc, 1, 1, 10, 10);
                hdcBits=::CreateCompatibleDC(hdc);
                SelectObject(hdcBits,startBitmap);
                BitBlt(hdc, 0, 0, 50, 20, hdcBits, 0, 0, SRCCOPY);
                DeleteDC(hdcBits);
        EndPaint(hWnd, &ps);
        break;
case WM_DESTROY:
        PostQuitMessage(0);
        break;
default:
        return DefWindowProc(hWnd, message, wParam, lParam);
}
return 0;
}
```

To begin painting, we should know where we'll do this. Each window has a context, in which you can paint with Windows tools. To get the context for the current window, call the BeginPaint function. This function returns a handle for the context of the window specified as the first parameter.

To display the image of the **Start** button, we should prepare a picture. There is no function among WinAPI functions that could draw a bitmap image. However, there is an option for selecting an image in a context and copying between contexts. To do this, first create a painting context compatible with that used by the window so that you can copy the image without problems. Call the CreateCompatibleDC function and pass it the window context. It will return a new context to you, one which is compatible with that specified.

Next you should select our picture in the new context. To do this, you can use the SelectObject function that takes two parameters:

❐ A context, in which an object is to be selected. Here, we specify the new context based on the window context.

❐ An object that should be selected. Here, we specify the picture.

Now, you can copy the image with the BitBlt function. It takes the following parameters:

❐ The context, to which copying should be done (the destination). Specify the window context.

❏   The next four parameters are integers. They determine a rectangle, to which the image should be copied. These are the upper and left coordinates, the width, and the height. In our case, the first two are equal to zero, so that the picture is positioned in the upper left-hand corner of the window. The width and height are equal to those of the picture (50×20).

❏   The source. Specify the `hdcBits` context, which contains the picture.

❏   The next two parameters specify the coordinates in the upper and left-hand side of the rectangle in the context, from which the image is copied. The image will be taken from this point. We need the entire button, so specify zeroes.

❏   The last parameter determines the type of copying. Since we are going to create a copy of the source in the destination context, specify the `SRC_COPY` flag.

After painting, we will no longer need the context we created. It is a good practice to delete it. To do this, call the `DeleteDC` function and pass it our painting context as a parameter.

Finally, you should finish painting by calling the `EndPaint` method. Thus, you'll complete the process started with the `BeginPaint` function.

From this point on, the **Start** button will be drawn in our window in the upper left-hand corner. All that remains is to adjust the size of the window to that of the picture (so that a user sees only the picture) and to make the window move. To achieve this, we should call the `DrawStartButton` function before the `_tWinMain` function, as shown in Listing 2.3.

☺ **Listing 2.3. A function that moves a window**

```
void DrawStartButton()
{
 int i;
 HANDLE h;
 int toppos = GetSystemMetrics(SM_CYSCREEN)-23;

 // Set the window position in the lower left corner of the screen
 SetWindowPos(hWnd, HWND_TOPMOST, 4, toppos, 50, 20, SWP_SHOWWINDOW);
 UpdateWindow(hWnd);
 // Create an empty pointer h that will be used for a delay
 h = CreateEvent(0, TRUE, FALSE, "et");

 // Now, we'll lift the button
 for (i=0; i<50; i++)
 {
```

```
            toppos = toppos-4;
            SetWindowPos(hWnd, HWND_TOPMOST, 4, toppos, 50, 20,
                SWP_SHOWWINDOW);
            WaitForSingleObject(h,15); // A delay for 15 milliseconds
}

// Put the button down
for (i=50; i>0; i--)
{
            toppos = toppos+4;
            SetWindowPos(hWnd, HWND_TOPMOST, 4, toppos, 50, 20,
                SWP_SHOWWINDOW);
            WaitForSingleObject(h,15);// A delay for 15 milliseconds
}
}
```

To place the window with our button on the computer screen properly, we need to know the vertical resolution. It is obtained with the following line of code:

```
int toppos = GetSystemMetrics(SM_CYSCREEN)-23;
```

Here, the GetSystemMetrics function is called that returns the value of a particular system setting. The setting we need is specified in parentheses (in this case, SM_CYSCREEN, the screen height). The result is decreased by 23 (the picture height plus three pixels) and stored in the toppos variable.

Thus, we computed the upper coordinate of the window with the button. Now, we should move the window there. We should also ensure that our window is always on top of the others. Both operations can be done with one function, SetWindowPos. It takes seven parameters:

❑ Movement of the window. Specify accordingly.
❑ Then, the specified window should be positioned. We want it to be on top, so specify the HWND_TOPMOST flag.
❑ The next four parameters define the rectangle, in which the window should be positioned. Set the left coordinate to 4 and the upper one to the toppos variable. The width and height of the window should be equal to those of the picture. You might need to adjust the left and upper positions a little, depending on the picture you actually have.
❑ The last parameter is a flag specifying how the window should be displayed. We just want to display it, so specify SWP_SHOWWINDOW.

After this, we redraw the window in a new position using the `UpdateWindow(hWnd)` function. Its parameter is the window that should be updated.

The final step is the creation of an empty event using the `CreateEvent` function. We'll use this event a bit later, and we are satisfied that it is empty, and that nothing will trigger it.

Our window is positioned properly, and we can proceed with animating it (moving it around the screen). To do this, we wrote the following loop:

```
for (i=0; i<50; i++)
  {
        toppos = toppos-4;
        SetWindowPos(hWnd, HWND_TOPMOST, 4, toppos, 50, 20,
          SWP_SHOWWINDOW);
        WaitForSingleObject(h,15); // A delay for 15 milliseconds
  }
```

First, this code decreases the `toppos` variable by four pixels. This is done to make the window move upwards. Then the window is actually moved into the new position.

The most interesting piece of this code is the last line, in which the `WaitForSingleObject` function is called. It waits for a particular event specified as the first parameter. The second parameter is a time interval, during which the function should wait. Since the event is empty, it will never occur, and the function will wait for the time set as the second parameter. As a result, there will be a delay between the window's movements that won't take up system resources.

A huge advantage of the `WaitForSingleObject` function is that it doesn't take up system resources. Some programmers use loops with mathematical operations to implement delays. This is inadvisable because it overloads the processor with useless work. My experience shows that the use of the `WaitForSingleObject` function almost doesn't overload the processor and works well.

Thus, the loop moves the window upwards. After that, we should return the button to its place. To do this, the other loop is written, which moves the button back in a similar manner.

Everything is ready now, and it is necessary to return to the `_tWinMain` function and write a call to the `DrawStartButton` function there. I recommend that you place this call both before the main message loop and inside it:

```
        DrawStartButton();

        // Main message loop:
        while (GetMessage(&msg, NULL, 0, 0))
        {
                DrawStartButton();
```

```
if (!TranslateAccelerator(msg.hwnd, hAccelTable,&msg))
{
        TranslateMessage(&msg);
        DispatchMessage(&msg);
}
}
```

When the program starts, our false button will fly up and then go back and cover the actual button. If a user tries to put the mouse pointer on the actual button, the pointer will touch the false button, and the program will receive an event from the mouse. As a result, the DrawStartButton function will throw up the false button again.

This is very effective, and I advise you to watch how it works. The program isn't destructive, and your friends will like the prank.

Fig. 2.5. Example of the program's work

The source code and executable files of this example are in the Demo\Chapter2\ Start Button directory on the accompanying CD-ROM. To start the program, select **Debug/Start**.

NOTE

Many jokes can be based on the substitution effect where a window with the image of an object is moved rather than the object itself. For example, you can display a dialog box with a message such as "Format disk C:," and the user will be frightened. If you display ten messages "Virus Alert!!!," even a professional will be fooled and make his colleagues smile.

I remember the good old 1990s when even viruses were light-hearted. They just displayed funny messages, played music through the PC speaker, or displayed some graphics made of ASCII characters. The worst thing they did was to replicate themselves from one computer to another. Of course, viruses are viruses, but at least those were inventive. Today viruses are neither interesting nor decent. Their only goals are to infect as many computers and to wreak as much havoc as possible. They are both silly and ineffective.

2.2. Start Your Work with the *Start* Button

If you installed Windows by yourself, you mostly likely saw a message like "Start your work with this button" with an arrow pointing to the **Start** button. I've worked as a network administrator for a long time, and consequently, users have bothered me with questions like "Where is such-and-such application?" Once I was so annoyed with one user that I wrote a program, which repeatedly opened the menu as displayed when you click the **Start** button. I'll show you a similar program now.

Create a new **Win32 Project** application. I named my project CrazyStart, but you can give yours any name you like. In the example, the project name isn't used, and everything will be clear.

Open the file with your project's code. It should have the name of your project and the CPP extension (my file is CrazyStart.cpp). Locate the _tWinMain function and change it so that it looks like that shown in Listing 2.4. The comments in the listing will guide you.

☺ **Listing 2.4. The `_tWinMain` function**

```
int APIENTRY _tWinMain(HINSTANCE hInstance,
                       HINSTANCE hPrevInstance,
                       LPTSTR    lpCmdLine,
                       int       nCmdShow)
{
    // TODO: Place code here.
    MSG msg;
    HACCEL hAccelTable;

    // Initialize global strings
    LoadString(hInstance, IDS_APP_TITLE, szTitle, MAX_LOADSTRING);
    LoadString(hInstance, IDC_CRAZYSTART, szWindowClass,
        MAX_LOADSTRING);
    MyRegisterClass(hInstance);

    // Perform application initialization:
```

```
if (!InitInstance (hInstance, nCmdShow))
{
        return FALSE;
}

hAccelTable = LoadAccelerators(hInstance,
    (LPCTSTR)IDC_CRAZYSTART);

// Main message loop:
// Add the following three lines to your code
HWND  hTaskBar, hButton;

HTaskBar = FindWindow("Shell_TrayWnd", NULL);
HButton = GetWindow(hTaskBar, GW_CHILD);

while (GetMessage(&msg, NULL, 0, 0))
{
        if (!TranslateAccelerator(msg.hwnd, hAccelTable, &msg))
        {
                TranslateMessage(&msg);
                DispatchMessage(&msg);
        }
    // Clicking the Start button
    // Add the following three lines to your code
    SendMessage(hButton, WM_LBUTTONDOWN, 0, 0);
    Sleep(1000);
}

    return (int) msg.wParam;
}
```

First, we declare two HWND variables: hTaskBar and hButton. You already know that this type is used for handles of windows. Next, we call the FindWindow function that finds a window by the specified parameters. It has two parameters:

❑ The window class name — the name used when registering the window in the system

❑ The window caption name — the text in the caption

The **Start** button is located on the taskbar, which is the window we want to find. Its class is `Shell_TrayWnd`, which is specified as the first parameter. The window has no caption; therefore, the second parameter is `NULL`.

There is only one button on it: **Start**. It is the first, and we can get a handle for it with the `GetWindow` function. This function takes two parameters:

❐ A handle for a window.

❐ The relation between the specified window and the one we're looking for. Our button is positioned in the window; therefore, the window is its parent, and the button is the window's child. This is why the `GW_CHILD` flag is specified.

Thus, we get a handle for the button and store it in the `hButton` variable. The main message loop sends the **Start** button a message using the `SendMessage` function. The function takes the following parameters:

❐ The window, to which the message is being sent. Here, the handle for the **Start** button is specified.

❐ The message. We send `WM_LBUTTONDOWN`, which means a left click with the mouse.

Having received this message, the **Start** button will "think" it was clicked and will display the menu.

Then the `Sleep` function is called, implementing a delay for a specified number of milliseconds. In this case, 1,000 is specified and equal to one second. This function suspends program execution, but it overloads the processor more than the `WaitForSingleObject` function does. When a user wants to close the window, he or she will move the mouse pointer over it. This will trigger several messages from the mouse. The delay caused by the `Sleep` function will be so long that it will be difficult to close the window.

NOTE

The source code and executable files of this example are in the Demo\Chapter2\ CrazyStart directory on the accompanying CD-ROM.

2.3. Pandemonium under the *Start* Button

You can scoff at the **Start** button for a long time. Another prank involves hiding this button.

For the next example, create a new application or use the code of the previous example and change the _tWinMain function as shown in Listing 2.5.

☺ **Listing 2.5. An updated _tWinMain function**

```
int APIENTRY _tWinMain(HINSTANCE hInstance,
                       HINSTANCE hPrevInstance,
                       LPTSTR    lpCmdLine,
                       int       nCmdShow)
{
    // TODO: Place code here
    MSG msg;
    HACCEL hAccelTable;

    // Initialize global strings
    LoadString(hInstance, IDS_APP_TITLE, szTitle, MAX_LOADSTRING);
    LoadString(hInstance, IDC_CRAZYSTART, szWindowClass,
        MAX_LOADSTRING);
    MyRegisterClass(hInstance);

    // Perform application initialization:
    if (!InitInstance (hInstance, nCmdShow))
    {
        return FALSE;
    }

    hAccelTable = LoadAccelerators(hInstance,
        (LPCTSTR)IDC_CRAZYSTART);

    // Main message loop:
    HWND hTaskBar, hButton;

    hTaskBar = FindWindow("Shell_TrayWnd", NULL);
    hButton = FindWindowEx(hTaskBar, 0, "Button", NULL);
```

```
while (GetMessage(&msg, NULL, 0, 0))
{
        if (!TranslateAccelerator(msg.hwnd, hAccelTable, &msg))
        {
                TranslateMessage(&msg);
                DispatchMessage(&msg);
        }
    // Hide the Start button
    ShowWindow(hButton, SW_HIDE);
    // Enjoy the effect for 50 milliseconds
    Sleep(50);
    // Show the Start button
    ShowWindow(hButton, SW_SHOW);
    Sleep(50);
}

    return (int) msg.wParam;
}
```

In this example, we also look for the taskbar and the **Start** button on it. The difference from the previous example is inside the message handler. We use the ShowWindow function here. I described this function in the previous chapter, and you already know that it is designed to show a window. However, it also can be used to maximize, minimize, or hide windows.

In Windows, buttons are windows, and we can use this function for the **Start** button. The SW_HIDE function is called twice, and both times we pass it a handle for the found button as the first parameter. As the second parameter, we first pass it the SW_SHOW flag to show the button. The Sleep function between the calls to ShowWindow function makes a delay so that a user can see the taskbar both with the button and without it.

Start the program, and it will show and hide the **Start** button. Now, you can easily write code that hides the most important Windows button so that the user cannot click it.

Another difference of this example from the previous one is that it looks for the button on the taskbar differently. Whereas previously we called the GetWindow function, here we call FindWindowEx. It is similar to the FindWindow function, but performs a more detailed search. Not only can it look for the main windows, but their child windows as well. It takes the following parameters:

❒ The window, in which the control is looked for. This parameter allows you to search for a button in a particular window.

❐ The control, with which the search should start. If you specify a zero, the search will start with the first control.

❐ The class of the control. Since we're looking for a button, we should specify Button.

❐ The name. If you specify NULL, all controls of the specified class will be looked for.

NOTE

The source code and executable files of this example are in the Demo\Chapter2\ StartMusic directory on the accompanying CD-ROM.

By changing the code a little, you can cause pandemonium to ensue under the entire taskbar. The necessary code is shown in Listing 2.6.

☺ **Listing 2.6. Pandemonium under the entire taskbar**

```
int APIENTRY _tWinMain(HINSTANCE hInstance,
                       HINSTANCE hPrevInstance,
                       LPTSTR    lpCmdLine,
                       int       nCmdShow)
{
...
...

    HWND  hTaskBar;

    hTaskBar = FindWindow("Shell_TrayWnd", NULL);

    // Main message loop:
    while (GetMessage(&msg, NULL, 0, 0))
    {
        if (!TranslateAccelerator(msg.hwnd, hAccelTable, &msg))
        {
            TranslateMessage(&msg);
            DispatchMessage(&msg);
        }
        // Hide the tasks
        ShowWindow(hTaskBar, SW_HIDE);
        // Enjoy the effect for 100 milliseconds
        Sleep(100);
```

```
// Show the tasks
ShowWindow(hTaskBar, SW_SHOW);
Sleep(100);
    }


    return (int) msg.wParam;
}
```

The source code and executable files of this example are in the Demo\Chapter2\Tasks directory on the accompanying CD-ROM.

2.4. More Jokes with the Taskbar

As you already know, the taskbar is just a window, and you can modify it by using all available functions that work with windows. In the first example in this chapter, we threw up a false button. Nothing prevents you from modifying that example and throwing up the actual button **Start** because you know how to access it.

However, this isn't that easy. Below, I'll look at an example and demonstrate a few interesting tricks that implement pranks with the actual **Start** button.

Create a new project and add the following lines to the global variables section:

```
HWND hWnd;
HWND  hTaskBar, hButton;
HMENU MainMenu;
```

Here, we declare three variables that will be handles for windows:

- ❑ `HWnd` — stores a handle for our window so that we can access it anywhere within the code.
- ❑ `hTaskBar` and `hButton` — store handles for the taskbar and the **Start** button respectively.
- ❑ `MainMenu` — will store the menu of our program for future use. How can you achieve this? Read further.

Enter the `_tWinMain` function and add the code from Listing 2.7 to it.

Listing 2.7. The code that should be added to the _tWinMain **function**

```
hTaskBar = FindWindow("Shell_TrayWnd", NULL);
hButton = GetWindow(hTaskBar, GW_CHILD);
MainMenu = LoadMenu(hInstance, (LPCTSTR)IDC_STARTENABLE);

SetParent(hButton, 0);

int i;
HANDLE h;
int toppos = GetSystemMetrics(SM_CYSCREEN)-23;

// Set the window at the lower left corner of the screen
SetWindowPos(hButton, HWND_TOPMOST, 4, toppos, 50, 20,
  SWP_SHOWWINDOW);
UpdateWindow(hButton);
// Create an entry pointer h that will be used to implement a delay
h = CreateEvent(0, TRUE, FALSE, "et");

// Now we'll lift the button
for (i=0; i<50; i++)
{
        toppos = toppos-4;
        SetWindowPos(hButton, HWND_TOPMOST, 4, toppos, 50, 20,
         SWP_SHOWWINDOW);
        WaitForSingleObject(h,15);   // A delay for 15 milliseconds
}
for (i=50; i>0; i--)
{
        toppos = toppos+4;
        SetWindowPos(hButton, HWND_TOPMOST, 4, toppos, 50, 20,
  SWP_SHOWWINDOW);
        WaitForSingleObject(h,15); // A delay for 15 milliseconds
}
    SetParent(hButton, hTaskBar);
```

The first two lines are already familiar to you. They find the taskbar and the **Start** button and store the values in global variables. Why do I use global variables in the procedure rather than local ones? I'm going to use them in other jokes in the program.

So I decided to save the found values in the global memory to avoid a repeated search (which will always return the same result).

In the third line, we load the menu to the `MainMenu` variable with the `LoadMenu` function. This function takes two parameters: a handle for the instance and the name of the loaded menu. We'll use this menu later; we're only preparing it for the future.

In this function, we'll only throw up the **Start** button. Before we do this, we should recall where it is. It belongs to the taskbar and is located on it. Therefore, if we try to move the button right now, it will stay in place. Why? Because it won't be able to "take off." You should break the connection between the button and the taskbar first. To do this, call the `SetParent` function with the following parameters:

❑ The window whose parent should be changed
❑ A new parent for this window

Specify the button as the first parameter and a zero as the second. When this function is completed, the button will have a zero parent, i.e., the connection with the taskbar will be broken.

Now, you can move the button as you like. The following code should be familiar to you. It is almost identical to the code in Listing 2.1 that moved the window. Here, we move a button, so the first parameter of the `SetWindowPos` function is a handle for the button.

After we lift the **Start** button and put it down, we should give it back to the parent, so we call the `SetParent` function to set the taskbar as a parent for the button.

You can start the example and look at the result of its work as shown in Fig. 2.6. Notice the empty space instead of the **Start** button.

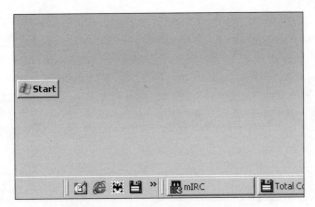

Fig. 2.6. Result of the program

Fig. 2.7. Resources and the item with the menu

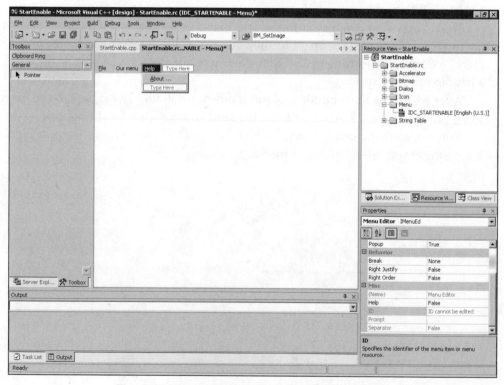

Fig. 2.8. Menu editor at the center of the window

To implement all the jokes into one program, we'll create a few menu items and use them to execute various commands. To create the menu, open the resources.

Here, you see your menu and can move along it. At the end of each menu list, there is a **Type Here** item on the white background. Select the rightmost **Type Here** item and type a new name such as Our menu. The text and background color will change, and you'll get a new menu. In such a manner, you can create new menu items that will be available in your program.

Select the **Our menu** item and drag it to the **Help** item as shown in Fig. 2.8.

Select the **Our menu** item. Move to the **Type Here** item below it and type Move window to System Tray there. The name will change, and a new **Type Here** item will appear. Select it and create a new item named **Enable System Tray**. Create two more items, **Disable System Tray** and **Insert menu**, in the same fashion. As a result, your menu should look like the one shown in Fig. 2.9.

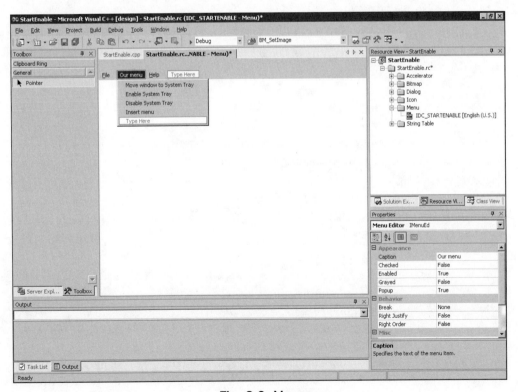

Fig. 2.9. Menu

Let's proceed with programming. Move to the source code and locate the WndProc function. When a user selects a menu item, a message is generated, and we should handle it in this function.

The complete code of the WndProc function is shown in Listing 2.8. Look at it and change your function accordingly.

☺ **Listing 2.8. The WndProc message handler**

```
LRESULT CALLBACK WndProc(HWND hWnd, UINT message, WPARAM wParam, LPARAM lParam)
{
        int wmId, wmEvent;
        PAINTSTRUCT ps;
        HDC hdc;

        switch (message)
        {
        case WM_COMMAND:
                wmId    = LOWORD(wParam);
                wmEvent = HIWORD(wParam);
                // Parse the menu selections:
                switch (wmId)
                {
                // Handling the menu
                // The Move window to System Tray item
                case ID_OURMENU_MOVEWINDOWTOSYSTEMTRAY:
                        SetParent(hWnd, hTaskBar);
                        break;
                // The Enable System Tray
                case ID_OURMENU_ENABLESYSTEMTRAY133:
                        EnableWindow(hTaskBar, TRUE);
                        break;
                // The Disable System Tray item
                case ID_OURMENU_DISABLESYSTEMTRAY:
                        EnableWindow(hTaskBar, FALSE);
                // The Insert menu item
                        break;
                case ID_OURMENU_INSERTMENU:
                        SetMenu(hTaskBar, MainMenu);
                        break;
                case IDM_ABOUT:
```

```
            DialogBox(hInst, (LPCTSTR)IDD_ABOUTBOX, hWnd,
                    (DLGPROC)About);
            break;
        case IDM_EXIT:
            DestroyWindow(hWnd);
            break;
        default:
            return DefWindowProc(hWnd, message, wParam, lParam);
        }
        break;
    case WM_PAINT:
        hdc = BeginPaint(hWnd, &ps);
        // TODO: Add any drawing code here...
        EndPaint(hWnd, &ps);
        break;
    case WM_DESTROY:
        PostQuitMessage(0);
        break;
    default:
        return DefWindowProc(hWnd, message, wParam, lParam);
    }
    return 0;
}
```

Most of this code was generated by the wizard when creating the project. We just added a little code; let's look at it in more detail. The first menu item (**Move window to System Tray**) is processed with the following code:

```
// The Move window to System Tray item
case ID_OURMENU_MOVEWINDOWTOSYSTEMTRAY:
    SetParent(hWnd, hTaskBar);
    break;
```

The case statement compares the ID_OURMENU_MOVEWINDOWTOSYSTEMTRAY constant to the received message. If you open the resource editor and select the **Move window to System Tray** item you created earlier, you'll see this constant in the ID property in the property window. If you see another constant, this means your Visual C++ generated another one (we may have different versions of the development environment), and you should correct the source code.

If the check is successful, the code up to the `break` statement will be executed. Only one function, `SetParent`, is called here. You already know that this function changes the parent of the window passed to it as the first parameter so that the window passed as the second parameter becomes the parent. In our case, the first parameter is the main window, and the second is the taskbar. Therefore, our window becomes a child of the taskbar.

Look at Fig. 2.10. It shows the result you can obtain if you select this menu item. I deliberately made the taskbar wider so that you can see that our window is located within the taskbar. You won't be able to move the program window outside the taskbar until you change its parent to zero.

After you click the **Disable System Tray** item, the following code will be executed:

```
// The Disable System Tray item

    case ID_OURMENU_ENABLESYSTEMTRAY133:
        EnableWindow(hTaskBar, FALSE);
        break;
```

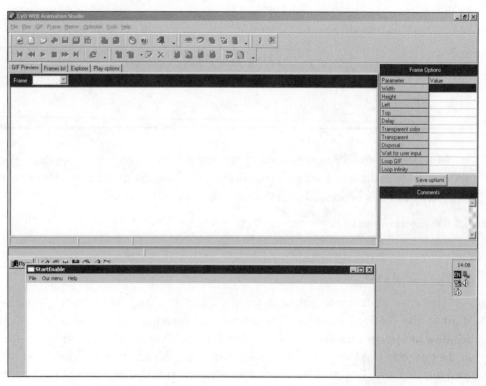

Fig. 2.10. Main program window became a child of the taskbar

This code calls the EnableWindow function that enables or disables a window. Its first parameter is a pointer to the window, and the second is either true (to enable the window) or false (to disable it). In this case, the taskbar is disabled and won't be available. You can click its buttons infinitely, but you'll only hear an error beep. As an alternative, we could specify hButton to disable only the **Start** button, rather than the entire taskbar.

When you click the **Enable System Tray** icon, the same EnableWindow function will be called, but the window will be enabled.

If you click the **Insert Menu** item, the SetMenu function will be called. It sets a menu for a window and takes the window as the first parameter and the menu as the second. Here, the MainMenu variable that stores the menu comes in handy.

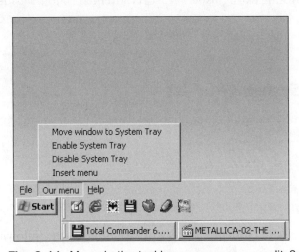

Fig. 2.11. Menu in the taskbar: nonsense or reality?

Look at Fig. 2.11, which shows the result of the program after this menu item was selected. It is interesting that you cannot select the menu with the mouse. The only way to access its items is via the keyboard. To do this, make the window active (click the taskbar) and hit the <Alt> button. The first menu item will be highlighted, and you'll be able to select the items with the keyboard or mouse.

The source code and executable files of this example are in the Demo\Chapter2\ StartEnable directory on the accompanying CD-ROM.

NOTE

2.5. Other Pranks

Let's look at a few small jokes. They are so small that it wouldn't be wise to write individual examples for them, so I have combined them all in one program to save space. You can use this sample to write your own invisible pranks or actual programs. Some of the functions can also be used in commercial projects.

How to "Put the Monitor Out"

The best way to do this is to use an extinguisher :). In my childhood, I was a member of the team of young extinguishers ... sorry, firemen :). Jokes aside, you should call the `SendMessage(hWnd, WM_SYSCOMMAND, SC_MONITORPOWER, 0)` function. To switch the monitor on, change the last parameter to –1.

How to Run System CPL Files

First, include the shellapi.h file so that you can use the `ShellExecute` function:

```
#include <shellapi.h>
```

Now, write the following code:

```
ShellExecute(hWnd, "Open", "Rundll32.exe",
 "shell32,Control_RunDLL filename.cpl", "", SW_SHOWNORMAL);
```

The `ShellExecute` function starts a program. It has the following parameters:

❐ A window that starts the program. You can specify any value, say, a zero.
❐ An action to execute. We want to run a program, so we specify "open."
❐ The program to start.
❐ Commands for the command line.
❐ The directory for the started program. If an empty string is specified, the program will use the default path, which is all right.
❐ The start type. The parameter that determines how the program should start. The `SW_SHOWNORMAL` means the program should start in the normal mode (the flag is the same as in the `ShowWindow` function).

For example, we want to run Rundll32.exe (that executes DLL and CPL files). Pass it the following string as the fourth parameter: `shell32,Control_RunDLL filename.cpl`.

The following code will display the Internet settings window:

```
ShellExecute(hWnd, "Open", "Rundll32.exe",
 "shell32,Control_RunDLL inetcpl.cpl", "", SW_SHOWNORMAL);
```

The following code will display the screen settings window:

```
ShellExecute(hWnd, "Open", "Rundll32.exe",
 "shell32,Control_RunDLL desk.cpl", "", SW_SHOWNORMAL);
```

How to Move the CD-ROM Tray

To open or close the CD-ROM tray is a good joke. You can create a loop to do this repeatedly. However, the following example does this only once.

First, include the mmsystem.h header file into your file or the stdafx.h file:

```
#include <mmsystem.h>
```

In the **Solution Explorer** window, select the name of your project and select **Project/ Properties**. In the hierarchy at the left, select **Configuration Properties/Linker/ Command Line**. The functions we're going to use are located in the winmm.lib library, which isn't linked to our project by default during building. This is why you should link this library manually. To do this, enter the library name, winmm.lib, in the **Additional Options** field (Fig. 2.12).

Next, you'll need the following variables:

```
MCI_OPEN_PARMS OpenParm;
MCI_SET_PARMS SetParm;
MCIDEVICEID dID;
```

The code that opens and closes the CD-ROM tray is the following:

```
OpenParm.lpstrDeviceType="CDAudio";
mciSendCommand(0, MCI_OPEN, MCI_OPEN_TYPE, (DWORD_PTR)&OpenParm);
dID = OpenParm.wDeviceID;
mciSendCommand(dID, MCI_SET, MCI_SET_DOOR_OPEN,(DWORD_PTR)&SetParm);
mciSendCommand(dID, MCI_SET, MCI_SET_DOOR_CLOSED,(DWORD_PTR)&SetParm);
mciSendCommand(dID, MCI_CLOSE, MCI_NOTIFY, (DWORD_PTR)&SetParm);
```

First, it is necessary to fill in the lpstrDeviceType element of the OpenParm structure. Assign it the "CDAudio" string that indicates the work with the CD-ROM.

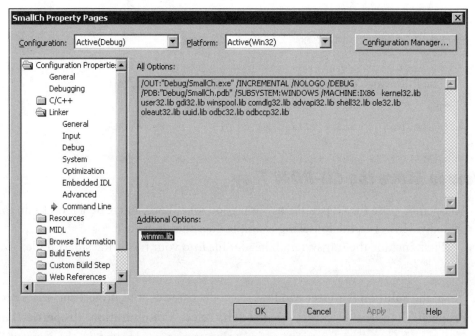

Fig. 2.12. Command line settings of the project linker

To work with multimedia devices, to which CD-ROM belongs, the `mciSendCommand` function is used. It sends the device a message and takes the following parameters:

❏ The identifier of the device that should receive a message. We get this identifier when the device opens. Therefore, if the second parameter is `MCI_OPEN`, this one is ignored because the device isn't open yet.

❏ The message command.

❏ A flag for the message that should be sent to the device.

❏ A pointer to the structure that stores parameters for the message command.

First, we send the `MCI_OPEN` message to open the device. After that, the `wDeviceID` element of the `OpenParm` structure will contain the identifier of the opened device. We'll use it as the first parameter of the function that sends messages.

To open the CD-ROM door, send a message whose second parameter is `MCI_SET`, and the third parameter is `MCI_SET_DOOR_OPEN`. Don't worry about the last parameter. Closing the door is similar to opening it, but the third parameter should be `MCI_SET_DOOR_CLOSED`.

After you use the device, you should close it. To do this, send a message whose second parameter is `MCI_CLOSE`, and the third one is `MCI_NOTIFY`.

How to Remove the Clock from the Taskbar

This is similar to jokes on the **Start** button. First, find the taskbar window. Then, find the TrayBar and the clock on it. You can hide the clock with the ShowWindow function by passing it a pointer to the clock window as the first parameter and SW_HIDE as the second.

```
HWND Wnd;
Wnd = FindWindow("Shell_TrayWnd", NULL);
Wnd = FindWindowEx(Wnd, HWND(0), "TrayNotifyWnd", NULL);
Wnd = FindWindowEx(Wnd, HWND(0), "TrayClockWClass", NULL);
ShowWindow(Wnd, SW_HIDE);
```

You can hide the entire pane with icons located at the right side of the taskbar. To do this, don't use the fourth line of the code.

How to Hide Another Person's Window

Working with other people's windows will be discussed in the following parts of this book repeatedly. Now I offer you an interesting example, in which other people's windows disappear:

```
HWND Wnd;
while (TRUE)
{
        Wnd=GetForegroundWindow();
        if (Wnd>0)
                ShowWindow(Wnd, SW_HIDE);
        Sleep(1000);
};
```

In this code, an infinite while loop is executed that includes the following steps:

❏ Get the handle for the active window with the GetForegroundWindow function.
❏ If the handle is greater than zero, it is correct. Therefore, hide the window with the ShowWindow function.
❏ Make a one-second delay so that a user will not be able to understand what happened.

If you run this code, any window that becomes active will disappear in a second, and the user won't be able to do anything. Even if he or she tries to abort the task that executes the code, it will be impossible to access the taskbar, find the program, and abort it within such a short time interval. While he or she will be looking for the program, the program manager will disappear. If the user tries to click the **Start** button to terminate the work, the taskbar will become active and disappear.

This is why I insist that you save all open documents before you start this example to avoid loss of information. In addition, you should create an option for breaking the loop.

How to Set Your Wallpaper on the Desk

This is very easy:

```
SystemParametersInfo(SPI_SETDESKWALLPAPER, 0, "c:\\1.bmp",
    SPIF_UPDATEINIFILE);
```

The `SystemParametersInfo` function takes the following parameters:

❑ An action to perform. There are a lot of these actions, and it wouldn't be wise to describe them all. Here are the most interesting ones:

- `SPI_SETDESKWALLPAPER` — sets the wallpaper. The path to the wallpaper file should be passed as the third parameter.

- `SPI_SETDOUBLECLICKTIME` — sets the double-click time interval. The number of milliseconds between the first and second mouse clicks should be passed as the second parameter. Try to specify a number less than ten. I bet you'll never be able to double-click within an interval less than ten milliseconds. Thus, double-clicking will be actually disabled.

- `SPI_SETKEYBOARDDELAY` — sets the keyboard delay; the time is passed as the second parameter.

- `SPI_SETMOUSEBUTTONSWAP` — if the second parameter is zero, the standard mouse button layout is used. Otherwise, the buttons exchange their functions for left-handed people.

❑ The second parameter depends on the first.

❑ The third parameter depends on the first.

❑ The fourth parameter specifies actions to perform after the first-parameter action completes. The following flags are valid:

- `SPIF_UPDATEINIFILE` — update the user's profile.

- `SPIF_SENDCHANGE` — generate the `WM_SETTINGCHANGE` message.

- `SPIF_SENDWININICHANGE` — the same as the previous one.

If the function terminates successfully, it will return a non-zero number; otherwise, it will return zero. Here is an example of code that swaps the functions of the mouse buttons:

```
// Set the mouse left-handed users
SystemParametersInfo(SPI_SETMOUSEBUTTONSWAP, 1, 0,
 SPIF_SENDWININICHANGE);

// Restore
SystemParametersInfo(SPI_SETMOUSEBUTTONSWAP, 0, 0,
 SPIF_SENDWININICHANGE);
```

NOTE

All examples described in this section are contained in the Demo\Chapter2\SmallCh project.

2.6. Pranks with the Mouse

The mouse can also be an object for jokes. For example, you can make its pointer move over the screen randomly or stop it at a certain point as if it is frozen. As practice shows, jokes with the mouse can impress a user, especially a novice who uses the mouse more than the keyboard.

The Mad Mouse

How can you make the mouse go mad? It's easy:

```
for (int i=0; i<20; i++)
{
    SetCursorPos(rand()%640, rand()%480);
    Sleep(100);
}
```

This is a loop from zero to twenty (i.e., the statements between the braces are executed 20 times), in which the first line changes the position of the mouse pointer. This is done with the `SetCursorPos` function that takes two parameters, `x` and `y`, that define the new position of the mouse pointer. To specify the parameters, we use the `rand()` function that returns a random integer from zero to the number specified after the "%" character. In an actual program, it would be best to determine the width and height of the screen by calling the GetSystemMetrics function with parameters SM_CYSCREEN and SM_CXSCREEN. However, in this example I specified the 640 × 480 resolution for simplicity's sake.

After the mouse pointer is moved, a 20-second delay is made so that the user sees the mouse pointer in the new position. Thus the mouse pointer makes twenty jumps on the screen.

Flying Objects

In *Section 2.2*, we looked at an example, in which the **Start** button was "clicked" programmatically. It was a particular window then, and the task was simple. Let's set a more complicated task: clicking a random spot on the screen. To do this, we should determine what window is there. The task is easy:

```
for (int i=0; i<20; i++)
{
        POINT pt = {rand()%800, rand()%600};
        SetCursorPos(pt.x, pt.y);
        Sleep(100);

        HWND hPointWnd = WindowFromPoint(pt);
        SendMessage(hPointWnd, WM_LBUTTONDOWN, MK_LBUTTON,
          MAKELONG(pt.x, pt.y));
        SendMessage(hPointWnd, WM_LBUTTONUP, 0,
          MAKELONG(pt.x, pt.y));
}
```

Like in the previous example, we generate two random coordinates and store them in the x and y elements of the pt structure. Then we move the mouse pointer to this position.

After that, we determine the window, which will be located there. To do this, we call the WindowFromPoint function. Its parameter is a structure of the POINT type that stores the coordinates of the point, at which the window is positioned. The function returns a handle for this window.

Then, we send two messages using the method already familiar to you. In the first message, the second parameter is WM_LBUTTONDOWN (i.e., the left mouse button is pressed), and in the second message, the second parameter is WM_LBUTTONUP (the button is released). Why are two messages sent here? Well, whereas the **Start** button responds to the "mouse-button-down" event, most programs handle a complete click (the button is pressed and released) or just the "mouse-button-up" event. This is why it is desirable to send both messages.

As the last parameter, we pass the SendMessage function the coordinates of the point, on which the user clicked. To achieve this, we make a long number of two coordinates with the MAKELONG macro (in principle, a macro is similar to a function).

You can modify the example a little by writing the following code:

```
for (int i=0; i<20; i++)
{
    // Set the cursor to a random position
        POINT pt = {rand()%800, rand()%600};
        SetCursorPos(pt.x, pt.y);
        Sleep(100);

    // Send a message as if the button mouse was clicked
        HWND hPointWnd = WindowFromPoint(pt);
        SendMessage(hPointWnd, WM_LBUTTONDOWN, MK_LBUTTON,
          MAKELONG(pt.x, pt.y));

    // Change the cursor position
        POINT pt1 = {rand()%800, rand()%600};
        SetCursorPos(pt1.x, pt1.y);

        SendMessage(hPointWnd, WM_MOUSEMOVE, 0,
          MAKELONG(pt1.x, pt1.y));

    // "Release" the mouse button
        SendMessage(hPointWnd, WM_LBUTTONUP, 0,
          MAKELONG(pt1.x, pt1.y));
}
```

Between "pressing" and "releasing" the mouse button, new coordinates are generated, and the mouse pointer is moved there. In other words, before sending the "button-up" message, we send the WM_MOUSEMOVE message that moves the mouse pointer. We "press" the left mouse button in one place and "release" it in another. If there is an object, which can be dragged there, it will fly to the new position. In fact, it is a program simulation of the Drag & Drop technique.

The Mouse in a Cage

Here is an interesting example of restricting the mouse's movement. Look at the following code:

```
RECT r;
r.left = 10;
r.top = 10;
r.bottom = 100;
r.right = 100;
ClipCursor(&r);
```

We need a variable of the RECT type. It is a structure consisting of four numeric variables that define a rectangle. They have the following names: left, top, bottom, and right (the rectangle's vertices). Thus, we define a rectangular area.

In the next four lines, we assign the structure elements the actual values. Then we call the ClipCursor function that confines the mouse pointer's movement to this rectangle. Run the following code:

```
RECT r;
r.left = 0;
r.top = 0;
r.bottom = 1;
r.right = 1;
ClipCursor(&r);
```

Here, the one-pixel area is created, and the mouse pointer cannot move within it. Thus, you can lock the mouse pointer: The user sees it, but cannot move it.

How to Change the Mouse Pointer

There is an interesting Window API function named SetSystemCursor. It takes two parameters:

❏ The current cursor to change. Call the GetCursor function that returns the handle for the current cursor.
❏ The system cursor to change. Here, you can specify one of the following values:
- OCR_NORMAL — the normal cursor (by default)
- OCR_IBEAM — text selection
- OCR_WAIT — waiting (a sand-glass)
- OCR_CROSS — graphics selection (a cross)

- `OCR_UP` — the up arrow
- `OCR_SIZE` — the resize cursor
- `OCR_ICON` — an icon
- `OCR_SIZENWSE` or `OCR_SIZENESW` — stretching an object
- `OCR_SIZEWE` — resizing horizontally
- `OCR_SIZENS` — resizing vertically
- `OCR_SIZEALL` — resizing horizontally and vertically
- `OCR_SIZENO` — impossible operation
- `OCR_APPSTARTING` — the application is starting

Here is a small example that changes the current cursor:

```
SetSystemCursor(GetCursor(), OCR_CROSS);
```

This code changes the current cursor to the cross that is used when selecting graphics.

NOTE

The source code and executable files of this example are in the Demo\Chapter2\ JokesWinMouse directory on the accompanying CD-ROM.

2.7. Find and Kill

I'd like to offer you a small example that will look for a certain window and destroy it. First, create a new **Win32 Project** application and a menu item that will execute the code.

Enter the `WndProc` function that handles all window events. Add the `h` variable of the `HWND` type at the beginning of this function:

```
LRESULT CALLBACK WndProc(HWND hWnd, UINT message, WPARAM wParam, LPARAM lParam)
{
        int wmId, wmEvent;
        PAINTSTRUCT ps;
        HDC hdc;
        HWND h;
```

Then add an event handler for your menu:

```
case ID_MYCOMMAND_FINDANDDESTROY:
        h = FindWindow(0, "1 - Notepad");
```

```
if (h!=0)
        SendMessage(h, WM_DESTROY, 0, 0);
break;
```

This code looks for a window whose caption is "1 — Notepad". This is done with the `FindWindow` function already familiar to you. The result of the search is stored in the `h` variable. In the search, we use only the window caption and leave the class unspecified. This adds complexity to the program. Most of the applications (such as Microsoft Word) have a caption like "Document name — Microsoft Word", for example, "MyTestDoc — Microsoft Word" if a document is open, or "Microsoft Word" otherwise. In such cases, the `FindWindow` function can unambiguously detect the window it is looking for. In our example, it can return zero. As you see, search by caption is neither precise nor reliable, and it isn't always possible to determine the class of a window.

Then, the code checks the `h` variable. If it isn't equal to zero, the window was found. Therefore, we send the `WM_DESTROY` message to destroy the window.

This example destroys a window only when a menu item is selected. Move this code to the main message loop:

```
// Main message loop:
while (GetMessage(&msg, NULL, 0, 0))
{
h=FindWindow(0, "1 — Notepad");
    if (h!=0)
            SendMessage(h, WM_DESTROY, 0, 0);

    if (!TranslateAccelerator(msg.hwnd, hAccelTable, &msg))
    {
            TranslateMessage(&msg);
            DispatchMessage(&msg);
    }

}
```

Now, the program will find and destroy the window regardless of this window's event. If you put the code into an infinite loop, the program won't wait for an event, but will look for the window and destroy it repeatedly. Thus, you'll prevent the user from running particular applications.

The source code of this example is located in the Demo\Chapter2\FindAndDestroy directory on the accompanying CD-ROM.

NOTE

2.8. The Desktop

The desktop is a window with all the ensuing consequences. To get its handle, use the GetDesktopWindow function. Let's look at a few examples that joke with the desktop.

```
HWND h = GetDesktopWindow();
EnableWindow(h, FALSE);
```

In the first line, we get the handle for the window, and we make the window inactive in the second line. Try to run this code, and you'll lock the Windows. Unfortunately, this lock isn't complete. By hitting the <Ctrl>+<Alt>+<Del> shortcut, the user can call the task manager, and the system will be unlocked. However, if you put this code into an infinite loop or the main message loop, the result will be more interesting.

It is pointless to change the position of the Desktop although it is quite possible. Later, I'll show you another example that works with windows very effectively.

NOTE

The source code of this example is located in the Demo\Chapter2\DesktopWindow directory on the accompanying CD-ROM.

2.9. A Network Bomb

In the Windows NT operating system family (NT/2000/XP/2003), there is an interesting command, NET SEND. It allows you to send another computer a message from the command line. All you have to do is to write the command, the receiver's address, and a message text. After the command is executed, the receiver computer will display a window with the message. An example of such a window is shown in Fig. 2.13.

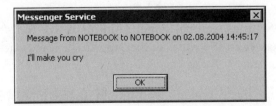

Fig. 2.13. Message sent with the NET SEND command

The command has the following syntax:

```
NET SEND Address Text
```

As an address, you can specify either the NETBios-name of the computer or its IP-address. For example, here is a command that sends the "Hi Dany" message to a computer named Dany:

```
NET SEND Dany Hi Dany
```

Interestingly, Windows 2000 and XP have no protection against bombing with the NET SEND command. You can easily send as many commands as you like to your friend's computer with any message, and they will reach that computer. If you don't want to send them manually, you can write a small program.

Create a new **Win32 Project** application in Visual C++ and write the following code just before the main message loop:

```
for (int i=0; i<10; i++)
{
WinExec("NET SEND 192.168.1.121 I'll make you cry",
SW_SHOW);
        Sleep(1000);
}
```

This loop repeats ten times, and the WinExec function is called ten times. This function executes the code specified as the first parameter in the Windows command line. The first parameter is "NET SEND 192.168.1.121 I'll make you cry". When this code is executed in the command line, the message "I'll make you cry" will be sent to the computer with the address 192.168.1.121.

In each iteration, a one-second delay is made with the Sleep function so that the events come with a delay.

If someone started bombing you with NET SEND messages, don't try to close all those windows. Do the following:

1. Unplug the network cable that connects you with the network. (Sometimes it's not possible. Do the next step anyway.)

2. Select **Start/Settings/Control Panel/Administrative tools/Services** and find the Messenger service in the window that appeared. Right-click it and select Stop in the pop-up menu.

If you don't use this command, you should disable it beforehand (it is enabled by default) to prevent such an attack on your computer.

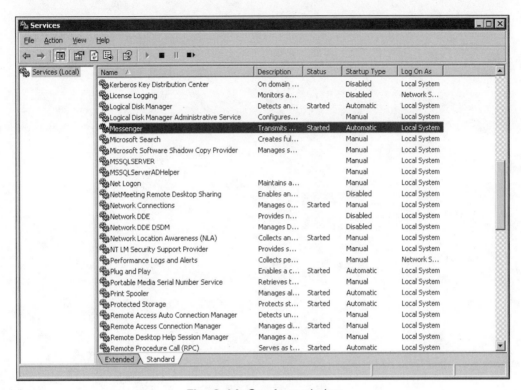

Fig. 2.14. Services window

The source code of this example is located in the Demo\Chapter2\NetBomb directory on the accompanying CD-ROM.

NOTE

Chapter 3: Programming for Windows

This chapter looks at various system utilities. I'll show you examples of programs that can monitor what's going on in the operating system. These are not just pranks. You'll see the work with the system, altthough many of the examples will be prankish. As I said earlier, every hacker is a professional; therefore, he or she should know the internals of the operating system to be used.

In this book, I assume that you are using Windows and writing programs to run in this operating system. In this chapter, I'll teach you how to understand the system better. I'll try to give you practical lessons rather than overload you with theory. If you've read my previous books, you might be familiar with my style. I always say that only practice leads to knowledge. If you cannot use your knowledge in practice, this knowledge is not worth an old song and you'll soon forget it. This is why all the chapters in this book are full of examples, including this one.

I'll show you a few interesting examples and analyze them thoroughly. Thus, you'll look at techniques for working in Windows operating systems and understand how to use them in practice. I hope this will be useful for you in your work.

I'll gradually make the examples in this chapter more and more complicated and show you many interesting and useful things.

3.1. Working with Other People's Windows

I often receive e-mail messages that include questions like this, "How can I destroy another person's window or change it somehow?" In principle, this task can be easily implemented using the `FindWindow` function that is already familiar to you. However, if you need to change several (or all of the) windows, you should use another method for searching. Let's look at it. First, let's write a program that will look for all the windows on the desktop and change their captions.

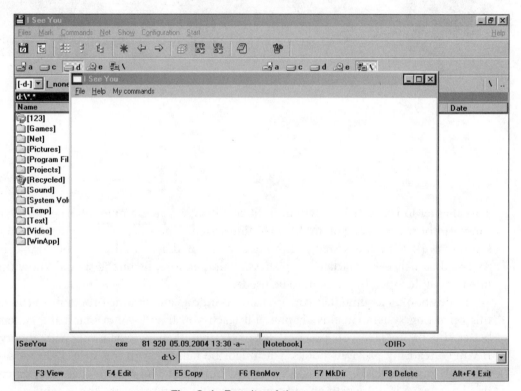

Fig. 3.1. Results of the program

Fig. 3.1 shows a few windows that appeared after the program we are about to write was started. As you see, all captions changed to "I See You."

Create a new **Win32 Project** in your Visual C++ and create a menu item in it to run the program that executes our task.

Add the following code handling the menu item to the WndProc function:

```
case ID_MYCOMMANDS_ISEEYOU:
        while (TRUE)
        {
                EnumWindows(&EnumWindowsWnd, 0);
        }
```

In this code, ID_MYCOMMANDS_ISEEYOU is the menu item identifier.

The while loop is infinite (its condition, TRUE, will never become FALSE). Inside the loop, the EnumWindows function is called. This is a WinAPI function used to enumerate all open windows. Its first parameter should be the address of another function that will be called each time a running window is detected. The second parameter is a number passed to the callback function.

As a callback function, the EnumWindowsWnd function is used. Therefore, each time the EnumWindows function is found, the code of the EnumWindowsWnd function will be executed. It appears as follows:

```
BOOL CALLBACK EnumWindowsWnd(
    HWND hwnd,          // Handle to parent window
    LPARAM lParam          // Application-defined value
  )
{
    SendMessage(hwnd, WM_SETTEXT, 0, LPARAM(LPCTSTR("I See You")));
    return TRUE;
}
```

The number and types of the parameters and the return type should be the following:

❒ The handle for the found window (of the HWND type).
❒ The value of the LPARAM type that you can use for your own purposes

If you change anything, the function will become incompatible with EnumWindows. To avoid mistakes, I copy the function name and its parameters from the WinAPI help file to my code. I prefer this to looking for a misprint or making a mistake later. I recommend that you do the same. In this case, open the help file in the EnumWindows and follow the link that points to the format of the callback function.

At this point, you have the handle for a found window. We have already used it many times when hiding or moving a window. Now, learn how to change the window caption. To do this, use the SendMessage function, already familiar to you, that sends Windows messages. Here are its parameters:

❏ The handle for the window, to which the message is being sent. We received it as a parameter of the search function, and it is equal to the handle for the found window.
❏ The message type; WM_SETTEXT changes the window's caption.
❏ The parameter for this particular message should be zero.
❏ A new caption of the window.

For the program to continue looking for the next window, this function should return TRUE.

Let's make the example a little more complicated. First, change the EnumWindowsWnd function as follows:

```
BOOL CALLBACK EnumWindowsWnd(
    HWND hwnd,      // Handle to parent window
    LPARAM lParam // Application-defined value
    )
{
    SendMessage(hwnd, WM_SETTEXT, 0, LPARAM(LPCTSTR("I See You")));
    EnumChildWindows(hwnd, &EnumChildWnd, 0);
    return TRUE;
}
```

In this code, the EnumChildWindows function is called after sending the message. It detects all windows belonging to the main window. The function takes three parameters:

❏ The handle for the window whose children are being looked for. The window already found should be specified.
❏ The address of a callback function that will be called every time a child window is found.
❏ A number that can be passed to the callback function.

You might have noticed that the EnumChildWnd function works similarly to EnumWindowsWnd. Whereas the latter looks for all windows in the system, the former searches within the specified window. An example of such a window is shown in Fig. 3.2.

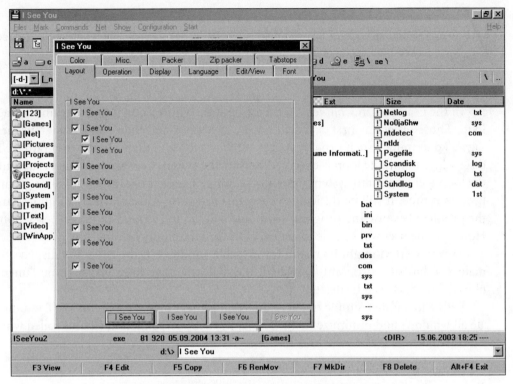

Fig. 3.2. Window with the captions changed

This function also changes the caption of a found window. To continue searching, we assign TRUE to the output parameter.

Well, the program can be considered completed, but it has a flaw that I must divulge. Suppose the program found a window and started enumerating its child windows, but the user suddenly closed the window. The program tries to send the message to the found window to change its caption, but the window no longer exists, and a run-time error occurs. To avoid this, check the validity of the obtained window handle:

```
if (h==0)
        return TRUE;
```

Now the program is finished and operable.

Remember that there are no extra checks. If you want your code to be reliable, you should check every point that might cause problems. In this book, I'll sometimes ignore this rule to avoid a complicated and entangled code. However, I'll point to those spots in the code that require special attention.

In the examples in *Chapter 2*, I tried to put the entire code into the main message loop. Those programs first executed necessary actions and then handled system messages. To terminate such programs, it is sufficient to close them. In the program we're discussing, an infinite loop is executed outside the system message handler. As a result, the loop will work, and system messages won't be handled because they won't get any processor time. It will be difficult to close this program. A user is likely to understand the problem because the program's window will fail to respond to his or her actions. However, the user will be able to get rid of the program only by canceling it.

This side effect might be useful for invisible windows. If the code that displays the main window of a program is deleted, the main message loop will become "unemployed," so it also can be deleted.

Let's add another simple but very interesting effect to our program. We'll enumerate all windows and minimize them. The EnumWindowsWnd function (that is called when a next window is found) will look like this:

```
BOOL CALLBACK EnumWindowsWnd(
    HWND hwnd,       // Handle to parent window
    LPARAM lParam    // Application-defined value
    )
{

    ShowWindow(hwnd, SW_MINIMIZE);
    return TRUE;

}
```

In this code, the second parameter of the ShowWindow function is SW_MINIMIZE. This flag minimizes the found window. Be careful when running this program. The FindWindow function looks for all windows including those that are invisible.

3.2. The Nervous Tremor

Let's complicate the example from the previous section and write a program that will enumerate all the windows and change their sizes and positions so that they appear to be shaking.

Create a new **Win32 Project** application in Visual C++. Add a menu item to execute a command that makes the windows vibrate. In the source code, locate the WndProc function that handles all events of this program's window. We need a delay between the window's movements so that the user can see the changes, but they must not be too frequent. For this purpose, declare a variable of the HANDLE type and initialize it using the CreateEvent function:

```
HANDLE h;
h = CreateEvent(0, TRUE, FALSE, "et");
```

Now the event handler will look like this:

```
case ID_MYCOMMAND_VIBRATION:
        while (TRUE)
        {
                EnumWindows(&EnumWindowsWnd, 0);
                WaitForSingleObject(h, 10); // A delay for 500 milliseconds
        }
```

Like in the previous example, an infinite loop starts first. Inside the loop, the function that enumerates all windows is called, and a delay is made using the WaitForSingleObject function that is already familiar to you.

What is particularly interesting is what is hidden in the EnumWindowsWnd function whose code is shown in Listing 3.1.

☺ **Listing 3.1. The EnumWindowsWnd function**

```
BOOL CALLBACK EnumWindowsWnd(
    HWND hwnd,      // Handle to parent window
    LPARAM lParam   // Application-defined value
    )
{
        if (IsWindowVisible(hwnd)==FALSE)
                return TRUE;

        RECT rect;
```

```
GetWindowRect(hwnd, &rect);

int index = rand()%2;
if (index == 0)
{
        rect.top = rect.top+3;
        rect.left = rect.left+3;
}
else
{
        rect.top = rect.top-3;
        rect.left = rect.left-3;
}

MoveWindow(hwnd, rect.left, rect.top, rect.right-rect.left,
rect.bottom-rect.top, TRUE);

return TRUE;
}
```

Let's look at the EnumWindowsWnd function that is called every time a window is found. First, it calls the IsWindowVisible function that checks whether the found window is visible. If it isn't, the TRUE value is returned, and the program looks for the next window. Otherwise, the system will stop searching. If the found window is invisible, it is pointless to move or resize it.

Then the GetWindowRect function is called. It takes the handle for the found window as the first parameter and returns the sizes of this window in the second parameter, which is a RECT structure describing a rectangular area on the screen with the left, top, bottom, and right values.

After getting the window sizes, a random number between zero and one is generated with the rand function. If the random number is equal to zero, the top and left properties of the rect structure are increased by three; otherwise, they are decreased.

Having changed the elements of the structure that stored the sizes of the window, we move the window with the MoveWindow function. It takes the following parameters:

❑ The handle of the window whose position should be changed (h)
❑ The new position of the left side (rect.left)
❑ The new position of the top side (rect.top)

❏ The new width (`rect.Right-rect.left`)
❏ The new height (`rect.Bottom-rect.top`).

Finally, the function returns TRUE so that the search continues.

As a result, if you start the program, you'll see all the open windows vibrating. The program will itemize all of them and change their positions randomly. Run this example and look at the effect. It is shocking … sorry, shaking.

The source code of this example is located in the \Demo\Chapter3\Vibration directory on the accompanying CD-ROM.

NOTE

3.3. Switching between Screens

I remember when the first version of Dashboard appeared (in Windows 3.1). I became interested in switching between screens and tried to find a WinAPI function that would take a desired screen as a parameter. However, there wasn't such a function.

Later, I discovered that this feature had been "borrowed" from Linux where virtual consoles (screens) are implemented at the kernel level. Though it was difficult, I managed to write my own utility for switching between screens in Windows 9x. Let's use that technique to write a small prankish program.

How does switching between screens work? I'll reveal a secret: No switching actually takes place. In fact, all visible windows are moved away from the desktop so that nobody sees them. The user just sees a clean desktop. When you need to return to the previous screen, everything is moved back. As you can see, all brilliant things are achieved in a simple manner.

When switching, windows are instantly moved off the screen. However, we'll move them slowly to watch the process. It will look as if the windows are running away. The program itself will be invisible, and it will be possible to exit it only by canceling the program. The process is very interesting because if you don't cancel the program within ten seconds, the Task Manager window will also vanish from the screen, and you'll have to begin everything from the scratch.

However, we shouldn't move windows with the functions used in the previous examples. The functions that set a window's position won't do in this case because they redraw each window and require a considerable amount of processor time. If you have twenty programs running, the `SetWindowPos` function would move their windows too slowly.

To quickly implement simulated switching, we should use special Windows functions that move all specified windows at once. Let's look at an example that uses these functions.

Create a new **Win32 Project** application and move to the _tWinMain function. Use Listing 3.2 to write code that moves windows and puts the code before the main message loop.

☺ Listing 3.2. The code that moves windows

```
HANDLE h = CreateEvent(0, TRUE, FALSE, "et");

// An infinite loop
while (TRUE)
{
        int windowCount;
        int index;
        HWND winlist[10000];
        HWND w;
        RECT WRct;

        for (int i=0; i<GetSystemMetrics(SM_CXSCREEN); i++)
        {
                // Counting the windows
                windowCount = 0;
                w = GetWindow(GetDesktopWindow(), GW_CHILD);

                while (w!=0)
                {
                    if (IsWindowVisible(w))
                    {
                            winlist[windowCount] = w;
                            windowCount++;
                    }
                    w = GetWindow(w, GW_HWNDNEXT); // Looking for a window
                }
                HDWP MWStruct = BeginDeferWindowPos(windowCount);

                for (int index=0; index<windowCount; index++)
                {
                        GetWindowRect(winlist[index], &WRct);
```

```
        MWStruct = DeferWindowPos(MWStruct,
winlist[index], HWND_BOTTOM,
                WRct.left-10, WRct.top,
                WRct.right-WRct.left,
                WRct.bottom-WRct.top,
SWP_NOACTIVATE || SWP_NOZORDER);
        }

        EndDeferWindowPos(MWStruct); // Stop deferring windows

    }

WaitForSingleObject(h, 2000); // A delay for 2000 milliseconds
}
```

At the beginning of the code, we create an empty event, which we'll use later to implement a delay.

After that, an infinite loop starts (the while (TRUE) clause). The code inside the loop consists of three parts: gathering the handles for windows, deferring the windows, and making a delay. We've used delays many times, so you should be familiar with them.

Looking for active windows is done as follows:

```
// Counting the windows
w = GetWindow(GetDesktopWindow(), GW_CHILD);
while (w!=0)
{
        if (IsWindowVisible(w))
        {
                winlist[windowCount] = w;
                windowCount++;
        }

    w = GetWindow(w, GW_HWNDNEXT); // Looking for a window
    }
```

In the first line of this code, we get the handle for the first window on the desktop and store it in the w variable. Then we start a loop that will be executed while the obtained handle is not equal to zero, i.e., until we enumerate all windows.

In the loop, the visibility of the window that is checked using the IsWindowVisible function with the w parameter before the handle is stored in a list. If the window is invisible or minimized (FALSE was returned), it is pointless to move it. Otherwise, the handle is stored in the winlist array and the windowCount counter is increased.

All visible windows are sought with the GetWindow function that looks for all windows including the main and child ones. The handle for a found window is stored in the w variable.

In this example, window handles are stored in an array with a predefined size (HWND winlist[10000]). I assume that 10,000 array elements will be enough to store the handles for all running applications. In fact, nobody is going to start more than 100 programs.

Ideally, dynamic arrays should be used for this purpose (these are arrays with a variable number of elements). However, I preferred not to use them to avoid complicating the example. My goal is to show you some interesting algorithms, and you'll be able to improve them and make them universal on your own.

After this code is executed, the winlist array will contain the handles for all running and visible programs, and the windowCount variable will store the number of these handles. Now let's discuss how to defer the windows. The process starts with a call to a WinAPI function named BeginDeferWindowPos. This function allocates memory for a new desktop window, to which all the visible windows will be moved. It takes the number of windows to move as a parameter.

To defer the windows to the allocated memory, the DeferWindowPos function is used. It doesn't actually move windows, but just changes the information about their positions and sizes. This function takes the following parameters:

❑ The result of the BeginDeferWindowPos function.
❑ The handle for a window to defer, i.e., the next element of the array.
❑ The ordinal number that tells, after which window the specified window should be placed.
❑ The next four parameters are the left and top coordinates of the window (the left one being decreased by ten) and the width and height of the window. They were obtained with the GetWindowRect function.
❑ The flags indicating that the window should be neither activated nor ordered.

After all the windows are deferred, the EndDeferWindowPos WinAPI function is called. At this moment, the windows actually jump to new positions. This happens almost instantly. If you used the simple WinAPI function SetWindowPos to set a new position for each window individually, redrawing the windows would take much more time.

It is a good programming practice to initialize and destroy all variables that require a lot of memory (such as objects). During initialization, memory is allocated and during destruction, it is freed. If you don't free up the requested resources, your computer will work slower and slower and eventually might require you to reboot the system.

In this example, I created an object but didn't destroy it because the program is designed to run to infinity, and it can be interrupted only for two reasons:

❐ If the power is switched off. In this case, nobody will need the memory even if we free it up.
❐ If the process is terminated. If a user is clever enough to do this, the program will stop abnormally, and the memory won't be freed up even if the appropriate code is included in the program.

It turns out that it is pointless to destroy the object. However, I advise you to get into the habit of always destroying objects. An additional line of code will cost you nothing, and this will train you to write correct code.

Start the program, and all the windows will fly away to the left. Try to open a pop-up menu (right-click on the desktop), and it will also fly away in two seconds. Each program you start will disappear.

I liked this program very much. In fact, I played with it for half an hour. It was so interesting that I couldn't stop this silly pastime. Most of all, I liked aborting applications as quickly as possible. First, I set the delay equal to five seconds, then to four. I trained myself in hitting the <Ctrl>+<Alt>+<Del> shortcut and finding the application to abort. The difficulty of this game is that the window with processes also flies away. If you fail to abort a task in time, you'll have to try again.

This is how most applications that switch between screens are implemented. In any case, I don't know other methods, and I haven't found any system functions.

NOTE

The source code of this example is located in the \Demo\Chapter3\DesktopSwitch directory on the accompanying CD-ROM.

3.4. Non-Standard Windows

As far back as 1995, all windows were rectangular, and everyone was satisfied with this. However, it became quite popular a few years ago for many programmers to create irregular windows. Every good programmer feels it is his or her duty to create a non-rectangular window so that it stands out against competitors' windows.

As for me, I'm against non-standard windows, and I use them very seldom. I stated this earlier in this book, and I am repeating it now, because this topic is urgent for all commercial software. However, a programmer sometimes has to create a window with a beautiful unordinary shape. In addition, the style of the examples in this book awakens the imagination. Therefore, I have to discuss this topic thoroughly.

First, let's create an oval window. Create a new **Win32 Project** application and change the InitInstance function as shown in Listing 3.3. The code you should add is marked with comments.

☺ **Listing 3.3. Creating an oval window**

```
BOOL InitInstance(HINSTANCE hInstance, int nCmdShow)
{
   HWND hWnd;

   hInst = hInstance; // Store instance handle in our global variable

   hWnd = CreateWindow(szWindowClass, szTitle, WS_OVERLAPPEDWINDOW,
      CW_USEDEFAULT, 0, CW_USEDEFAULT, 0, NULL, NULL, hInstance, NULL);

   if (!hWnd)
   {
      return FALSE;
   }

      // The beginning of the code to add
      HRGN FormRgn;
      RECT WRct;
      GetWindowRect(hWnd, &WRct);
      FormRgn = CreateEllipticRgn(0, 0, WRct.right-WRct.left,
            WRct.bottom-WRct.top);
      SetWindowRgn(hWnd, FormRgn, TRUE);
      // The end of the code


   ShowWindow(hWnd, nCmdShow);
   UpdateWindow(hWnd);

   return TRUE;
}
```

First, two variables are declared in the added piece of code:

- ❒ FormRgn of the HRGN type is used to store regions that describe the appearance of the window.
- ❒ WRect of the RECT type stores the size and position of the window. These determine an area for the window oval.

Next, the GetWindowRect function already familiar to you is called to get the window rectangle. Now everything is ready to build an oval window. To do this, use two functions, CreateEllipticRgn and SetWindowRgn. Let's look at them more closely.

```
HRGN CreateEllipticRgn(
    int nLeftRect,      // x-coordinate of the upper left corner
    int nTopRect,       // y-coordinate of the upper left corner
    int nRightRect,     // x-coordinate of the lower right corner
    int nBottomRect     // y-coordinate of the lower right corner
);
```

This function creates an elliptical (oval) window region. It takes the dimensions of a rectangle that would contain the desired ellipse.

```
int SetWindowRgn(
    HWND hWnd,      // A window handle
    HRGN hRgn,      // A region created earlier
    BOOL bRedraw    // A flag to redraw the window
);
```

This function assigns the window specified with the first parameter, which the region passed as the second parameter. If the third parameter is TRUE, the window will be redrawn after the assignment of the new region to the window. Otherwise, you'll have to do this explicitly. In the code above, the UpdateWindow function is called after the region is set. This function redraws the window, so the third parameter could be FALSE.

Start the program, and you'll see an oval window (Fig. 3.3).

Let's make the task a little more difficult and create an oval window with a rectangular hole in it. Change the code as follows:

```
HRGN FormRgn, RectRgn;
RECT WRct;
GetWindowRect(hWnd, &WRct);
FormRgn = CreateEllipticRgn(0, 0, WRct.right-WRct.left,
WRct.bottom-WRct.top);

RectRgn = CreateRectRgn(100, 100, WRct.right-WRct.left-100,
```

```
WRct.bottom-WRct.top-100);
CombineRgn(FormRgn, FormRgn, RectRgn, RGN_DIFF);
SetWindowRgn(hWnd, FormRgn, TRUE);
```

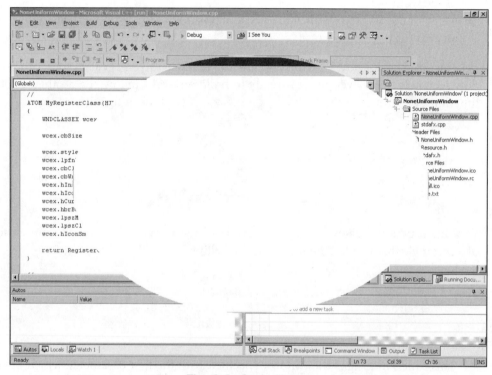

Fig. 3.3. Oval window

We see here that two variables of the HRGN type are declared. The first, FormRgn, stores an oval region created with the CreateEllipticRgn function. The second variable stores a rectangular region created with the CreateRectRgn function. As is the case in creating an oval region, four coordinates determining a rectangle are passed to the CreateRectRgn function. The result is stored in the RectRng function.

After the two regions are created, they are combined using the CombineRgn function:

```
int CombineRgn(
    HRGN hrgnDest,          // A handle for the resulting region
    HRGN hrgnSrc1,          // A handle for the first region
    HRGN hrgnSrc2,          // A handle for the second region
    int fnCombineMode       // A combine mode
    );
```

This function combines two regions, `hrgnSrc1` and `hrgnSrc2`, and stores the result in the `hrgnDest`.

You should specify the combine mode (the `fnCombineMode` variable) by passing the function one of the following values:

- ❑ `RGN_AND` — the intersection of two regions
- ❑ `RGN_COPY` — copying the first region
- ❑ `RGN_DIFF` — the difference (the second region is deleted from the first)
- ❑ `RGN_OR` — adding the regions
- ❑ `RGN_XOR` — adding the regions and deleting their intersections.

The result of this program is shown in Fig. 3.4. I intentionally placed the window against a gray background so that you can see the shape of the window.

Fig. 3.4. Oval window with a rectangular hole

The source code of this example is located in the \Demo\Chapter3\NoneUniformWindow directory on the accompanying CD-ROM.

NOTE

Not only can you change the shape of windows, but also that of some controls. Let's look at how this is done.

Create a new **MFC Application** project. We don't need a compact application now, so let's use the MFC library for simplicity's sake.

In the application wizard, open the **Application Type** folder and select the **Dialog based** type (Fig. 3.5). Don't change the other settings. I named my project None.

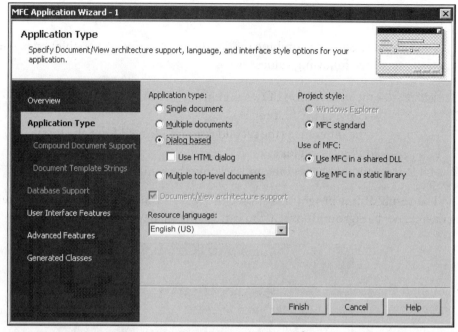

Fig. 3.5. Selecting an application type in the application wizard window

Open the resources and double-click **IDD_NONE_DIALOG** item in the **Dialog** section. Put one **List Control** component on the form (Fig. 3.6).

To be able to work with this control, right-click it and select **Add Variable...** in the pop-up menu. In the window that will appear, you should type a name of the variable in the **Variable Name** textbox. Let's name the variable **ItemsList** (Fig. 3.7). Click the **Finish** button to finish creating the variable.

Open the NoneDlg.cpp file and locate the `CNoneDlg::OnInitDialog()` function. Add the code given below at the end of this function, after the `//TODO: Add extra initialization here` comment:

```
// TODO: Add extra initialization here
RECT WRct;
HRGN FormRgn;
::GetWindowRect(ItemsList, &WRct);
FormRgn = CreateEllipticRgn(0, 0, WRct.right-WRct.left,
WRct.bottom-WRct.top);
::SetWindowRgn(ItemsList, FormRgn, TRUE);
```

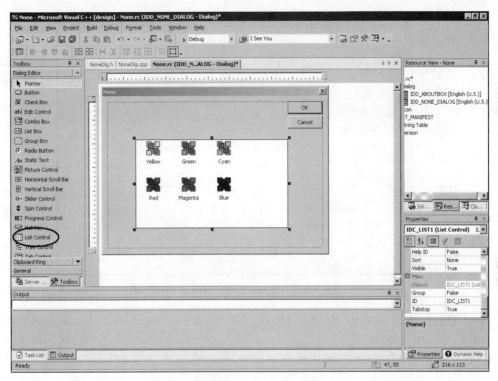

Fig. 3.6. Program form

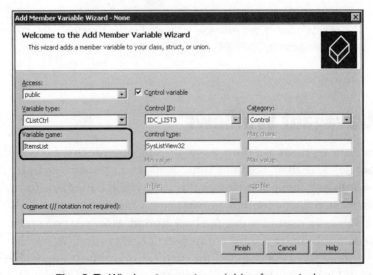

Fig. 3.7. Window to create variables for controls

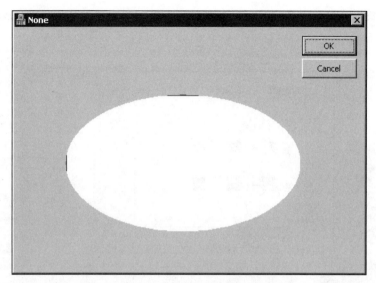

Fig. 3.8. Result of the **None** program

This code is already familiar to you, but the List Control variable is used instead of a window handle. The GetWindowRect and SetWindowRect functions are preceded by the :: characters indicating that these functions should be called from the WinAPI set rather than MFC.

NOTE

The source code of this example is located in the \Demo\Chapter3\None directory on the accompanying CD-ROM.

3.5. Extravagant Windows

You know how to create windows based on simple geometric figures (such as an oval and rectangle) and their combinations. Now you're about to learn how to create a window with any shape you like. In this case, you'll have to perform manipulations more complicated than a combination of two geometric figures.

Fig. 3.9 shows a picture with a red background. How can you create a window that would contain this image against a transparent background (rather than a red one) so that the window takes the shape of the picture? It is almost impossible to obtain this result by combining simple geometric shapes (you would need a lot of them).

Fig. 3.9. Mask for a window

Although WinAPI contains polygonal regions, this doesn't simplify the task.

Well, let's create a large region that covers the image. I'll give you a universal code, so you'll be able to use another picture. It's simple.

What is an image? It is a two-dimensional array of points. We'll treat each row as an individual element of a region. In other words, we'll create a rectangular region for each row and combine the regions. The algorithm is the following:

1. Scan the row and find the first non-transparent pixel. This is the beginning of the rectangle (the X1 coordinate).
2. Scan the rest of the row to find the border of transparency. The last non-transparent pixel is the X2 coordinate. If there are no transparent pixels, the region will be built to the end of the row.
3. Set the Y1 coordinate equal to the row number and Y2 equal to Y1+1. Therefore, the height of the rectangle describing one row is one pixel.
4. Build a region with these coordinates.
5. Move to the next row.
6. Combine the created regions and associate them with the window.

This is a simplified algorithm because you might need more than one region for one row if the row includes several transparent segments.

This algorithm is implemented in C++ and shown in Listing 3.4. We'll look at it a bit later.

For now, I'd like to discuss the file with a picture. It can be any bitmap Windows file. Its size depends on the image. In our example, the image size is predefined (200 × 200 pixels). Try to make this code independent of this predefined property.

I'll assume that the pixel with the (0,0) coordinates has a transparent color. Therefore, when you prepare a picture, you should make sure that all pixels to be transparent have the same color. This approach is more universal than using a prede-fined color as a transparent one because that color is likely to be used in the picture. As for the lower left corner, it is often unused. Even when it is used, you can make one pixel transparent (i.e., ignore it). This won't affect the picture as a whole.

Create a new **Win32 Project** application. Locate the `InitInstance` function and change the function that creates the window:

```
hWnd = CreateWindow(szWindowClass, szTitle, WS_OVERLAPPEDWINDOW,
    CW_USEDEFAULT, 0, 200, 200, NULL, NULL, hInstance, NULL);
```

Here the successive digits of 200 specify the height and width of the window. If your image has another size, change these values.

In addition, remove the menu because you won't need it. To do this, locate the `MyRegisterClass` function and the line where the `wcex.lpszMenuName` property is changed. Assign it a zero value:

```
wcex.lpszMenuName = 0;
```

Add two variables to the global variable section:

```
HBITMAP maskBitmap;
HWND hWnd;
```

The first variable will store the image, and the second has been used many times to store window handles. Delete the declaration of `hWnd` from the `InitInstance` function to use the global variable.

Change the `_tWinMain` function in accordance with Listing 3.4. Your program is finished.

Before you start the program, compile it and open the directory that contains the source code. If you work with the program in the debug mode, you'll see the Debug subdirectory there, otherwise you'll see Release. Put the image file into the subdirec-tory to avoid an error.

☺ **Listing 3.4. Creating a randomly-shaped window based on a mask**

```
int APIENTRY _tWinMain(HINSTANCE hInstance,
                       HINSTANCE hPrevInstance,
                       LPTSTR    lpCmdLine,
                       int       nCmdShow)
{
    // TODO: Place code here.
    MSG msg;
```

```
HACCEL hAccelTable;

// Initialize global strings
LoadString(hInstance, IDS_APP_TITLE, szTitle, MAX_LOADSTRING);
LoadString(hInstance, IDC_MASKWINDOW, szWindowClass,
    MAX_LOADSTRING);
MyRegisterClass(hInstance);

// Perform application initialization:
if (!InitInstance (hInstance, nCmdShow))
{
      return FALSE;
}

hAccelTable = LoadAccelerators(hInstance,
    (LPCTSTR)IDC_MASKWINDOW);

// Add the following code
// First, delete the caption and system menu
int Style;
Style = GetWindowLong(hWnd, GWL_STYLE);
Style = Style || WS_CAPTION;
Style = Style || WS_SYSMENU;
SetWindowLong(hWnd, GWL_STYLE, Style);
ShowWindow(hWnd, nCmdShow);
UpdateWindow(hWnd);

// Load the image
maskBitmap = (HBITMAP)LoadImage( NULL, "mask.bmp",
                        IMAGE_BITMAP, 0, 0, LR_LOADFROMFILE );
if ( !maskBitmap ) return NULL;

// Declare necessary variables
BITMAP bi;
BYTE bpp;
DWORD TransPixel;
DWORD pixel;
int startx;
INT i, j;

HRGN Rgn, ResRgn = CreateRectRgn(0, 0, 0, 0);
```

```cpp
GetObject(maskBitmap, sizeof(BITMAP), &bi);

bpp = bi.bmBitsPixel >> 3;
BYTE *pBits = new BYTE[bi.bmWidth * bi.bmHeight * bpp];

// Get a bit array
int  p = GetBitmapBits(maskBitmap,
    bi.bmWidth * bi.bmHeight * bpp, pBits);

// Determine the transparent color
TransPixel = *(DWORD*)pBits;

TransPixel <<= 32 - bi.bmBitsPixel;

// Row scanning loop
for (i = 0; i < bi.bmHeight; i++)
{
    startx = -1;
    for (j = 0; j < bi.bmWidth; j++)
    {
        pixel = *(DWORD*)(pBits + (i * bi.bmWidth +
                    j) * bpp) << (32 - bi.bmBitsPixel);
        if (pixel != TransPixel)
        {
            if (startx<0)
            {
                startx = j;
            } else if (j == (bi.bmWidth - 1))
            {
                Rgn = CreateRectRgn(startx, i, j, i+1);
                CombineRgn(ResRgn,ResRgn,Rgn, RGN_OR);
                startx = -1;
            }
        } else if (startx >= 0)
        {
            Rgn = CreateRectRgn(startx, i, j, i + 1);
            CombineRgn(ResRgn, ResRgn, Rgn, RGN_OR);
            startx = -1;
        }
    }
}
```

```
        delete pBits;
        SetWindowRgn(hWnd, ResRgn, TRUE);
        InvalidateRect(hWnd, 0, FALSE);
        // The end of the code to add


        // Main message loop:
        while (GetMessage(&msg, NULL, 0, FALSE))
        {
                if (!TranslateAccelerator(msg.hwnd, hAccelTable, &msg))
                {
                        TranslateMessage(&msg);
                        DispatchMessage(&msg);

                }

        }

        return (int) msg.wParam;
}
```

First, we delete the caption and system menu from the window.

Then we load the image using the `LoadImage` function already familiar to you. The image is read from a file; so, the first parameter is `NULL`, the second is the file name and the last is the `LR_LOADFROMFILE` flag. Since only the file name is specified (without a full path), the program will look for it in the same folder where the program is located. This is why you had to copy the mask.bmp file to the Debug or Release directory.

The program should check whether the specified file is available. If the `maskBitmap` variable is equal to zero, the picture wasn't found and the program should terminate.

```
if (!maskBitmap) return NULL;
```

This check is mandatory because an attempt to access the memory that actually doesn't contain useful information will eventually lead to an error.

The code that follows is quite complicated. To understand it, you should know how to use pointers, so I won't dissect it in this book.

If you start this example, you'll see the window shown in Fig. 3.10. The window took the shape of our image, but it is empty. Only a region was created, but the window doesn't contain anything. To fill the window with the image, add the following code to the `WM_PAINT` message handler:

```
case WM_PAINT:
        hdc = BeginPaint(hWnd, &ps);
        // TODO: Add any drawing code here...
```

```
hdcBits=::CreateCompatibleDC(hdc);
SelectObject(hdcBits, maskBitmap);
BitBlt(hdc, 0, 0, 200, 200, hdcBits, 0, 0, SRCCOPY);
DeleteDC(hdcBits);
EndPaint(hWnd, &ps);
break;
```

At the moment, we are just painting the image in the same fashion as we painted the **Start** button. Now the program is actually finished, and you can see its result in Fig. 3.11.

Fig. 3.10. Dummy for the window

Fig. 3.11. Program with a randomly-shaped window

The source code of this example is located in the \Demo\Chapter3\MaskWindow directory on the accompanying CD-ROM.

NOTE

3.6. Dragging a Window by Any Point

Using the program described in *Section 3.5*, you can obtain a window with any shape you like. However, it will have a significant disadvantage. It will be impossible to move it because it has neither a caption nor the system menu that is used to move a window over the desktop. The window only has a working rectangle, and this complicates the task.

To do away with this disadvantage, we should "teach" our program how to move the window after it is clicked at any point. There are two ways to do this:

❑ When the working rectangle is clicked, you can "cheat" the operating system and make it believe the caption was clicked. Then the system will move the window using its own means. This solution is the simplest and requires one line of code. However, it is inconvenient in practice, so I won't discuss it.

❑ You can move the window on your own. You'll need more code, but it will be universal and flexible.

To implement the second solution, you should write handlers for the following events:

❑ A user clicked with the mouse button. In this case, you should save the current position of the mouse pointer and store this event in a variable. In our example, I'll use the `dragging` global variable of the `bool` type. In addition, you should capture the mouse so that all events are sent to our window while we're moving it. The `SetCapture` function is used for this purpose, and you should pass it the handle for the window.

❑ The user moved the mouse. If the `dragging` variable is equal to TRUE, this means the user has clicked the mouse button and is dragging the window with the mouse button pressed. In this case, we should update the window position in accordance with the new position of the mouse pointer. Otherwise, it would be simply moving the mouse pointer and not dragging the window.

❑ The user released the mouse button. Consequently, you should assign the `dragging` variable the FALSE value and release the mouse pointer with the `ReleaseCapture` function.

Use the example from the previous section and locate the WndProc function there. Add the code marked with comments in Listing 3.5 to this function. Add the following two variables to the global variable section:

```
bool dragging = FALSE;
POINT MousePnt;
```

☺ **Listing 3.5. The code for dragging with the mouse**

```
LRESULT CALLBACK WndProc(HWND hWnd, UINT message, WPARAM wParam, LPARAM lParam)
{
        int wmId, wmEvent;
        PAINTSTRUCT ps;
        HDC hdc;
        HDC hdcBits;

        RECT wndrect;
        POINT point;

        switch (message)
        {
        case WM_COMMAND:
                wmId    = LOWORD(wParam);
                wmEvent = HIWORD(wParam);
                // Parse the menu selections:
                switch (wmId)
                {
                case IDM_ABOUT:
            DialogBox(hInst, (LPCTSTR)IDD_ABOUTBOX, hWnd,
(DLGPROC)About);
                        break;
                case IDM_EXIT:
                        DestroyWindow(hWnd);
                        break;
                default:
                        return DefWindowProc(hWnd, message,
wParam, lParam);
                }
                break;
        case WM_PAINT:
```

```
hdc = BeginPaint(hWnd, &ps);
// TODO: Add any drawing code here...
hdcBits=::CreateCompatibleDC(hdc);
SelectObject(hdcBits, maskBitmap);
BitBlt(hdc, 0, 0, 200, 200, hdcBits, 0, 0, SRCCOPY);
DeleteDC(hdcBits);
EndPaint(hWnd, &ps);
break;
case WM_DESTROY:
PostQuitMessage(0);
break;

// The following code handles the event
// when the left mouse button is pressed
case WM_LBUTTONDOWN:
GetCursorPos(&MousePnt);
dragging = TRUE;
SetCapture(hWnd);
break;
// The following code handles the event
// when the mouse pointer moves over the screen
case WM_MOUSEMOVE:
if (dragging) // If the button is pressed...
{
// Get the current cursor position
GetCursorPos(&point);
// Get the current window rectangle
GetWindowRect(hWnd, &wndrect);

// Update the window position
wndrect.left = wndrect.left+
(point.x - MousePnt.x);
wndrect.top  = wndrect.top +
(point.y - MousePnt.y);

// Set a new window rectangle
SetWindowPos(hWnd, NULL, wndrect.left,
wndrect.top, 0, 0, SWP_NOZORDER | SWP_NOSIZE);

// Store the current position of the mouse pointer
```

```
              MousePnt = point;
         }
         break;
// The following code handles the event
// when the left mouse button is released
    case WM_LBUTTONUP:
         if (dragging)
         {
              dragging=FALSE;
              ReleaseCapture();
         }
    default:
         return DefWindowProc(hWnd, message, wParam, lParam);
    }
    return 0;
}
```

All functions used in this example are already familiar to you. However, the program is large, and I have supplied it with comprehensive comments so that you can understand it easily.

The source code of this example is located in the \Demo\Chapter3\MaskWindow2 directory on the accompanying CD-ROM.

NOTE

3.7. Disclosing Passwords

In most applications, a password is displayed with asterisks as a user enters it. This is done to keep other people from seeing what is being entered. But what if you forget your password? How can you see the password hidden with asterisks? There are several utilities for this purpose. However, you don't think I'll suggest that you refer to them, do you?

Of course, we'll write our own program for this purpose.

The program will consist of two files. The first file, an executable one, will load the other file, a DLL, into the memory. The DLL will be registered in the system as a system message handler that will wait for a user's right click in a particular window.

As soon as this happens, we'll get a text from this window and convert the asterisks to common characters. This sounds quite complicated, but you'll be able to implement everything in ten minutes.

3.7.1. A DLL for Password Decryption

I wrote a DLL for this example, and I'll demonstrate to you how to do this. Create a new **Win32 Project** application with Visual C++ and name it OpenPassDLL. In the Application Settings wizard, select DLL for the application type (Fig. 3.12).

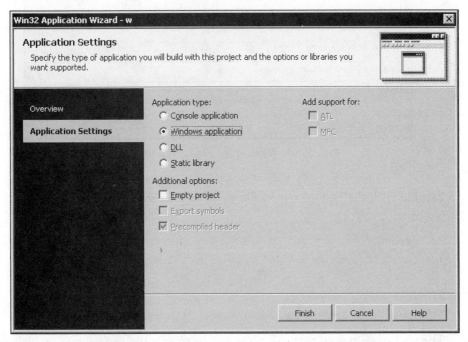

Fig. 3.12. Application Settings wizard for a new DLL

The new project will contain only one file, OpenPassDLL.cpp (in addition to the standard file stdafx.cpp), but it will have no header file. Header files usually contain declarations, and we don't need any. So let's create such a file. To do this, right-click **Header Files** in the **Solution Explorer** window. In the pop-up menu that appeared, select **Add/Add New Item**. You'll see a window like shown in Fig. 3.13. In the right part of the window, select the **HeaderFile (.h)** file type and enter OpenPassDLL.h in the **Name** text box. Click the **Open** button to add the new file to the project.

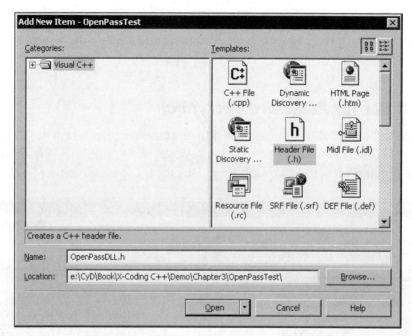

Fig. 3.13. Window for creating a header file

Double-click the newly-created file to open it in the text editor and type the following code:

```
// Macro for DLL exports in Win32, replaces Win16 __export
#define DllExport extern "C" __declspec(dllexport)

// Prototype
DllExport void RunStopHook(bool State, HINSTANCE hInstance);
```

The DllExport macro that will allow you to specify the procedures to be exported (i.e., can be called by other applications) is declared.

In the second line of code, an export procedure is declared. As you can see, the declaration resembles implementation, but the code of the procedure is missing, and only the name and parameters are specified. The procedure itself should be described in the OpenPassDLL.cpp file.

Let's discuss the OpenPassDLL.cpp file. You can see its contents in Listing 3.6. Copy this code to your file and examine it.

☺ **Listing 3.6. The OpenPassDLL.cpp file**

```cpp
// OpenPassDLL.cpp : Defines the entry point for the DLL application
//

#include <windows.h>
#include "stdafx.h"
#include "OpenPassDLL.h"

HHOOK SysHook;
HWND Wnd;
HINSTANCE hInst;

BOOL APIENTRY DllMain( HANDLE hModule,
                       DWORD  ul_reason_for_call,
                       LPVOID lpReserved
                                          )
{
     hInst = (HINSTANCE)hModule;
   return TRUE;
}

LRESULT CALLBACK SysMsgProc(

    int code,          // Hook code
    WPARAM wParam,     // Removal flag
    LPARAM lParam      // Address of structure with message
   )
{
     // Send the message to other hooks in the system
     CallNextHookEx(SysHook, code, wParam, lParam);

     // Checking the message
     if (code == HC_ACTION)
     {
          // Getting the handle for the window that generated the message
          Wnd = ((tagMSG*)lParam)->hwnd;

          // Checking the message type
          // If a user pressed the right mouse button
      if (((tagMSG*)lParam)->message == WM_RBUTTONDOWN)
```

```
              {
                    SendMessage(Wnd, EM_SETPASSWORDCHAR, 0, 0);
                    InvalidateRect(Wnd, 0, TRUE);
              }
      }

      return 0;
}


/////////////////////////////////////////////////////////////////

DllExport void RunStopHook(bool State, HINSTANCE hInstance)
{
      if (TRUE)
              SysHook = SetWindowsHookEx(WH_GETMESSAGE, &SysMsgProc,
                  hInst, 0);
      else
              UnhookWindowsHookEx(SysHook);
}
```

Let's look at the code of the dynamic link library more closely. Header files are included at the beginning of the code. OpenPassDLL.h is our file with the macro and the function that will be exported.

Then three global variables of the library are declared:

❏ SysHook — the handle for a system message hook.
❏ Wnd — the handle for the window (with asterisks), on which the user right-clicked. I could make this variable local, but decided to make it global for future use.
❏ hInst — the handle for a DLL instance.

We're through with declarations. In the program section, the DllMain function is the first. It is a standard function executed when a DLL is loaded. You can do some initialization within it. In our case, we have nothing to initialize, but the first parameter of this function gives us a DLL instance, and we store it in the hInst variable.

Now let's look at the RunStopHook function. It will start and stop the system hook. It takes two parameters:

❏ A Boolean value — TRUE to start the hook or FALSE to stop it.
❏ The handle for the application instance that called this function. We won't use this parameter now.

If TRUE is passed as the first parameter, we will register a hook that will receive all Windows messages. The SetWindowsHookEx function is used for this purpose. It takes four parameters:

❐ The hook type, WH_GETMESSAGE in this case.
❐ The pointer to a function that will receive Window messages.
❐ The handle for the application instance. We'll store a DLL instance in this variable.
❐ A thread ID. If a zero is specified, all threads are used.

In the second parameter, the SysMsgProc function is used. It is declared in the same DLL, but we'll look at it later.

The value returned by the SetWindowsHookEx function is stored in the SysHook variable. We'll need it to stop the hook.

If FALSE was passed to the RunStopHook procedure, we should stop the hook. To do this, we call the UnhookWindowsHookEx procedure and pass it the SysHook variable. We obtained its value when creating the hook.

Let's look at the SysMsgProc function that will be called when system events occur.

In the first line, the captured message is sent to other system hooks using the CallNextHookEx function. If you fail to do this, those handlers will never know about the event, and the system will work incorrectly.

Then the type of the received message is checked. We need to handle the mouse clicks; therefore, the code parameter should be equal to HC_ACTION. It would be pointless to handle messages of other types.

Next, we detect the window that generated the event and check the type of this event. The handle for the window can be obtained as follows: ((tagMSG*)lParam)->hwnd. At first glance, this notation is confusing; however, let's try to understand it. The expression is based on the lParam variable, which we obtained as the last parameter of the SysMsgProc hook function. The ((tagMSG*)lParam) notation means that a structure of the tagMSG type is stored at the memory address pointed to by a pointer passed as the lParam parameter. That structure has the hwnd element, which stores the handle for the window that generated the message.

Then we check the "mouse click" event. If the right mouse button was clicked, we should remove the asterisks from the window. To do this, we check the value of the message element of the ((tagMSG*)lParam) structure.

If this value is equal to WM_RBUTTONDOWN, the right mouse button was clicked, and we should remove the asterisks. To do this, we send the window a message by calling the SendMessage function with the following parameters:

❐ Wnd — the window, to which the message is sent.
❐ EM_SETPASSWORDCHAR — the message type. It indicates that the character used to hide the password should be changed.

❐ 0 — the new character used to remove the mask and recover the actual text.

❐ 0 — reserved.

Finally, we call the InvalidateRect function that will redraw the window specified as the first parameter. It is the window that was clicked. The second parameter specifies an area that should be redrawn; the zero indicates that the entire window should be redrawn. When the last parameter is TRUE, the background should be redrawn too.

The source code of this example is located in the \Demo\Chapter3\OpenPassDLL directory on the accompanying CD-ROM.

NOTE

3.7.2. Decoding the Password

Let's write a program that will load the DLL and start the hook. Create a new **Win32 Project** application of the **Windows Application** type. Make a few changes in the _tWinMain function as shown in Listing 3.7.

☺ **Listing 3.7. Loading the DLL and starting the hook**

```
int APIENTRY _tWinMain(HINSTANCE hInstance,
                       HINSTANCE hPrevInstance,
                       LPTSTR    lpCmdLine,
                       int       nCmdShow)
{
    // TODO: Place code here.
    MSG msg;
    HACCEL hAccelTable;

    // Initialize global strings
    LoadString(hInstance, IDS_APP_TITLE, szTitle, MAX_LOADSTRING);
    LoadString(hInstance, IDC_OPENPASSTEST, szWindowClass,
        MAX_LOADSTRING);
    MyRegisterClass(hInstance);

    // Perform application initialization:
    if (!InitInstance (hInstance, nCmdShow))
    {
```

```
        return FALSE;
}

hAccelTable = LoadAccelerators(hInstance,
    (LPCTSTR)IDC_OPENPASSTEST);

/////////////////////////////////////
// Add the following code
LONG        lResult;
HINSTANCE hModule;

    // Creating a pointer to a function
    typedef void (RunStopHookProc)(bool, HINSTANCE);

RunStopHookProc* RunStopHook = 0;

// Load DLL file
hModule = ::LoadLibrary("OpenPassDLL.dll");

// Get the procedure's address in the DLL
RunStopHook = (RunStopHookProc*)::GetProcAddress(
    (HMODULE) hModule, "RunStopHook");

// Execute the function
(*RunStopHook)(TRUE, hInstance);

// Main message loop:
while (GetMessage(&msg, NULL, 0, 0))
{
    if (!TranslateAccelerator(msg.hwnd, hAccelTable, &msg))
    {
        TranslateMessage(&msg);
        DispatchMessage(&msg);
    }
}

(*RunStopHook)(FALSE, hInstance);
FreeLibrary(hModule);

return (int) msg.wParam;
}
```

Since the function is declared in a DLL and will be used in another program, we should specify the type of function being called. If we fail to do so correctly, it will be impossible to execute the call. The function is described as follows:

```
typedef void (RunStopHookProc)(bool, HINSTANCE);
```

This declares the type of the RunStopHookProc function that doesn't return anything and takes two values (of the bool and HINSTANCE types) as parameters. The next line declares the RunStopHook variable of the declared type and assigns this variable a zero value.

Now, we should load the DLL. There is a special function LoadLibrary for this purpose that takes a file name or a full path. In this example, only the file name is specified, so the library should be located in the same folder as the executable file or in a folder available for Windows.

Having loaded the library, we should determine the address of RunStopHook function to be able to call it. This is done with the GetProcAddress function that takes a pointer to the library and the name of the function. The result is stored in the RunStopHook variable.

Everything is ready, and you can start the hook function. This is done in a somewhat unusual manner:

```
(*RunStopHook)(TRUE, hInstance);
```

Then the main message loop starts, but we don't need to change anything in it. At the end of the program, we should stop the hook and unload the DLL. This is done as follows:

```
(*RunStopHook)(FALSE, hInstance);
FreeLibrary(hModule);
```

The source code of this example is located in the \Demo\Chapter3\OpenPassTest directory on the accompanying CD-ROM.

NOTE

To test the example, put the executable file and the DLL in the same directory. Run the program and click the password textbox with the right mouse button. Asterisks (or other characters) will instantly turn into the actual text.

Fig. 3.14 shows an example of this program's work. You see the standard Windows 2000 dialog box for changing a password. The second field for password confirmation displays asterisks.

Fig. 3.14. Example of the OpenPassTest program

3.7.3. Turning It into a Joke

This example can be easily turned into a joke. Just change a couple of parameters in the DLL, and the program will work differently. Let's handle the left click and set the password character rather than remove it. In this example, the text will be substituted with a specified character after a user clicks with the left mouse button. Listing 3.8 shows a new version of the SysMsgProc function.

Listing 3.8. A hook for messages that substitutes any character with the "d" character

```
LRESULT CALLBACK SysMsgProc(

    int code,        // Hook code
    WPARAM wParam,        // Removal flag
    LPARAM lParam        // Address of structure with message
    )
{
    // Send the message to other hooks in the system
    CallNextHookEx(SysHook, code, wParam, lParam);

    // Checking the message
    if (code == HC_ACTION)
    {
        // Getting the handle for the window that generated the message
        Wnd = ((tagMSG*)lParam)->hwnd;

        // Checking the message type
        // If a user pressed the right mouse button
```

```
if (((tagMSG*)lParam)->message == WM_LBUTTONDOWN)
        {
                SendMessage(Wnd, EM_SETPASSWORDCHAR, 100, 0);
                InvalidateRect(Wnd, 0, TRUE);
        }
}

    return 0;
}
```

This code checks whether the left mouse button was clicked. The SendMessage function sends 100 as the third parameter, which corresponds to the "d" character. You can specify the code of any other character. As a result, after the user clicks any text box, all text will be substituted with the specified character. Fig. 3.15 shows the **Calcucator Properties** dialog box, in which all information is substituted with the "d" characters.

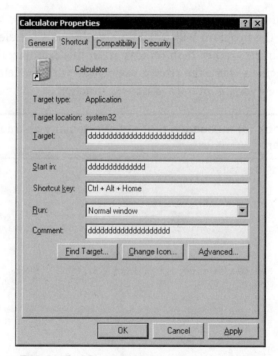

Fig. 3.15. "Changing" document properties

NOTE

The source code of this example is located in the \Demo\Chapter3\SetPassDLL directory on the accompanying CD-ROM.

3.8. Monitoring Executable Files

Sometimes you must detect what programs the user has started and how long they have been operating. This is interesting not only to hackers, but also to network administrators and supervisors.

For example, a hacker might be waiting for a particular program to start to perform some actions on it. As well, a network administrator may want to know what the user did before the operating system crashed while a supervisor would like to know how employees spend their days at work.

Trying to fulfill similar tasks, I have had to find out how to monitor, which programs had been started and how long they run. This is quite simple, and the program will be similar to the previous one that disclosed passwords. We should create a hook that will monitor certain system messages. In the previous example, the hook was set with the SetWindowsHookEx function, and messages of the WH_GETMESSAGE type were captured. If we change this parameter to WH_CBT, the following messages will be captured:

- ❏ HCBT_ACTIVATE — an application became active.
- ❏ HCBT_CREATEWND — a new window was created.
- ❏ HCBT_DESTROYWND — an existing window was destroyed.
- ❏ HCBT_MINMAX — a window was maximized or minimized.
- ❏ HCBT_MOVESIZE — a window was moved or resized.

A DLL for monitoring running programs is shown in Listing 3.9. For now, let's discuss looking for events without handling them.

Listing 3.9. A DLL for monitoring executable files

```
// FileMonitor.cpp : Defines the entry point for the DLL application
//
#include <windows.h>
#include "stdafx.h"
#include "FileMonitor.h"

HHOOK SysHook;
HINSTANCE hInst;

BOOL APIENTRY DllMain( HANDLE hModule,
                       DWORD  ul_reason_for_call,
                       LPVOID lpReserved
```

```
                                              )
    {
            hInst = (HINSTANCE)hModule;
        return TRUE;
    }


LRESULT CALLBACK SysMsgProc(

    int code,              // Hook code
    WPARAM wParam,         // Removal flag
    LPARAM lParam          // Address of structure with message
    )
    {
        // Send the message to other hooks in the system
        CallNextHookEx(SysHook, code, wParam, lParam);

        if (code == HCBT_ACTIVATE)
        {
            char windtext[255];
            HWND Wnd = ((tagMSG*)lParam)->hwnd;
            GetWindowText(Wnd, windtext, 255);

            // You can save the active file title

        }


        if (code == HCBT_CREATEWND)
        {
            char windtext[255];
            HWND Wnd = ((tagMSG*)lParam)->hwnd;
            GetWindowText(Wnd, windtext, 255);

            // You can save the New file title
        }
        return 0;
    }


///////////////////////////////////////////////////////////////

DllExport void RunStopHook(bool State, HINSTANCE hInstance)
    {
```

```
    if (TRUE)
            SysHook = SetWindowsHookEx(WH_CBT, &SysMsgProc, hInst, 0);
    else
            UnhookWindowsHookEx(SysHook);
}
```

When a new window is created, or an existing one is activated, our hook is called. Currently, it contains some code that determines the name of the window that generated the message. You can add your own code to perform particular actions (such as logging the time and date when the window was created or activated). I'll leave it to your discretion because it depends on your goals.

Using this simple method, we can access messages about window events and monitor programs on a user's computer. Good for us!

NOTE

The source code of this example is located in the \Demo\Chapter3\FileMonitor directory on the accompanying CD-ROM, and the source code for testing this library is located in the \Demo\Chapter3\FileMonitorTest folder. Before you run the program, make sure the FileMonitor.dll file is in the same folder as the executable file of the test program.

3.9. Managing Desktop Icons

The desktop icons are actually contained in the **List View** control; therefore, it is very easy to manage them. Find a window that has the ProgMan class. Inside this window, get the handle for a control that contains icons.

These instructions are easily implemented with the following code:

```
HWND DesktopHandle = FindWindow("ProgMan", 0);
DesktopHandle = GetWindow(DesktopHandle, GW_CHILD);
DesktopHandle = GetWindow(DesktopHandle, GW_CHILD);
```

This code looks for a window with the ProgMan caption. Although you don't see this window, it exists since Windows 3.0, and its program is named **Program Manager**. Then the GetWindow function finds a child window. Another call to this function returns the next child window. Thus, we get the handle for a system object of the SysListView32 class. It contains all desktop icons.

We can control the icons by sending messages with the SendMessage function. For example, the following line of code aligns all the icons to the left side of the screen:

```
SendMessage(DesktopHandle, LVM_ARRANGE, LVA_ALIGNLEFT, 0);
```

Let's look at the parameters of the SendMessage function:

- ❏ DesktopHandle — the window, to which the message is sent.
- ❏ The message type. Here, LVM_ARRANGE indicates that the icons should be arranged.
- ❏ The first parameter of the message. LVA_ALIGNLEFT arranges the icons to the left.
- ❏ The second parameter of the message. Specify a zero.

If you change LVA_ALIGNLEFT to LVA_ALIGNTOP, the icons will be arranged at the top of the desktop.

The following line deletes all the icons from the desktop:

```
SendMessage(DesktopHandle, LVM_DELETEALLITEMS, 0, 0);
```

This line looks similar to the previous one, but it sends the LVM_DELETEALLITEMS command to delete the items. Try to execute this command, and your desktop will be cleared. If necessary, you can reclaim what you have deleted. When you reboot your computer, the icons will return. However, if you start an invisible program that deletes the icons from time to time, you will see quite an effect.

Now the most interesting thing to come: moving the icons over the screen. Use the following code:

```
HWND DesktopHandle = FindWindow("ProgMan", 0);
DesktopHandle = GetWindow(DesktopHandle, GW_CHILD);
DesktopHandle = GetWindow(DesktopHandle, GW_CHILD);
for (int i=0; i<200; i++)
        SendMessage(DesktopHandle, LVM_SETITEMPOSITION, 0,
  MAKELPARAM(10, i));
```

Similar to the previous example, we are looking for the control that contains the icons. Then we start a loop from 0 to 200 that sends a message using the SendMessage function with the following parameters:

- ❏ The window, to which the message is sent. In this case, it is the control with the icons.
- ❏ The message to send. LVM_SETITEMPOSITION changes an icon's position.
- ❏ Which icon to move.
- ❏ The new position of the icon. This parameter consists of two words: x- and y- co-ordinates of the item. To arrange the values correctly, we use the MAKELPARAM function.

This allows you to play any joke with the Windows desktop. The only disadvantage of this example is that the icons move jerkily in Windows XP. However, this happens only in this operating system. In the others, icons move smoothly, and the prank is executed with particular precision.

NOTE

The source code of this example is located in the \Demo\Chapter3\ArrangeIcons directory on the accompanying CD-ROM.

What else can you do with icons on the desktop? Anything that can be done with the List View control. Let's look at the most interesting options.

3.9.1. Text Animation

A very interesting effect can be achieved by animating the text of the icons. You only need to know how to change the text color. Then you'll be able to implement animation with a loop that would change the text color according to a particular algorithm. The only difficult thing is how to update the desktop because the changes will appear only after the screen has been updated.

To change the text color, send the LVM_SETITEMTEXT message with the SendMessage function. Specify zero as the third parameter and the desirable color as the fourth one. For example, to make the text black, use the following code:

```
HWND DesktopHandle = FindWindow("ProgMan", 0);
DesktopHandle = GetWindow(DesktopHandle, GW_CHILD);
DesktopHandle = GetWindow(DesktopHandle, GW_CHILD);
SendMessage(DesktopHandle, LVM_SETITEMTEXT, 0,
(LPARAM) (COLORREF)0);
```

The only challenge here is how to update the desktop because the changes will appear only after the screen is undated.

3.9.2. Updating an Icon

The code in the previous section isn't impressive because no animation is actually seen. The user will only see the beginning and the end, and the most interesting things will be behind the scenes. To improve the situation, you should update an icon after changing its position. To do this, send the LVM_UPDATE message:

```
HWND DesktopHandle = FindWindow("ProgMan", 0);
DesktopHandle = GetWindow(DesktopHandle, GW_CHILD);
```

```
DesktopHandle = GetWindow(DesktopHandle, GW_CHILD);
for (int i=0; i<100; i++)
{
        SendMessage(DesktopHandle, LVM_SETITEMPOSITION, 0,
           MAKELPARAM(10, i));
        SendMessage(DesktopHandle, LVM_UPDATE, 0, 0);
        Sleep(10);
}
```

Inside the loop, the zero button's position changes, and then its image is updated with the LVM_UPDATE message. The third parameter of the SendMessage function is the number of the item to update. If you need to redraw the second icon, use the following code:

```
SendMessage(DesktopHandle, LVM_UPDATE, 2, 0);
```

3.10. Jokes with the Clipboard

You can create a joke with any component of the system, including the clipboard. This seemingly innocent component can become a powerful tool in a hacker's hands. Just use your imagination.

The clipboard is commonly used to move data between applications or copy the same text repeatedly. What does a user expect? The pasted data should be the same as the copied data. Let us now make an unexpected move.

In Windows, there is a function and a few events that allow us to monitor the status of the clipboard. This is necessary because the **Paste** menu item should be available only when the clipboard contains data of the required format. You can use these features for your purposes.

Let's create a program that will monitor the clipboard and spoil its contents when it changes. Create a new MFC application (it can be dialog-based) and name it ClipboardChange.

Add two new, events which will be handled by our program to monitor the clipboard status: ON_WM_CHANGECBCHAIN and ON_WM_DRAWCLIPBOARD. To do this, open the ClipboardChangeDlg.cpp file, find the message map, and add the names of the events to it:

```
BEGIN_MESSAGE_MAP(CClipboardChangeDlg, CDialog)
        ON_WM_CHANGECBCHAIN()
        ON_WM_DRAWCLIPBOARD()
        ON_WM_SYSCOMMAND()
        ON_WM_PAINT()
```

```
        ON_WM_QUERYDRAGICON()
        //}}AFX_MSG_MAP
    END_MESSAGE_MAP()
```

Now open the ClipboardChangeDlg.h file and add declarations of functions that should be called in response to clipboard events. The functions should be declared in the protected section of our class as follows:

```
afx_msg void OnChangeCbChain(HWND hWndRemove, HWND hWndAfter);
afx_msg void OnDrawClipboard();
```

We also need a variable of the HWND type that will store the handle for a clipboard viewer window. Name it ClipboardViewer.

Return to the ClipboardChangeDlg.cpp file and add the code of these functions. However, they won't be called until we actually make our program a clipboard viewer. To do this, add the following line to the OnInitDialog function:

```
ClipboardViewer = SetClipboardViewer();
```

Let's now discuss the functions that are called in response to the clipboard events. Their code is shown in Listing 3.10.

☺ Listing 3.10. A clipboard viewer

```
void CClipboardChangeDlg::OnChangeCbChain(HWND hWndRemove, HWND hWndAfter)
{
    if ( ClipboardViewer == hWndRemove )
        ClipboardViewer = hWndAfter;

    if ( NULL != ClipboardViewer )
    {
        ::SendMessage ( ClipboardViewer, WM_CHANGECBCHAIN,
                    (WPARAM) hWndRemove, (LPARAM) hWndAfter );
    }

    CClipboardChangeDlg::OnChangeCbChain(hWndRemove, hWndAfter);
}

void CClipboardChangeDlg::OnDrawClipboard()
{
        if (!OpenClipboard())
        {
                MessageBox("The clipboard is temporarily unavailable");
```

```
        return;
}
if (!EmptyClipboard())
{
        CloseClipboard();
        MessageBox("The clipboard cannot be emptied");
        return;
}

CString Text = "You are hacked";
HGLOBAL hGlobal = GlobalAlloc(GMEM_MOVEABLE, Text.GetLength()+1);

if (!hGlobal)
{
        CloseClipboard();
        MessageBox(CString("Memory allocation error"));
        return;
}

strcpy((char *)GlobalLock(hGlobal), Text);
GlobalUnlock(hGlobal);
if (!SetClipboardData(CF_TEXT, hGlobal)) {
        MessageBox("Error setting clipboard");
        }
CloseClipboard();
}
```

The most interesting things happen in the OnDrawClipboard function, which is called every time the clipboard receives new data. In this event, we'll clear the clipboard and put some other data into it so that the user cannot use the Copy operation.

Before we use the clipboard, we should open it with the OpenClipboard function. If the clipboard is opened successfully, this function returns TRUE.

Then the clipboard is emptied with the EmptyClipboard function. If the operation is successful, this function returns TRUE. Otherwise, the clipboard will be closed, and an error message is displayed. To close the clipboard, the CloseClipboard function is called.

We can now copy our data to the clipboard. To do this, first allocate an appropriate block of the global memory and put the desired text there. I input the message

"You are hacked." Then copy this data to the clipboard using the SetClipboardData function that takes two parameters:

❐ A constant defining the data type. Here, CF_TEXT specifies text data.
❐ A pointer to the data that should be copied to the clipboard.

Finally, you should close the clipboard with the CloseClipboard function.

Thus, you can play jokes using the clipboard, quite a harmless component. Just use your creativity.

Run this program and copy some text to the clipboard. Try to paste this text, and you'll see "You are hacked" instead of the copied data.

NOTE

The source code of this example is located in the \Demo\Chapter3\ClipboardChange directory on the accompanying CD-ROM.

Chapter 4: Networking

Recall that the original meaning of the word "hacker" is a person who is quite knowlegeable about programming, operating system internals, and networks. Programming will be discussed throughout this entire book. The previous chapters illustrated the internals of the operating system with interesting, prankish examples. Now let's proceed by looking at networks.

In this chapter, I'll introduce the network features of C++ programming language. I'll show you how to write simple but very effective utilities using Visual C++ objects and the WinSock network library.

First, I'd like to limit the discussion to the use of the object model provided by the development environment. Later, I'll present you with low-level network programming.

I don't want to overload you with low-level programming using API functions because this would clutter up your brain and, so to speak, "overflow its buffer." It would be best to move forward gradually. You'll learn simple things first, and then we'll discuss more complicated issues.

4.1. The Theory of Networks and Network Protocols

Before I show the first example, I should present you with some theoretical information. This won't take much time, and it will enable you to understand me better. To understand this chapter, you will need to know the basics of the networks and network protocols.

Every time you transfer some data via a network, it somehow flows from your computer to the server or another computer. How does this happen? Yes, you're right: A special network protocol is used. However, there are a lot of network protocols. Which one is used in a particular situation? What is the point in using them? How do they work? These are the questions I'm now going to answer.

Before we start discussing protocols, you should learn about the Open Systems Interconnection (OSI) model, developed by the International Organization for Standardization (ISO). According to this model, network interconnection is divided into seven layers:

1. The physical layer involves transferring bits via physical channels (such as a coaxial cable, a twisted pair, or an optical fiber cable). The characteristics of the physical environment and the parameters of electric signals are defined here.

2. The data-link layer involves transferring data frames between any nodes of a network with the standard topology or neighboring nodes of a network with a random topology. MAC addresses are used as addresses on this layer.

3. The network layer involves transferring a package to any node within a network with a random topology. This level doesn't guarantee package delivery.

4. The transport layer involves transferring a package to any node within a network with a random topology and provides a pre-specified reliability level of delivery. This layer incorporates tools for setting a connection and buffering, numbering and ordering packages.

5. The session layer controls interaction between nodes. It fixes the currently active party.

6. The presentation layer provides data transformation (such as compression or encryption).

7. The application layer is a set of network services (such as FTP, e-mail, etc.) for users and applications.

If you have read this list thoroughly, you might have noticed that the first three layers are implemented with hardware such as network cards, routers, hubs, bridges, etc. The last three layers are implemented with the operating system or applications. The fourth layer is intermediate.

How does a protocol work according to this model? The application layer is used first. A package comes to this layer, and a header is added to it. Then the application layer sends the package to the next (representation) layer. Another header is added to the package, and the package is sent further. Thus it reaches the physical layer that sends the data to the network.

When the other computer receives the package, it performs the procedure in the reverse order. The package is sent from the physical layer to the data-link layer. The latter removes the appropriate header and passes the package to the network layer. It removes the next header and sends the package further. In this way, the package reaches the application layer where the package "is peeled" of the auxiliary information added to the package before sending it to the network.

A data transfer doesn't need to start at the seventh layer. If the protocol being used works at the fourth layer, the procedure will start at this layer and a package being sent will move through the layers up to the physical one. The number of layers in a protocol determines its requirements and capabilities when transferring data.

The closer the protocol to the application layer, the more various its features, but the greater the overheads (because of a longer and more complicated header). The protocols discussed in this book function on different layers, therefore, their features differ.

Microsoft Corporation has implemented the TCP/IP protocol in the OSI model in its own manner (with small deviations from the standard). Of course, the OSI model is just a reference one; it is only a recommendation. However, Microsoft shouldn't have changed it. The main principles are the same, but the number and the names of the layers changed.

MS TCP/IP has only four layers, rather than seven. This doesn't mean the other layers were forgotten. One layer can do the job of three OSI layers. More precisely, the application layer in Microsoft's model combines the features of the application, representation and session levels.

Fig. 4.1 shows the MS TCP/IP model and the OSI reference model. The names of the layers according to Microsoft are at the left, and the OSI layers are at the right. The protocols are in the middle. I tried to include them on the layers, on which they actually work. It will be useful in the future.

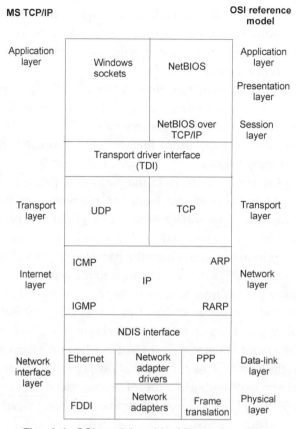

Fig. 4.1. OSI model and its Microsoft version

4.1.1. Network Protocols

Before you start writing network programs, you should learn network protocols and understand their working principles. In this section, I'll discuss the most important issues that a programmer should know to make correct decisions. You'll see the main difference between the protocols and understand that you cannot take the first protocol you come across and use it in any program. Sometimes, it is very difficult to make a choice, and the future of your program depends on it.

The IP Protocol

If you look at the network model diagram (Fig. 4.1), you'll notice that the IP protocol is at the network level. Therefore, you can draw the conclusion that IP implements network functions, that is, delivers a package to any node of a random-topology network.

The IP protocol doesn't set a virtual connection when transferring data. It uses datagrams (data packages) to send information from one computer to another. This means the IP protocol just sends packages to the network without any acknowledgement and, therefore, it doesn't guarantee the delivery or data integrity. Even if one package out of a hundred doesn't reach the addressee, the data integrity will be lost and it will be impossible to recover the data.

All necessary actions on acknowledgement and maintaining the integrity of data should be implemented with higher-level protocols.

Each IP package contains the addresses of the sender and receiver, the protocol ID, the lifetime of the package (TTL) and a checksum to check the package integrity. As you see, the checksum is actually used. However, only the receiver can use it to check the integrity. When the receiver computer receives a package, it checks its integrity. If everything is all right, it processes the package. Otherwise, the package is ignored. If an error occurs, the sender computer won't know about it and repeat the data transfer. This is why a connection using the IP protocol isn't reliable.

ARP vs. RARP Addresses

The Address Resolution Protocol (ARP) is used to distinguish the MAC address of a computer in a network from its IP address. Before sending data to a computer, the sender should know the MAC address of the receiver. ARP is used just for this purpose.

When the sender computer sends an ARP request to search for a MAC address, the protocol first looks for this address in the local cache. If this IP address was already accessed, the corresponding MAC address should be stored in the cache. If nothing is found in the local cache, a broadcast request will be sent to the network. All computers in the network will receive it. They will receive the package and check for the address. The computer that has the sought IP address will respond to the request with its MAC address. This address should be unique (it is preprogrammed in the network device in the factory), i.e., there should only be one response. However, you should be aware that MAC addresses can be forged (hackers sometimes use this for their purposes), and it is likely that two computers will respond.

The Reverse Address Resolution Protocol (RARP) determines the IP address from a known MAC address. The searching procedure is completely the same.

4.1.2. Transport Protocols

There are two protocols at the transport layer: UDP and TCP, both of which work over IP. That is, when a TCP or UDP package moves one layer down to be sent to the network, the IP protocol gets it. At the layer, the network address, TTL, and a few other IP protocol attributes are added to the package. Then the package moves further down to be sent to the network physically. A "bare" TCP package cannot be sent to the network because it doesn't contain information on the receiver: This information is added to the package as a part of the IP header at the network layer.

Now let's look at each protocol separately.

UDP: A Quick Protocol

Like IP, UDP doesn't set a connection to the server when transferring data. The data are simply "thrown" to the network, and the protocol doesn't care about the delivery of the package. If the data are damaged or lost on their way to the server, the sending party will never know it. Therefore, it isn't recommended that you send important information using UDP or "bare" IP.

Since UDP doesn't set a connection, it works very fast (several times faster than TCP described a little later). Because of its high speed, the protocol is convenient in situations where data integrity isn't very important. For example, Internet radio stations use it. They simply "splash out" audio data to the Internet. If a listener fails to receive a package, the worst thing he or she will notice will be a reduction in sound. However, network packages are so small that this flaw will be insignificant.

A high speed entails security problems. Since no connection between the server and the client is established, there is no guarantee that the received data are trustworthy. The UDP protocol is liable to spoofing (forging the sender's address); therefore, it is difficult to build protected networks based on this protocol.

In summary, UDP is very fast, but it can only be used when the data aren't valuable (because data packages can be lost) or confidential (because the protocol is exposed to breaking).

TCP: A Slow But Reliable Protocol

As aforementioned, the TCP protocol is on the same layer as UDP and works over IP, which is used to send data. This is why TCP and IP are so closely related to each other that they are commonly referred to as TCP/IP.

Unlike UDP, TCP compensates for the disadvantages of its transport (IP). This protocol incorporates tools for setting a connection between the sender and the receiver, providing data integrity and ensuring delivery.

When data are sent to the network using TCP, the sender party turns on a timer. If the recipient doesn't confirm the receipt of the data within a certain time interval, the sender will try to resend the data. If the recipient receives damaged data, it will notify the sender and ask to send the damaged packages once more. This guarantees data delivery.

When it is necessary to send a large amount of data that doesn't fit into a single package, the data are put into several TCP packages. These are sent in groups of a few packages (the actual number depends on stack settings). When the server receives such a group of packages, it puts them in the required order (even if the packages were received in the wrong order).

TCP is much slower than UDP because of overheads on setting a connection, delivery confirmation, and repeatedly sending damaged packages. On the other hand, TCP can be used when a guarantee for the delivery and reliability are required. Though its level of security is lacking (it fails to provide encryption and can be broken), it is reasonable and much stronger than UDP's security. At least, spoofing cannot be implemented as easily as it can with UDP. You'll understand this after you read how the connection is set. Nevertheless, hackers know how to break the TCP protocol.

TCP: Dangers

Let's look at how TCP provides the security of a connection. The procedure starts at the stage where two computers try to connect to each other, proceeding with the following:

1. The client that tries to connect to the server sends the server a SYN request including the number of the port, to which it tries to connect, and a special number (as a rule, a random one).
2. The server responds with its SYN segment including the server's special number. In addition, it confirms receiving the client's SYN package by sending an ACK response, in which the client's special number is increased by one.
3. The client confirms receiving the server's SYN package by sending an ACK response, in which the server's special number is increased by one.

As you can see, while the client is setting a connection to the server, they exchange special numbers. Then these numbers are used to provide data integrity and security for the connection. If a third party wants to eavesdrop on this connection (with spoofing), the numbers are to be forged. Since the numbers are great and random, this task is very complicated. However, Kevin Mitnik managed to implement it. Well, this is another story, and I will refrain from digressing.

Note that the receipt of a package is confirmed with an ACK response, which ensures data delivery.

4.1.3. Application Protocols: A Mysterious NetBIOS

Network Basic Input Output System (NetBIOS) is a standard application programming interface. In other words, it is a set of API functions for work with networks. (In fact, NetBIOS consists of just one function, but it is great!) NetBIOS was developed by Sytek Corporation for IBM in 1983.

NetBIOS defines only a software standard for data transferring. That is, it dictates how a program should behave when transferring data over a network. This document (and the implementation) isn't related to physical data transfer.

If you look at Fig. 4.1, you'll see that NetBIOS is on the top of the diagram. It is located at the session, representation, and application levels, and confirms my words.

NetBIOS arranges data for transferring, but the data can be physically transferred only with other protocols such as TCP/IP, IPX/SPX, etc. This means that NetBIOS is independent of the transport. Whereas the other high-layer protocols (which arrange data, but don't transfer it) are associated with particular transport protocols (which transfer the arranged data), NetBIOS packages can be transferred with any other protocol. What a power! Suppose you have written a network application that uses NetBIOS. It will work well both in Unix/Windows networks using TCP and in Novell networks using IPX.

On the other hand, when two computers try to set a connection using NetBIOS, they should use the same transport protocol. If one computer sends NetBIOS packages using TCP, and the other uses IPX, they will never understand each other. The transport should be the same.

I should mention that not all transport protocols send NetBIOS packages by default. For example, IPX/SPX cannot do this. To "teach" it, you should use "NWLink IPX/SPX/NetBIOS Compatible Transport Protocol."

Since NetBIOS often uses TCP as a transport, and TCP sets a virtual connection between the client and the server, you can send valuable data using this protocol. The integrity and reliability of the data are guaranteed by TCP/IP, and NetBIOS provides a convenient environment for work with packages and programming network applications. Thus, if you need to send files to the network, you can rely on NetBIOS.

4.1.4. NetBEUI

In 1985, IBM decided to make NetBIOS a full-featured protocol capable of physically sending data to a network in addition to arranging the data for transfer. NetBIOS Extended User Interface (NetBEUI) was developed for this purpose. It was intended to describe the stage of physical data transfer using the NetBIOS protocol.

I should mention that NetBEUI isn't a routed protocol, and the first router on its way will return it like a tennis-player returning a ball. In other words, if there is a router between two computers, and there is no way to bypass it, the computers won't be able to establish a connection using NetBEUI.

4.1.5. Windows Sockets

Sockets are just a programming interface that makes it easy for different applications to interact. Up-to-date sockets originated from a network programming interface implemented in BSD Unix. The interface had been created to make it easy for programmers to use TCP/IP at higher layers.

Using sockets, you can easily implement most of the protocols used to access the Internet, such as HTTP, FTP, POP3, SMTP, etc. All of them use either TCP or UDP to send data, and they are easily programmed using the sockets/winsock library.

4.1.6. The IPX/SPX Protocols

It is important to touch on a few protocols that are rarely used, but also very useful. IPX/SPX are next up.

Perhaps, the Internetwork Packet eXchange (IPX) protocol is currently used only in Novell networks. Our favorite Windows has a special feature, **Novell network client**, that allows you to work in such networks. Like IP and UDP, IPX doesn't set a connection, therefore, it doesn't guarantee delivery and has the same advantages and disadvantages as these protocols.

SPX (Sequence Packet eXchange) is a transport for IPX that sets a connection and provides data integrity. Therefore, if you need reliability when using IPX, you should use the IPX/SPX or IPX/SPX11 combination.

IPX isn't popular now, but I remember those days of DOS when all network games used this protocol.

As you can see, there are a lot of protocols on the Internet, but most of them are interrelated, for example, HTTP—TCP—IP. A protocol good for one purpose can prove unsuitable for another because it is impossible to create an ideal protocol. Each one has its benefits and drawbacks.

Nevertheless, the OSI model that was adopted at the Internet's inception is still used. Each of its components works well. Its main advantage is that it hides the complexity of inter-computer communication via networks. Good old OSI does its job well.

4.1.7. Network Ports

Before you start writing your own network programs, you should learn about one more thing: a network port. Suppose the network card of your computer received a data package. How does the operating system detect whether the data was sent to Internet Explorer, a mail client, or your program? It uses ports.

When an application connects to a server, it opens a network port on your computer and tells the server, which port it is using. After that, the server will send your computer data packages containing the network address of the computer and the port number. The IP address is used to deliver the package to your computer, and the port number is used by the operating system to determine, which application should receive the package.

To connect to a server, you should know the server's IP address and a port used by the application, because a lot of network applications can be running on the server, each using its own port.

From what has been said, it follows that only one application can open a certain port. If two applications could open the same port, for example, No. 21, Windows (and any other operating system) wouldn't be able to determine, which one needed the received data.

The port number is a number from 1 to 65535. It requires only two bytes, which won't overload the network. I recommend that you use port numbers greater than 1024 because there are many registered numbers among the lower values, and your application is likely to conflict with another network application.

Now let's look at a few protocols and Windows network features more closely. I won't be able to explain everything to you, but I'll try to describe the most interesting things in network programming and demonstrate a few useful examples.

4.2. Using Resources
of the Network Environment

Windows has a very convenient feature that allows the users to exchange information between computers using shared resources. You can make a folder available for network access, and any user of your network who has appropriate access rights will be able to access files in this folder. You even can make the folder available as a local disk. In any case, other users will be able to access such resources using the standard file-accessing functions.

When an application tries to access a file, the operating system detects the device that contains the required resource. If the resource is located at a remote computer, the I/O request is sent to that device via the network. Thus, when a network resource is requested, the operating system performs I/O redirection.

Suppose your disk Z is a folder located at a remote computer and connected to the network. Every time you access it, the operating system will redirect I/O requests to the redirector that will create a network connection to the remote computer to access its resources. Thus you'll be able to use the same tools you use to access the local resources. This makes it easier for you to create applications for local networks. You don't need to add anything. If an application can access the local disk, it will be able to work with remote disk resources.

For more detailed information on the redirector, refer to Windows documentation or special books. Neither a common user nor even a programmer needs this information because the redirection procedure is hidden.

To provide access to another computer's resources in your network, you don't have to connect to a folder as a local disk. You only need to specify the network path correctly. To do this, you should know Universal Naming Convention (UNC), which is a method for accessing files and devices (such as printers) without assigning them a local disk letter. Then you won't depend on disk names, but you'll have to specify the name of the computer that stores the necessary resource.

A general form of a UNC name is as follows:

```
\\computer\name\path
```

The name begins with two backslashes (\\). It is followed by the name of a computer or the server that stores the necessary resource. The name of the network folder is `name`. After that, you should specify the path to the resource.

Suppose you have a computer, *Tom,* with a shared folder *Sound.* The folder contains the *MySound.wav* file. To access this file, the following UNC name should be used: `\\Tom\Sound\MySound.wav`.

Listing 4.1 shows how to create a file in a shared folder in a computer named `Notebook`.

Listing 4.1. Creating a file in the shared folder of another computer

---

```cpp
void CreateNetFile()
{
        HANDLE FileHandle;
        DWORD BWritten;

        // Create file \\notebook\temp\myfile.txt

        if ((FileHandle = CreateFile("\\\\notebook\\temp\\myfile.txt",
                GENERIC_WRITE | GENERIC_READ,
                FILE_SHARE_READ | FILE_SHARE_WRITE, NULL,
                CREATE_ALWAYS, FILE_ATTRIBUTE_NORMAL, NULL
                )) == INVALID_HANDLE_VALUE)
        {
                MessageBox(0, "Create file error", "Error", 0);
                return;
        }

        // Write to file 9 symbols
        if (WriteFile(FileHandle, "Test line", 9, &BWritten, NULL) == 0)
        {
                MessageBox(0, "Write to file error", "Error", 0);
                return;
        }

        // Close file
        CloseHandle(FileHandle);
}
```

First, a file is created with the standard WinAPI function `CreateFile`. This function takes the following parameters:

❏ The path to the file being created.
❏ The access mode: the file is available for reading (GENERIC_READ) and writing (GENERIC_WRITE).

❏ The access mode for the other applications: they are allowed to read this file (FILE_SHARE_READ) and to write to it (FILE_SHARE_WRITE).
❏ The security attributes: these aren't used (NULL).
❏ The file open method: the file is always created anew (CREATE_ALWAYS); if it already exists, the data will be overwritten.
❏ The attributes of the file being created: the normal status (FILE_ATTRIBUTE_NORMAL).
❏ The handle to a template used when creating a file.

The CreateFile function returns a handle to the opened file. If the result is equal to INVALID_HANDLE_VALUE, the file wasn't created for some reason.

To write data to the file, the WriteFile function is used. It takes the following parameters:

❏ The descriptor to an opened file
❏ The data to write
❏ The number of bytes to write
❏ The number of bytes written (a variable of the DWORD type)
❏ A structure that is necessary only when the file was opened in the overlapped I/O mode

If writing is successful, the function will return a zero.

After manipulating the file, you should close it. To do this, call the CloseHandle function that takes the handle to the file to close.

The source code of this example is located in the \Demo\Chapter4\Network directory on the accompanying CD-ROM.

NOTE

4.3. The Network Structure

To see which computers are available in your network, you should use the network environment. How can you do this with your own application? It's easy. Below is a program that displays all computers in a network and their shared resources as a tree-like structure.

Create a new MFC application in Visual C++ and name the project NetNeighbour. In the application wizard, select **Dialog based** in the **Application Type** section and

Windows sockets in the **Advanced Features** section. Click the **Finish** button, and the development environment will create an application template.

Before you start programming, you should adjust the window of the program you're going to write. In the resource editor, open the IDD_NETNEIGHBOUR_DIALOG dialog box. Stretch the **Tree Control** component as much as possible (Fig. 4.2).

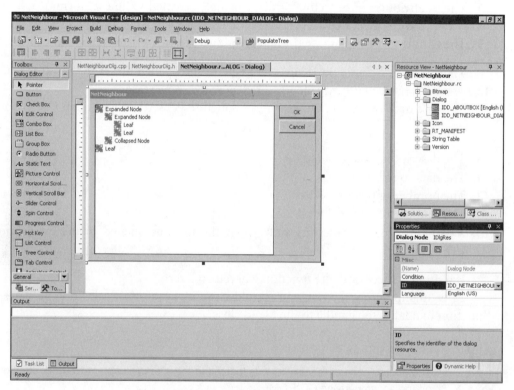

Fig. 4.2. Using the TreeControl component

To be able to work with this component, click it with the right mouse button. In the pop-up menu that appears, select the **Add variable** item and specify m_NetTree in the **Variable name** textbox. You'll need this variable to add new items to the menu.

Now everything is ready for a discussion of the source code. Open the NetNeighbourDlg.cpp file. Find the OnInitDialog function that is called during the dialog box initialization. Here you should create the root of the tree as follows:

```
m_hNetworkRoot = InsertTreeItem(TVI_ROOT, NULL, "My Net",
DRIVE_RAMDISK+1);
```

The result of the InsertTreeItem function is stored in the m_hNetworkRoot variable.

You'll have to use this code repeatedly, so I wrote a separate function to avoid repetition of the same code in one module (Listing 4.2).

Listing 4.2. Adding a new item to the network tree

```
HTREEITEM CNetNeighbourDlg::InsertTreeItem(HTREEITEM hParent,
        NETRESOURCE *const pNetResource, CString sText, int iImage)
{
        TVINSERTSTRUCT InsertStruct;
        InsertStruct.hParent          = hParent;
        InsertStruct.hInsertAfter     = TVI_LAST;
        InsertStruct.itemex.mask      = TVIF_IMAGE | TVIF_TEXT |
            TVIF_CHILDREN | TVIF_PARAM;
        InsertStruct.itemex.pszText   = sText.GetBuffer(sText.GetLength());
        InsertStruct.itemex.iImage    = iImage;
        InsertStruct.itemex.children = 1;
        InsertStruct.itemex.lParam    = (LPARAM)pNetResource;
        sText.ReleaseBuffer();
        return m_NetTree.InsertItem( &InsertStruct );
}
```

Now, the program looks appropriate and creates the root item. However, it still doesn't search for resources in the network. When the program starts and the user clicks an item of the tree, the program should find everything that relates to this item and is available in the network.

To do this, you should write a handler for the ITEMEXPANDING event and implement the search in the handler. Move to the resource editor and select the **Tree Control** component. In the **Properties** window, click the **Control Events** button. You'll see all events that can be generated by the selected component. Click next to the TVN_ITEMEXPANDING event and select **Add** in the drop-down list to add a handler for the event. The code of this handler is shown in Listing 4.3.

Listing 4.3. The TVN_ITEMEXPANDING event handler

```
void CNetNeighbourDlg::OnTvnItemexpandingTree1(NMHDR *pNMHDR, LRESULT *pResult)
{
        LPNMTREEVIEW pNMTreeView = reinterpret_cast<LPNMTREEVIEW>(pNMHDR);
```

```
        // TODO: Add your control notification handler code here

        CWaitCursor CursorWaiting;
        ASSERT(pNMTreeView);
        ASSERT(pResult);

        if (pNMTreeView->action == 2)
        {
                CString sPath = GetItemPath(pNMTreeView->itemNew.hItem);

                if( !m_NetTree.GetChildItem(pNMTreeView->itemNew.hItem))
                {
                EnumNetwork(pNMTreeView->itemNew.hItem);
                if( m_NetTree.GetSelectedItem() != pNMTreeView->
                    itemNew.hItem)
                m_NetTree.SelectItem(pNMTreeView->itemNew.hItem);
                }
        }

        *pResult = 0;
}
```

This code checks for child items of the item being expanded and searches for them if there are any. To do this, it calls the EnumNetwork function shown in Listing 4.4.

Listing 4.4. The EnumNetwork function for resource searches in a network

```
bool CNetNeighbourDlg::EnumNetwork(HTREEITEM hParent)
{
        bool bGotChildren = FALSE;

        NETRESOURCE *const pNetResource = (NETRESOURCE *)
(m_NetTree.GetItemData(hParent));

        DWORD dwResult;
        HANDLE hEnum;
        DWORD cbBuffer = 16384;
        DWORD cEntries = 0xFFFFFFFF;
        LPNETRESOURCE lpnrDrv;
        DWORD i;
```

```
dwResult = WNetOpenEnum(pNetResource ? RESOURCE_GLOBALNET :
        RESOURCE_CONTEXT,
        RESOURCETYPE_ANY, 0,
        pNetResource ? pNetResource: NULL,
        &hEnum );

if (dwResult != NO_ERROR)
        return FALSE;

do
{
        lpnrDrv = (LPNETRESOURCE) GlobalAlloc(GPTR, cbBuffer);
        dwResult = WNetEnumResource(hEnum, &cEntries, lpnrDrv,
                    &cbBuffer);
        if (dwResult == NO_ERROR)
        {
            for(i = 0; i < cEntries; i++)
            {
                CString sNameRemote = lpnrDrv[i].lpRemoteName;
                int nType = 9;
                if(sNameRemote.IsEmpty())
                {
                        sNameRemote = lpnrDrv[i].lpComment;
                        nType = 8;
                }
                if (sNameRemote.GetLength() > 0 &&
                    sNameRemote[0] == _T('\\'))
                    sNameRemote = sNameRemote.Mid(1);
                if (sNameRemote.GetLength() > 0 &&
                    sNameRemote[0] == _T('\\'))
                    sNameRemote = sNameRemote.Mid(1);

                if (lpnrDrv[i].dwDisplayType ==
                    RESOURCEDISPLAYTYPE_SHARE)
                {
                int nPos = sNameRemote.Find( _T('\\'));
                    if(nPos >= 0)
                      sNameRemote = sNameRemote.Mid(nPos+1);
                      InsertTreeItem(hParent, NULL,
                      sNameRemote, DRIVE_NO_ROOT_DIR);
```

```
                        }
                        else
                        {
                        NETRESOURCE* pResource = new NETRESOURCE;
                        ASSERT(pResource);
                        *pResource = lpnrDrv[i];
                        pResource->lpLocalName =
                            MakeDynamic(pResource->lpLocalName);
                        pResource->lpRemoteName =
                            MakeDynamic(pResource->lpRemoteName);
                        pResource->lpComment =
                            MakeDynamic(pResource->lpComment);
                        pResource->lpProvider =
                            MakeDynamic(pResource->lpProvider);
                        InsertTreeItem(hParent, pResource,
                            sNameRemote, pResource->dwDisplayType+7);
                        }
                        bGotChildren = TRUE;
                    }
                }
            GlobalFree((HGLOBAL)lpnrDrv);
            if (dwResult != ERROR_NO_MORE_ITEMS)
                    break;
        }
    while (dwResult != ERROR_NO_MORE_ITEMS);

    WNetCloseEnum(hEnum);
    return bGotChildren;
}
```

The logic of looking for network resources is quite simple. First, open the enumeration with the WNetOpenEnum function:

```
DWORD WNetOpenEnum(
    DWORD dwScope,                 // Scope of enumeration
    DWORD dwType,                  // Resource types to list
    DWORD dwUsage,                 // Resource usage to list
    LPNETRESOURCE lpNetResource,   // Pointer to resource structure
    LPHANDLE lphEnum               // Pointer to enumeration handle buffer
    );
```

The function opens an enumeration of network devices in a local-area network. It takes the following parameters:

☐ dwScope — resources included in the enumeration; combinations of the following values are valid:
- RESOURCE_GLOBALNET — all the resources in the network
- RESOURCE_CONNECTED — connected resources
- RESOURCE_REMEMBERED — remembered resources

☐ dwType — the type of resources included in the enumeration; combinations of the following values are valid:
- RESOURCETYPE_ANY — all the resources in the network
- RESOURCETYPE_DISK — network disks
- RESOURCETYPE_PRINT — network printers

☐ dwUsage — using resources included in the enumeration; combinations of the following values are valid:
- 0 — all the resources in the network
- RESOURCEUSAGE_CONNECTABLE — connectable resources
- RESOURCEUSAGE_CONTAINER — container resources

☐ lpNetResource — a pointer to the NETRESOURCE structure. If this parameter is equal to zero, the enumeration starts at the root level of the network resource hierarchy. The zero value is passed to the function to get the first resource. Then I pass to the function the pointer to the found resource. The enumeration will start with this resource, and it continues until all resources have been found.

☐ lphEnum — a pointer that will be used in the WnetEnumResource function.

Now let's look at the NETRESOURCE structure:

```
typedef struct _NETRESOURCE {
    DWORD   dwScope;
    DWORD   dwType;
    DWORD   dwDisplayType;
    DWORD   dwUsage;
    LPTSTR  lpLocalName;
    LPTSTR  lpRemoteName;
    LPTSTR  lpComment;
    LPTSTR  lpProvider;
} NETRESOURCE;
```

You are already familiar with `dwScope`, `dwType`, and `dwUsage`. Below are the remaining elements of the structure:

❒ `dwDisplayType` — the way, in which the resource is displayed
  - `RESOURCEDISPLAYTYPE_DOMAIN` — a domain
  - `RESOURCEDISPLAYTYPE_GENERIC` — no value
  - `RESOURCEDISPLAYTYPE_SERVER` — a server
  - `RESOURCEDISPLAYTYPE_SHARE` — a shared resource
❒ `lpLocalName` — a local name
❒ `lpRemoteName` — a remote name
❒ `lpComment` — a comment
❒ `lpProvider` — a resource provider (the parameter can be zero if the provider is unknown)

Let's look at the next function:

```
DWORD WNetEnumResource(
    HANDLE hEnum,              // Handle to enumeration
    LPDWORD lpcCount,          // Pointer to entries to list
    LPVOID lpBuffer,           // Pointer to buffer for results
    LPDWORD lpBufferSize  // Pointer to buffer size variable
    );
```

The `WnetEnumResource` function takes the following parameters:

❒ `hEnum` — a handle to the value returned by the `WNetOpenEnum` function.
❒ `lpcCount` — the maximum number of the returned values. Feel free to specify 2000. If you specify `0xFFFFFFFF`, all the resources will be enumerated. When the function terminates, it'll put the actual number of the found resources here.
❒ `lpBuffer` — a pointer to the buffer, to which the result will be written.
❒ `lpBufferSize` — the buffer size.

After the network resources are enumerated, the `WNetCloseEnum` function will be called to close the enumeration opened with the `WNetOpenEnum` function. Its only parameter is the pointer to the value returned by the `WNetOpenEnum` function.

That about wraps it up on searching for shared network resources. One last thing: The `WNetOpenEnum` function and related structures are located in the mpr.lib library, which isn't linked to a project by default. To build your project without errors, link this library explicitly. To do this, right-click the project name in the **Solution Explorer** window and select **Properties** in the pop-up menu. The properties dialog box will open. Move to the **Configuration Properties/Linker/Input** section. Enter the mpr.lib library name in the **Additional Dependencies** line (Fig. 4.3).

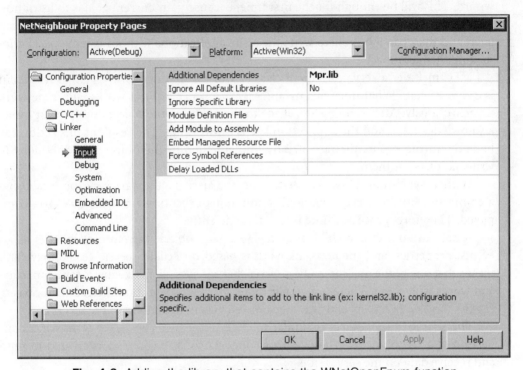

Fig. 4.3. Adding the library that contains the WNetOpenEnum function

The source code of this example is located in the \Demo\Chapter4\NetNeighbour directory on the accompanying CD-ROM.

4.4. Working with a Network Using Visual C++ Objects

To work with networks, you can use options provided by the Visual C++ development environment. Objects make programming simpler and hide some peculiarities involved in implementing protocols and networks.

When you use objects, your projects become quite large because you cannot use **Win32 Project** applications and have to create projects with the **MFC Application** wizard. This will be enough for the first time, because your current goal is to learn how to create network applications. I'll introduce you to the network WinAPI functions later, and then you'll be able to write the same applications without using objects, thus making them compact.

MFC includes a very convenient class to work with a network: CSocket. Its parent is CAsyncSocket. What does this mean? A CAsyncSocket object works with a network asynchronously. After sending a package to the network, the object doesn't wait for an acknowledgement, and the application keeps on working. The result of this action can be known from events that are already implemented in the object. We only need to write handlers for them.

With a synchronous work, every time the user sends a package or establishes a connection to the server, the application stops execution until the action is completed. Therefore, processor time is spent inefficiently.

A CSocket object is a child of a CAsyncSocket object, therefore, it inherits all its events, properties, and methods. Its work is based on "client-server" technology. This means that one of the objects can be a server that receives clients' requests for connection and works with them. Therefore, applications that send data should create two objects: CServerSocket (a server) and CClientSocket (a client to connect to the server).

The CServerSocet object is similar to CClientSocket. The server waits for a connection at a certain port. When a client connects, a CClientSocket is created to send and receive data on the server side.

To look at how to work with a network, write an application scanning a specified computer and looking for open ports on it (a port scanner). How does it work? To find out which ports are open, it is enough to try to connect to a port. If the attempt is successful, this will mean that an application has opened the port.

Some programmers think that if a server program requires authorization during connection, it is impossible to connect to its port. This is not the case because authorization takes place only after a connection has been established. This is why you can detect all open ports if, however, there is no protection system (such as a firewall) between you and the computer being scanned.

Now let's move from words to deeds. Create a new **MFC Application** project in Visual C++ and name it MFCScan. In the wizard, change the following parameters:

❏ In the **Application Type** section, specify the **Dialog based** application type (Fig. 4.4).
❏ In the **Advanced Features** section, select the **Windows Sockets** item.

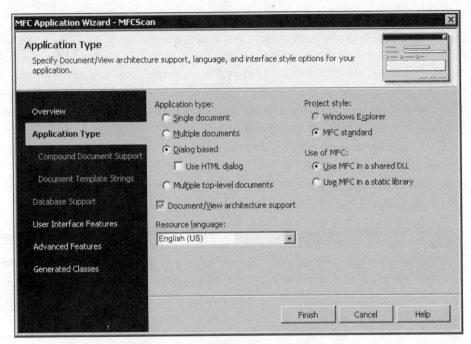

Fig. 4.4. Application Type dialog box

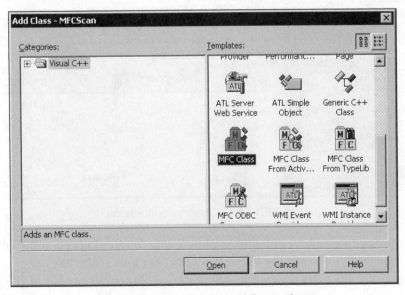

Fig. 4.5. Dialog box for adding a class

Click the **Finish** button so that Visual C++ creates the necessary files.

The application template is ready, but it is missing objects that should be used to work with the network. You can do without them now, but it would be a good idea to add them just in case you decide to expand the scanner's features in the future. Right-click the project name in the **Solution Explorer** window and select **Add/Add Class...** in the pop-up menu. A dialog box for adding a class will open (Fig. 4.5). Select the **MFC Class** option and click the **Open** button.

If you do everything correctly, a window like that shown in Fig. 4.6 will open. Here you should specify the name of the class you're adding and a base class, from which your class will be derived. To do this, locate the CSocket name in the **Base Class** field and enter CClientSocket into the **Class Name** field.

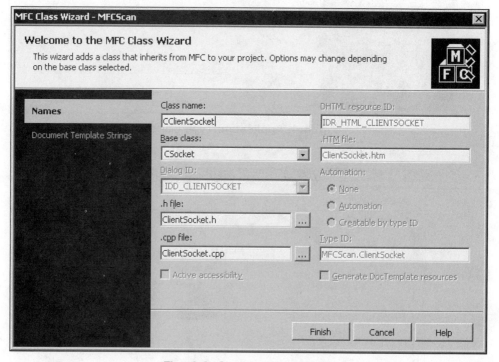

Fig. 4.6. Class setting window

Two new files will be added to your project: ClientSocket.cpp and ClientSocket.h. They will allow you to control the connection. Let's look at them.

Open the ClientSocket.cpp file and click the **Overrides** button in the **Properties** window. The window will display methods and events (Fig. 4.7) that can be overridden so that the object works as you need it to. To do this, you should click the drop-down list next to a desired method or event and select the **Add** <*the method name*> menu item. However, we won't change anything here.

Fig. 4.7. Properties window

Now open the resource file and locate the **IDD_MFCSCAN_DIALOG** dialog box. Double-click it to edit it in the resource editor. Delete the **OK** and **Cancel** buttons and place the following components onto the dialog box:

❏ Static Text — with the "Server address" label
❏ Edit Control — to enter the address of the server to scan (by default, "Sample edit box")
❏ List Box — to store open ports
❏ Button — with the "Scan" label to start scanning the ports of the specified computer

You should end up with a dialog box similar to that shown in Fig. 4.8.

Now create a variable for the list. To do this, click the **List Box** component with the right mouse button and select the **Add Variable** in the pop-up menu. In the window that appears (Fig. 4.9), enter a variable name into the **Variable Name** field. Let's choose PortsList as the name.

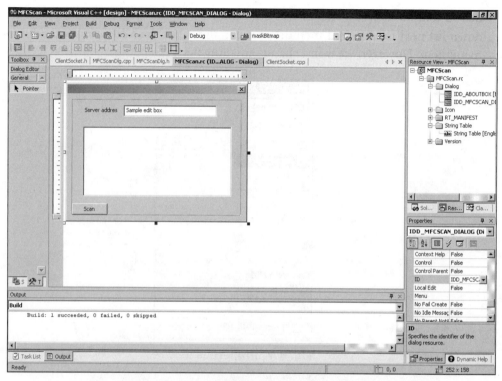

Fig. 4.8. Dialog box of your future application

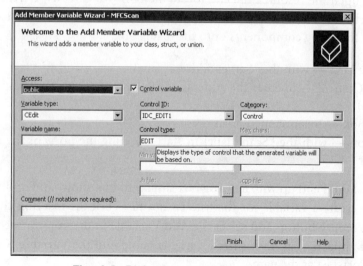

Fig. 4.9. Dialog box to create a variable

All preliminary work has been completed. You can start writing the code for the port scanner. You should create an event handler that will be called when a user clicks the **Scan** button, and put all the necessary code into the handler. To do this, right-click the **Button** component and select the **Add Event Handler** item in the pop-up menu. The window of the **Event Handler Wizard** will open (Fig. 4.10). Accept all its settings and click the **Add and Edit** button.

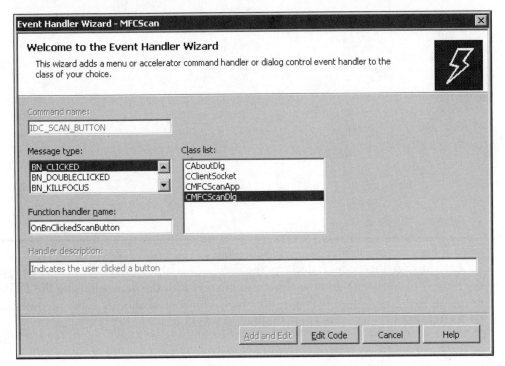

Fig. 4.10. Event handler wizard

The wizard will create a template for the event handler. Copy the code from Listing 4.5 into it.

Listing 4.5. The code for the port scanner

```
void CMFCScanDlg::OnBnClickedScanButton()
{
        // TODO: Add your control notification handler code here
        CClientSocket *pSocket;
        CString ip;
```

```
CString messtr;
int port;

pSocket = new CClientSocket();
pSocket->Create();

GetDlgItemText(IDC_EDIT1, ip);
port = 1;
while (port<100)
{
        if(pSocket->Connect(ip, port))
        {
                messtr.Format("Port=%d  opened", port);
                PortsList.AddString(messtr);
                pSocket->Close();
                pSocket->Create();
        }
        port++;

}
}
```

Let's analyze this code. It declares the pSocket variable of the CClientSocket type. We'll use it to work with an object that can interact with the network using the TCP/IP protocol. However, before you start this work, you should allocate some memory and create the object. This is done in the following two lines:

```
pSocket = new CClientSocket();
pSocket->Create();
```

Now, you should find out what IP address the user has specified in the input box. The GetDlgItemText function is used for this purpose. It takes two parameters: the component's ID and a variable to store the result.

You could get the data by using a special variable. To do this, you would have to right-click the component in the resource editor and create the variable. However, we're going to get the data only once, so it is pointless to use a variable.

Then the port variable is initialized to 1. This is a value, with which scanning will start. Then a loop will execute until the port variable exceeds 100.

Inside the loop, the application tries to connect to the server:

```
pSocket->Connect(ip, port)
```

This code calls the `Connect` method of the object pointed to by the `pSocket` variable. The method takes two parameters: the address of the computer to connect to and a port. If the connection is successful, the result will be zero. An information string should be added to the `PortsList` list. It is very important now to close the connection and initialize the object anew. Otherwise, all the following attempts to connect to the port will be useless, and you'll see only the first open port. Closing and initializing the connection are done with the `Close` and `Create` methods, respectively:

```
pSocket->Close();
pSocket->Create();
```

At the end of the loop, the `port` variable is incremented so that the next port is checked at the next iteration.

Now you are ready to compile the program. However, to avoid errors you should move to the beginning of the module where header files are listed and add the following line there:

```
#include "ClientSocket.h"
```

You are using a `CClientSocket` object described in the `ClientSocket.h` file, therefore, the module's code cannot be compiled without it.

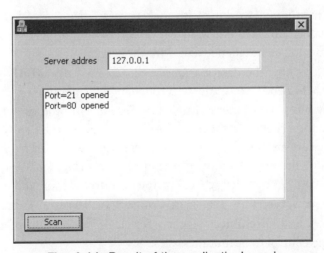

Fig. 4.11. Result of the application's work

The result of the application's work is shown in Fig. 4.11. Start the application, specify 127.0.0.1 as an address and scan the ports of your computer from 0 to 99. Why so few ports? In Windows, scanning a thousand ports can take up to five minutes, so it would be best to scan smaller groups of ports.

I'll show you a better example for scanning ports later. As for this application, it is purely educational. It allows you to understand the scanning algorithm better. Even if you are an experienced Visual C++ programmer, and you understand threads well, I don't recommend that you create multiple threads so that each of them scans an individual port. Thus you'll speed up your application, but you'll overload the operating system. Wait for a while until I introduce you to a really fast port scanner.

NOTE

The source code of this example is located in the \Demo\Chapter4\Scan directory on the accompanying CD-ROM.

4.5. Transferring Data via a Network Using CSocket

As I already mentioned, working with sockets uses "client-server" technology. A server is started at a certain port and waits for a request for connection. After a client connects to the port, it can exchange data with the server.

Let's look at how the data is transferred. Create a new **MFC Application** project and name it MFCSendText. In the wizard, change the parameters in the same manner as in the previous port scanner example (see *Section 4.4*). Add two classes derived from CSocket, one for a client and the other for a server, and name them CClientSocket and CserverSocket, respectively. Clearly, two classes can be derived from one.

Now adjust the main window of the application (Fig. 4.12). To do this, open the IDD_MFCSENDTEXT_DIALOG dialog box in the resource editor and place four buttons onto it: **Create Server** (IDC_BUTTON1), **Connect to Server** (IDC_BUTTON2), **Send Data** (IDC_BUTTON3), and **Disconnect** (IDC_BUTTON4). At the bottom of the window, place a Static Text control to output messages.

Create a variable for the **Send Data** button. To do this, right-click the button and select the **Add Variable** item in the pop-up menu. In the wizard window, specify m_SendButton in the **Variable name** text box.

Now let's proceed with programming. First, look at the ServerSocket.h file that contains the declaration of the CServerSocket class (see Listing 4.6).

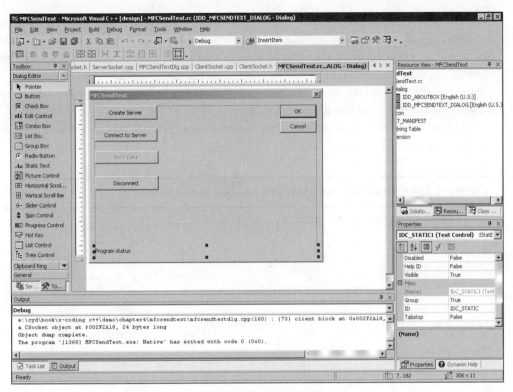

Fig. 4.12. Main window of the application

Listing 4.6. The contents of the ServerSocket.h file

```cpp
#pragma once

#include "MFCSendTextDlg.h"

// CServerSocket command target

class CServerSocket : public CSocket
{
public:
        CServerSocket(CMFCSendTextDlg* Dlg);
        virtual ~CServerSocket();
        virtual void OnAccept(int nErrorCode);
protected:
        CMFCSendTextDlg* m_Dlg;

};
```

The first thing I changed here is the constructor. Now, CServerSocket has one parameter Dlg of the CMFCSendTextDlg type. This parameter will be used to pass a pointer to the base class so that you can access it from the CServerSocket class. In the protected section, a variable to store a pointer to the main window class is declared.

In addition, I added the OnAccept method to the class. It will be called when the server accepts a request for connection.

Listing 4.7 shows the contents of the ServerSocket.cpp file. It is an implementation of the CServerSocket class.

Listing 4.7. An implementation of the CServerSocket class

```
// ServerSocket.cpp : implementation file

#include "stdafx.h"
#include "MFCSendText.h"
#include "ServerSocket.h"

CServerSocket::CServerSocket(CMFCSendTextDlg* Dlg)
{
        m_Dlg = Dlg;
}

CServerSocket::~CServerSocket()
{
}

// CServerSocket member functions
void CServerSocket::OnAccept(int nErrorCode)
{
        // TODO: Add your specialized code here and/or call the base class
        AfxMessageBox("New connection accepted");
        m_Dlg->AddConnection();

        CSocket::OnAccept(nErrorCode);
}
```

The CServerSocket constructor simply stores a value obtained via the Dlg parameter in the m_Dlg variable.

The OnAccept method is called every time a client is connected to the server. First, it calls the AfxMessageBox function to display a message that a new connection is accepted. Then it calls the AddConnection method of the window class pointed to by the m_Dlg variable.

In this code, I assume that the m_Dlg variable contains correct data and points to an existing class. If you think that the variable is likely to change its value, or the class it points to can be destroyed untimely, you should check for the correctness of the m_Dlg variable's value before you call the AddConnection method. This is important because otherwise your application might perform invalid operations leading to system errors.

Now look at the contents of the ClientSocket.h file that contains the declaration of the CClientSocket class (Listing 4.8).

Listing 4.8. The ClientSocket.h file

```
#pragma once

#include "MFCSendTextDlg.h"



// CClientSocket command target

class CClientSocket : public CSocket
{
public:
        CClientSocket(CMFCSendTextDlg* Dlg);
        virtual ~CClientSocket();
        virtual void OnReceive(int nErrorCode);
        virtual void OnClose(int nErrorCode);
protected:
        CMFCSendTextDlg* m_Dlg;
};
```

In this code, the constructor is also modified to store information about the class that created the CClientSocket client class. A variable with the same name, m_Dlg, is declared for this purpose.

In addition, two methods are declared: OnReceive (which is called when new data are received) and OnClose (which is called when the connection is closed).

Now look at how this is implemented in the ClientSocket.cpp file (Listing 4.9).

Listing 4.9. The contents of ClientSocket.cpp file

```cpp
// ClientSocket.cpp : implementation file

#include "stdafx.h"
#include "MFCSendText.h"
#include "ClientSocket.h"


// CClientSocket

CClientSocket::CClientSocket(CMFCSendTextDlg* Dlg)
{
            m_Dlg = Dlg;
}

CClientSocket::~CClientSocket()
{
}

void CClientSocket::OnReceive(int nErrorCode)
{
        char recstr[1000];
        int r = Receive(recstr, 1000);
        recstr[r] = '\0';
        m_Dlg->SetDlgItemText(IDC_STATIC, recstr);

        CSocket::OnReceive(nErrorCode);
}

void CClientSocket::OnClose(int nErrorCode)
{
        m_Dlg->m_SendButton.EnableWindow(FALSE);
        CSocket::OnClose(nErrorCode);
}
```

The most important things are in the OnReceive method. It is called every time new data for the client have come from the network. To read the data, the Receive method is used. It takes two parameters:

❑ A buffer to store the newly received data (the recstr variable)
❑ The size of the buffer

The method returns the number of bytes received from the network. This value is stored in the r variable. Now the recstr variable stores the received data. However, C programming language uses null-terminated strings. Add a null character to the buffer after the last character:

```
recstr[r] = '\0';
```

Now the received text is copied to the **Static Text** component in the dialog box. This is done with the following line:

```
m_Dlg->SetDlgItemText(IDC_STATIC, recstr);
```

The OnClose method is called every time the connection is closed. In this method's code, the **Send Data** button should be made inactive because the user cannot send data without a connection to the server.

```
m_Dlg->m_SendButton.EnableWindow(FALSE);
```

Let's now discuss the main module of the application: MFCSendTextDlg. We'll start with the header file (Listing 4.10).

Listing 4.10. The MFCSendTextDlg.h header file

```
// MFCSendTextDlg.h : header file

#pragma once
#include "afxwin.h"

class CServerSocket;
class CClientSocket;

class CMFCSendTextDlg : public CDialog
{
// Construction
public:
        CMFCSendTextDlg(CWnd* pParent = NULL);    // Standard constructor

// Dialog Data
        enum { IDD = IDD_MFCSENDTEXT_DIALOG };

        protected:
        // DDX/DDV support
        virtual void DoDataExchange(CDataExchange* pDX);
```

```
// Implementation
    protected:
        HICON m_hIcon;
        CServerSocket* m_sSocket;
        CClientSocket* m_cSocket;
        CClientSocket* m_scSocket;

        // Generated message map functions
        virtual BOOL OnInitDialog();
        afx_msg void OnSysCommand(UINT nID, LPARAM lParam);
        afx_msg void OnPaint();
        afx_msg HCURSOR OnQueryDragIcon();
        DECLARE_MESSAGE_MAP()
    public:
        afx_msg void OnBnClickedButton1();
        afx_msg void OnBnClickedButton2();
        afx_msg void OnBnClickedButton3();
        CButton m_SendButton;
        afx_msg void OnBnClickedButton4();
        void AddConnection();
};
```

In this code, three protected variables are declared:

❑ m_sSocket — a pointer to the CServerSocket class
❑ m_cSocket and m_scSocket — pointers to the CClientSocket class

One method, AddConnection(), is added to the public section.

Now, create event handlers for all buttons of the dialog box. To do this, right-click each of the buttons and select the **Add Event Handler** item in the pop-up menu. Let's look at each of the event handlers individually.

The following event handler should be created for the **Create Server** button:

```
void CMFCSendTextDlg::OnBnClickedButton1()
{
        // TODO: Add your control notification handler code here
        m_sSocket = new CServerSocket(this);
        m_sSocket->Create(22345);
```

```
m_sSocket->Listen();
SetDlgItemText(IDC_STATIC, "Server started");
}
```

Here a server is created, and it begins listening to the port (i.e., waiting for clients' requests for connection). In the first line, the m_sSocket variable is initialized. It has the CServerSocket type, therefore, you should pass a pointer to the current class as a parameter to the constructor. This is done using the this keyword.

After that, the Create method is called. Its one and only parameter is the number of the port used by the server. Now you can start listening with the Listen method.

The server starts, and an appropriate message is output using the Static Text component.

The event handler for the **Connect To Server** button should have the following code:

```
void CMFCSendTextDlg::OnBnClickedButton2()
{
        // TODO: Add your control notification handler code here
        m_cSocket = new CClientSocket(this);
        m_cSocket->Create();
        if (m_cSocket->Connect("127.0.0.1", 22345))
                m_SendButton.EnableWindow(TRUE);

}
```

In the first line, the m_cSocket variable is initialized. In the next line, the class is created. Now you can connect to the server with the Connect method. There are several implementations of this method that differ in number and types of parameters. In our example, the following parameters are used:

❐ The IP address as a string
❐ The port to connect to

If the connection is set successfully, the method will return a non-zero value. The return value is checked, and the **Send Data** button is made active if everything is all right. The data are sent when the user clicks the **Send Data** button. The code of the corresponding event handler should be the following:

```
void CMFCSendTextDlg::OnBnClickedButton3()
{
        // TODO: Add your control notification handler code here
        m_cSocket->Send("Hello", 100);
```

```
int err = m_cSocket->GetLastError();
if(err>0)
{
        CString ErrStr ;
        ErrStr.Format("errcode=%d", err);
        AfxMessageBox(ErrStr);
}
}
```

The data are sent with the Send method of the m_cSocket client object. It takes two parameters:

☐ The data to send (the "Hello" string).
☐ The data length. In this case, we should have specified 5, because the string being sent contains 5 characters (is 5 bytes long), but 100 is actually specified. This won't cause an error and will allow us to change the string. In actual applications, be sure to specify the actual lengths of strings.

So far I haven't checked operations for errors. However, this is required when starting a server because if the server has been started earlier, additional attempts to start it will cause an error. In addition, it is likely that the TCP protocol hasn't been installed on the client computer. If this is the case, an error will result.

Such a check is done when data are sent. The GetLastError method returns the error code of the last operation in the m_cSocket class. If it is greater than zero, therefore, an error will result.

The event handler of the **Disconnect** button has the following code:

```
void CMFCSendTextDlg::OnBnClickedButton4()
{
        // TODO: Add your control notification handler code here
        SetDlgItemText(IDC_STATIC, "Disconnected");
        m_cSocket->Close();
}
```

The first line outputs a message, informing you that the connection was broken, to the text box in the dialog box. The second line calls the Close method that closes the connection to the server.

Now, the most interesting thing to come: the AddConnection method that was already used when connecting to the server.

```
void CMFCSendTextDlg::AddConnection()
{
```

```
m_scSocket = new CClientSocket(this);
m_sSocket->Accept(*m_scSocket);
}
```

As you can see, a new object of the CClientSocket type is created here. Then it connects to the m_sSocket server using the Accept method. This is how a variable of the CClientSocket class is associated with a new connection. The server uses this variable to send data to and receive data from the client.

It turns out that the same class, CClientSocket, is used to connect to the server and send it data on the client side and to receive and send data on the server side. The CServerSocket class is only used to listen to the port and receive requests for connection.

This example will work well only when one client is connected to the server. If another client tries to connect, the m_scSocket variable will be associated with it. This is why you should have a dynamic array of classes of the CClientSocket type on the server. When a client connects, you should create a new class of the CClientSocket type and store it in the array. When the client disconnects, the corresponding class should be deleted from the array.

Finally, I should mention that I didn't specify the protocol that the client and the server will use. By default, the CSocket class uses TCP/IP.

The source code of this example is located in the \Demo\Chapter4\MFCSendText directory on the accompanying CD-ROM.

NOTE

4.6. Using Winsock Directly

Working with a network using MFC objects such as Csocket is very simple. However, if you wish to write a compact application, you'll have to do without standard libraries. This is why I'll discuss direct work with a network comprehensively.

In Windows, the Winsock library is used to work with a network. There are two versions of this library. The first one was based on the Berkeley socket model used in Unix systems. Starting with Windows 98, the second version has been built into the operating system.

The Winsock library is compatible with previous program versions. This means the older functions didn't change, and programs written for the first version will work in the second one. Microsoft added new functions to later versions, but they appeared to be incompatible with network functions of other platforms. The new functions first appeared in version 1.1. These were WSAStartup, WSACleanup, WSAGetLastError, and WSARecvEx (all names include the WSA prefix). The next version contained many more such functions.

If Winsock2 is available to you, you don't need to use it. First check whether the features of the first version are enough. If so, it will be easy to adapt your program to the compilation on the Unix platform.

Of course, computers with Windows 95 are rare, but they still exist. If you have this operating system on your computer, you can download a version of the library from **www.microsoft.com**.

If you decide to use the first version in your program, you should include the winsock.h header file, otherwise include winsock2.h.

I should warn you that I'll be using both WinSock and WinSock2.

4.6.1. Handling Errors

First, you should learn how to detect errors emerging when network functions are called. Handling errors correctly is very important in each application. Though network functions aren't crucial for the operating system, they can affect the program's work. In turn, this can weaken the security of the system.

Network applications exchange data with other computers, and a malicious person can act as a client. If you don't handle errors, he or she might access important data on your computer or system functions.

Consider a simple example. Suppose a function is called every time your application receives data to check the data for correctness and access rights. When everything is fine, the function executes some code that shouldn't be exposed to an intruder. Error handling should be done at each stage: When the data is received, when it is checked for correctness and access rights, and when any of the network functions is called. Remember that this will make your application more reliable and your system safer.

If an error occurs when a function is executed, the function will return the SOCKET_ERROR constant or -1. When you receive this value, you can use the WSAGetLastError function. You don't have to pass it parameters; it will just return the code of the error occurred when the last function was being executed. There are quite a lot of error codes, and they depend on the function that was called last. I'll discuss them as needed.

4.6.2. Loading the Library

Before you start working with a network, you should load the desired version of the library. The set of available functions will depend on this. If you load the first version of the library and call a function from the second version, a program failure will occur. If you don't load the library, any call to a network function will result in the WSANOTINITIALISED error.

To load the library, call the WSAStartup function that looks as follows:

```
int WSAStartup (
     WORD wVersionRequested,
     LPWSADATA lpWSAData
);
```

The first parameter (wVersionRequested) is the requested version of the library. The least significant byte of this parameter determines the major version number, and the most significant byte determines the minor version number. To make it easier for you to use this parameter, I recommend that you use the MAKEWORD(i,j) macro where i is the most significant byte, and j is the least significant byte.

The second parameter of the WSAStartup function is a pointer to the WSADATA structure that will store information in the library after the function completes.

If loading is successful, the result will be zero. Another result indicates an error.

Look at an example of how the WSAStartup function is used to load Winsock 2.0:

```
WSADATA wsaData;

int err = WSAStartup(MAKEWORD(2, 0), &wsaData);
if (err != 0)
{
    // Tell the user that WinSock is not loaded
    return;
}
```

Note that the returned value is checked immediately after an attempt is made to load the library. If the function terminates correctly, it returns a zero. Here are the most important error codes:

- ❏ WSASYSNOTREADY — the main network subsystem isn't ready for a network connection
- ❏ WSAVERNOTSUPPORTED — the requested library version isn't supported
- ❏ WSAEPROCLIM — the number of the tasks exceeds a certain limit
- ❏ WSAEFAULT — a wrong pointer to the WSAData structure

The WSADATA structure is as follows:

```
typedef struct WSAData {
        WORD                    wVersion;
        WORD                    wHighVersion;
        char                    szDescription[WSADESCRIPTION_LEN+1];
        char                    szSystemStatus[WSASYS_STATUS_LEN+1];
        unsigned short          iMaxSockets;
        unsigned short          iMaxUdpDg;
        char FAR *              lpVendorInfo;
} WSADATA, FAR * LPWSADATA;
```

Let's look at each of its elements individually:

- ❑ wVersion — the version of the loaded WinSock library.
- ❑ wHighVersion — the latest version.
- ❑ szDescription — a text description provided only in some versions.
- ❑ szSystemStatus — a text description of the status provided only in some versions.
- ❑ iMaxSockets — the maximum number of open connections. This information doesn't correspond to reality because the number depends only on available resources. The parameter was retained for compatibility with the initial specification.
- ❑ iMaxUdpDg — the maximum size of the datagram (package). This information doesn't correspond to reality because the size depends on the protocol.
- ❑ lpVendorInfo — information about the vendor.

Let's look at a simple example that loads the WinSock library from the WSAData structure. Create a new **MFC Application** project. In the application wizard, select **Dialog based** in the **Application Type** section and **Windows sockets** in the **Advanced Features** section. This application type is already familiar to you.

In the resource editor, open the application's dialog box and adjust it as shown in Fig. 4.13. The form should have four **Edit Control** components to output information about the loaded library and one **Get WinSock Info** button which loads the data when clicked.

Declare the following variables:

- ❑ mVersion — the version number
- ❑ mHighVersion — the latest version
- ❑ mDescription — the description
- ❑ mSystemStatus — the status

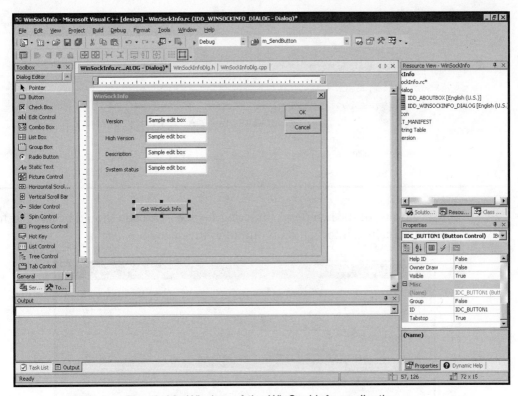

Fig. 4.13. Window of the WinSockInfo application

Create an event handler for the **Get WinSock Info** button and copy the code from Listing 4.11 into the handler.

Listing 4.11. Getting information about WinSock

```
void CWinSockInfoDlg::OnBnClickedButton1()
{
      // TODO: Add your control notification handler code here
      WSADATA wsaData;

      int err = WSAStartup(MAKEWORD(2, 0), &wsaData);
      if (err != 0)
      {
          // Tell the user that WinSock not loaded
             return;
```

```
    }

    char mText[255];
    mVersion.SetWindowText(itoa(wsaData.wVersion, mText, 10));
    mHighVersion.SetWindowText(itoa(wsaData.wHighVersion, mText, 10));
    if (wsaData.szDescription)
        mDescription.SetWindowText(wsaData.szDescription);
    if (wsaData.szSystemStatus)
        mSystemStatus.SetWindowText(wsaData.szSystemStatus);
}
```

At the beginning of the handler, WinSock is loaded (the code should be familiar to you). Then the obtained information is output to the dialog box.

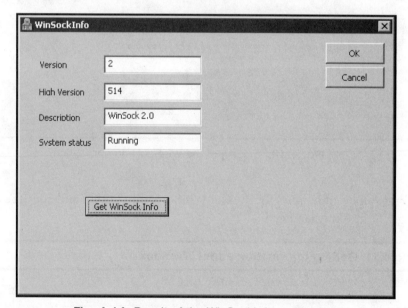

Fig. 4.14. Result of the WinSockInfo application

Fig. 4.14 shows how the application works on my computer.

NOTE

The source code of this example is located in the \Demo\Chapter4\WinSockInfo directory on the accompanying CD-ROM.

This example has one disadvantage: It doesn't unload the library. To do this, use the WSACleanup function:

```
int  WSACleanup(void);
```

The function takes no parameters; it just unloads the library. After this, the network functions become unavailable.

4.6.3. Creating a Socket

After you load the library, you should create a socket to work with the network. There is the socket function in the first version of the library:

```
SOCKET socket (
    int af,
    int type,
    int protocol
    );
```

In WinSock2, you can use the WSASocket function to create a socket.

```
SOCKET WSASocket (
    int af,
    int type,
    int protocol,
    LPWSAPROTOCOL_INFO lpProtocolInfo,
    GROUP g,
    DWORD dwFlags
    );
```

The first three parameters and the returned value are the same for both functions. In either case, the created socket is returned. You'll use it in your future work with the network. Let's look at the common parameters:

❑ af — a protocol family to use:
 - AF_UNSPEC — unspecified
 - AF_INET — the Internet protocols such as TCP, UDP, etc. (in this book, these protocols are used as the most common ones)
 - AF_IPX — the IPX and SPX protocols
 - AF_APPLETALK — the AppleTalk protocol
 - AF_NETBIOS — the NetBios protocol

❑ type — the specification for a new socket. The following values are valid:
- SOCK_STREAM — data transfer with setting a connection. When the Internet protocol family is specified, I'll use TCP.
- SOCK_DGRAM — data transfer without setting a connection. When the Internet protocol family is specified, I'll use UDP.

❑ protocol — a protocol to use. There are a lot of protocols, and you can get information on the constants used from the online help. Most often, I'll use the IPPROTO_TCP constant that denotes the TCP protocol.

The WSASocket function takes three more parameters:

❑ lpProtocolInfo — a pointer to the WSAPROTOCOL_INFO structure that determines characteristics of the socket being created
❑ g — a socket group identifier
❑ dwFlags — socket attributes

You'll learn more details on these parameters when analyzing the examples in the following sections. This will help you better understand the parameters as you see the results of the examples.

4.6.4. Server Functions

As already mentioned, TCP protocol uses "client-server" technology. For two computers to be able to establish a connection, one of them must start listening to a certain port. Only after that will the client be able to connect to the server.

Let's look at functions necessary to create a server. First, it is necessary to bind a local network address to the newly-created socket. To do this, use the bind function:

```
int bind (
    SOCKET s,
    const struct sockaddr FAR*  name,
    int namelen
    );
```

It takes the following parameters:

❑ A socket created previously
❑ A pointer to a structure of the sockaddr type
❑ The size of the sockaddr structure specified as the second parameter

The `sockaddr` structure is used to store the address, and different protocols use different addressing conventions. This is why the `sockaddr` structure can vary. For the Internet protocols, the structure is named `sockaddr_in` and is as follows:

```
struct sockaddr_in {
        short   sin_family;
        u_short sin_port;
        struct  in_addr sin_addr;
        char    sin_zero[8];
};
```

Below are its elements:

- ❑ `sin_family` — a protocol family. This element is similar to the first parameter of the `socket` function. For the Internet protocols, the `AF_INET` constant is used.
- ❑ `sin_port` — a port used by the application to receive data.
- ❑ `sin_addr` — the `SOCKADDR_IN` structure that stores the IP address.
- ❑ `sin_zero` — used to align the address stored in the `sin_addr` parameter. This is necessary because the size of the `SOCKADDR_IN` structure should be equal to the size of `SOCKADDR`.

Now I'd like to discuss the ports in more detail. You should be very careful when choosing a port because if it is already occupied by another application, your attempt to use it will cause an error. You should be aware that some ports are reserved for certain (the most common) services. The Internet Assigned Numbers Authority (IANA) assigns their numbers. There are three categories of ports:

- ❑ 0–1023 — are managed by IANA and reserved for standard services. It is inadvisable that you use the ports from this range.
- ❑ 1024–49151 — are reserved by IANA, but can be used by processes and programs. You can use most of them.
- ❑ 49152–65535 — are private, unreserved ports.

If the `bind` function detects that the port is used by a service, it will return the `WSAEADDRINUSE` error.

Look at an example that creates a socket and binds a local network address to it:

```
SOCKET s = socket(AF_INET, SOCK_STREAM, IPPROTO_TCP);

struct sockaddr_in addr;
addr.sin_family = AF_INET;
addr.sin_port = htons(4888);
```

```
addr.sin_addr.s_addr = htonl(INADDR_ANY);

bind(s, (SOCKADDR*)&addr), sizeof(addr);
```

In this example, a socket with the following parameters is created:

- ❏ AF_INET — indicates that the Internet protocol family will be used
- ❏ SOCK_STREAM — specifies a protocol that sets a connection
- ❏ IPPROTO_TCP — indicates that TCP will be used

Then, the addr structure of the sockaddr_in type is used. Its sin_family element also indicates the Internet protocol family (AF_INET). The sin_port element stores the port number. The bytes in the number should be arranged in an order other than the order of the bytes in a numeric variable in C programming language. This is why the htons function is called to convert the number.

The sin_addr.s_addr element stores a special address INADDR_ANY that will allow the application to wait for a connection to any network interface. This means that if you have two network cards for two different networks, the application will wait for a request for connection from both networks. Another address that could be specified, INADDR_BROADCAST, allows you to broadcast data to all computers on the network.

After you bind the local address and port to the socket, you can start listening to the port, i.e., waiting for a request for connection from a client. To do this, use the listen function:

```
int listen (
    SOCKET s,
    int backlog
);
```

Its first parameter is the socket that you created, and to which the address was bound. The function uses these data to determine, which port should be listened to.

The second parameter is the maximum number of requests waiting for processing. For example, if you had specified three requests, and five were received from different clients, only the first three would be queued. The rest would get the WSAECONNREFUSED error message. This is why when writing a client, you should check for this error.

When you call the listen function, the following main errors can occur:

- ❏ WSAEINVAL — the bind function wasn't called for this socket.
- ❏ WSANOTINITIALISED — the WinSock library wasn't loaded, i.e., the WSAStartup function wasn't called.
- ❏ WSAENETDOWN — the network subsystem is damaged.
- ❏ WSAEISCONN — the socket is already connected.

Other errors are less likely.

When a client is put in a queue to connect to the server, the connection should be accepted with the accept function. It appears as follows:

```
SOCKET accept (
    SOCKET s,
    struct sockaddr FAR* addr,
    int FAR* addrlen
    );
```

The WSAAccept function is in the second version of the library. Its first three parameters are the same as in the accept function. The WSAAccept is as follows:

```
SOCKET WSAAccept (
    SOCKET s,
    struct sockaddr FAR * addr,
    LPINT addrlen,
    LPCONDITIONPROC lpfnCondition,
    DWORD dwCallbackData
    );
```

Let's discuss the common parameters of these functions:

❏ The socket that was created and started for listening
❏ A pointer to a structure of the sockaddr type
❏ The size of the structure specified as the second parameter

When the accept function finishes, its second parameter (addr) will store information on the IP address of the client that has connected to the server. This information can be used to control access to the server using the IP address. You should be aware that an intruder can easily forge the IP address, therefore, such a protection isn't strong enough. However, it makes it more difficult to break into the server.

The accept function returns a pointer to a new socket that can be used for communication with the client. The older variable of the SOCKET type keeps on listening to the port and waiting for new connections, so it is pointless to use it. Thus, every connected client will have its own SOCKET, and you'll be able to work with any of them.

If you recall an example in which MFC objects were used for data exchange (see *Section 4.5*), you'll recall that the same method was used there. As soon as a client had connected to the server, we created a new socket that was used to working with the client. This socket received data from the network and could send data to a program on the client side.

4.6.5. Client Functions

In *Section 4.6.4*, I introduced server functions, and now you're able to write a server using WinAPI functions. However, we won't do this now because you don't know how to write a client and cannot test your application. Therefore, it's time to look at client functions and functions for data exchange.

Connecting to a server involves two stages: creating a socket and connecting to it. However, this is an ideal case. As a rule, the third stage is necessary. Which one? It is difficult for common users to use IP addresses, so they most often use symbolic server names. In such cases, you should convert a symbolic name to an IP address before connecting to the server.

You already know how to create a socket. Let's now try to understand how to determine an IP address. Depending on the WinSock version, one of two functions is used: `gethostbyname` or `WSAAsyncGetHostByName`. Let's look at `gethostbyname` first:

```
struct hostent FAR * gethostbyname (
    const char FAR * name
    );
```

Its one and only parameter is the symbolic name of the server. The function returns a structure of the `hostent` type that will be discussed later.

Now look at the `WSAAsyncGetHostByName` function:

```
HANDLE WSAAsyncGetHostByName (
    HWND hWnd,
    unsigned int wMsg,
    const char FAR * name,
    char FAR * buf,
    int buflen
    );
```

It works asynchronously. This means that the application isn't suspended when the function is called. The application will keep on working, and it will receive the result later via a Windows message specified as the second parameter. This is very convenient because the process of resolving the address can take long, and suspending the application would be unpractical. The processor time can be used for other purposes.

Let's take a close look at the parameters:

❑ `hWnd` — the handle to the window, which will receive the message after the asynchronous request is completed.
❑ `wMsg` — the Windows message, which will be sent after the IP address is resolved.

❏ `name` — the symbolic name of the computer whose address is being resolved.

❏ `buf` — a buffer to store the `hostent` structure. The buffer should be sufficiently large. Its maximum length can be specified with the MAXGETHOSTSTRUCT macro.

❏ `buflen` — the length of the buffer specified as the fourth parameter.

Now let's look at the `hostent` structure that is used to get the result:

```
struct hostent {
    char FAR *        h_name;
    char FAR * FAR *  h_aliases;
    short             h_addrtype;
    short             h_length;
    char FAR * FAR *  h_addr_list;
};
```

Its elements are the following:

❏ `h_name` — the full name of the computer. If the domain system is used in the network, this element will contain the full domain name of the computer.

❏ `h_aliases` — an additional name of the node.

❏ `h_addrtype` — the type of the address.

❏ `h_length` — the length of each address in an address list.

❏ `h_addr_list` — the address list of the computer.

A computer can have several addresses, so the structure stores a full null-terminated list of the computer's addresses. In most cases, it will suffice to select the first address in the list. If the `gethostbyname` function determines several addresses, any of them can be used to connect to the computer.

The `connect` function that connects to the server is next up. It is the following:

```
int connect (
    SOCKET s,
    const struct sockaddr FAR*  name,
    int namelen
    );
```

It takes three parameters:

❏ `s` — a socket created beforehand

❏ `name` — a SOCKADDR structure that stores the address of the server to connect to

❏ `namelen` — the length of the SOCKADDR structure specified as the second parameter

In the second WinSock version, there is an additional function WSAConnect:

```
int WSAConnect (
    SOCKET s,
    const struct sockaddr FAR * name,
    int namelen,
    LPWSABUF lpCallerData,
    LPWSABUF lpCalleeData,
    LPQOS lpSQOS,
    LPQOS lpGQOS
        );
```

The first three parameters are the same as in the connect function, so I'll introduce you to the other two:

☐ lpCallerData — a pointer to the user data that will be sent to the server while a connection is being established

☐ lpCalleeData — a pointer to the buffer to store the data received during the connection

Both parameters are pointers to a WSABUF structure that appears below:

```
typedef struct _WSABUF {
    u_long      len;
    char FAR *  buf;
} WSABUF, FAR * LPWSABUF;
```

Its first element is the buffer length, and the second is a pointer to the buffer. The last two parameters of the WSAConnect function (i.e., lpSQOS and lpGQOS) are pointers to structures of the QoS type. They define requirements to the channel's bandwidth when sending and receiving data. If you specify zeroes, this will indicate there are no requirements for service quality.

When trying to connect, the following errors are most likely:

☐ WSAETIMEDOUT — the server is unavailable. A problem somewhere on the route is likely.

☐ WSAECONNREFUSED — the service hasn't started listening to the specified port.

☐ WSAEADDRINUSE — the specified address is already in use.

☐ WSAEAFNOSUPPORT — the specified address cannot be used with this socket. This error occurs when the address is specified according to one protocol, and an attempt to connect uses another protocol.

4.6.6. Data Exchange

You learned how to create a server and became familiar with the connection functions. Now you should learn how to receive and send data, because this is our ultimate goal. We used all these functions just to implement data exchange.

First, I'd like to mention that the functions were created before UNICODE appeared. (This is a universal coding that makes it possible to use any language.) This is why to send some data in this coding, you should convert the data to the char* type and multiply its length by two because each UNICODE character takes two bytes (unlike ASCII, where a character takes one byte).

For data to be received, they should first be sent. Therefore, I'll start discussing data exchange functions with sending. To send data to a server, two functions can be used: send and WSASend (for WinSock2). The send function is as follows:

```
int send (
    SOCKET s,
    const char FAR * buf,
    int len,
    int flags
);
```

It takes the following parameters:

❑ s — a socket used to send data. An application can open a few connections with different servers, and you should explicitly specify the socket to use.
❑ buf — a buffer containing the data to send.
❑ len — the length of the buffer.
❑ flags — flags that determine a sending method. You can specify a combination of the following values:
- 0 — no flags are specified.
- MSG_DONTROUTE — the sent packages shouldn't be routed. If the transport protocol that sends the data doesn't support routing, the flag will be ignored.
- MSG_OOB — the data should be sent "out of band," i.e., it is urgent.

The WSASend function is the following:

```
int WSASend (
    SOCKET s,
    LPWSABUF lpBuffers,
    DWORD dwBufferCount,
```

```
    LPDWORD lpNumberOfBytesSent,
    DWORD dwFlags,
    LPWSAOVERLAPPED lpOverlapped,
    LPWSAOVERLAPPED_COMPLETION_ROUTINE lpCompletionROUTINE
);
```

Let's take a look at its parameters:

- s — a socket used to send data.
- lpBuffers — a structure or an array of structures of the WSABUF type. I introduced this structure when discussing the connect function. The same structure is used to send data during connection.
- dwBufferCount — the number of structures in the lpBuffers parameter.
- lpNumberOfBytesSent — the number of bytes sent by the I/O operation.
- dwFlags — determines a sending method and can take the same values as the dwFlags parameter of the send function.
- pOverlapped and pCompletionRoutine — are specified when an overlapped I/O is used. This is one of the asynchronous models supported by WinSock.

If the send (or WSASend) function has been completed successfully, it will return the number of the sent bytes, otherwise it will return –1 (or the SOCKET_ERROR constant that is equal to –1). If you receive such a value, you can analyze the error using the WSAGetLastError function:

- WSAECONNABORTED — the connection was broken, or the time-out has occurred, or another error occurred.
- WSAECONNRESET — the remote computer broke the connection, and you should close the socket.
- WSAENOTCONN — a connection wasn't established.
- WSAETIMEDOUT — the time-out has elapsed.

To receive data, use the recv or WSARecv (for the second version of WinSock) function. The recv function is as follows:

```
int recv (
    SOCKET s,
    char FAR* buf,
    int len,
    int flags
);
```

Its parameters are similar to those of the send function:

❏ s — a socket used to receive data.
❏ buf — a buffer containing the received data.
❏ len — the length of the buffer.
❏ flags — flags that determine a receiving method. You can specify a combination of the following values:
   ● 0 — no flags are specified.
   ● MSG_PEEK — read data from the system buffer without deleting. By default, the data are deleted from the buffer.
   ● MSG_OOB — process "out-of-band" data.

I don't recommend that you use the MSG_PEEK flag, because you may encounter a lot of problems. In such cases, you'll have to call the recv function for the second time (without the flag) to delete the data from the system buffer. When you read the data next time, the buffer may contain more data than previously (the computer may receive a few packages at this port), and you will risk processing the same data twice or fail to process all of it.

Another problem that is likely is that the system memory might not be freed up, and the space available for new data continually decreases. This is why you should use the MSG_PEEK flag very carefully, and only when you have to.

The WSARecv function is as follows:

```
int WSARecv (
    SOCKET s,
    LPWSABUF lpBuffers,
    DWORD dwBufferCount,
    LPDWORD lpNumberOfBytesRecvd,
    LPDWORD lpFlags,
    LPWSAOVERLAPPED lpOverlapped,
    LPWSAOVERLAPPED_COMPLETION_ROUTINE lpCompletionROUTINE
);
```

The similarity of its parameters to those of the WSASend function is obvious. Here they are:

❏ s — a socket used to receive data.
❏ lpBuffers — a structure or an array of structures of the WSABUF type. These buffers will store received data.
❏ dwBufferCount — the number of structures in the lpBuffers parameter.

❏   `lpNumberOfBytesSent` — the number of bytes received by the I/O operation.

❏   `dwFlags` — determines a receiving method and can take the same values as the `dwFlags` parameter of the `recv` function. There is one more flag: `MSG_PARTIAL`. You should specify it for protocols that read data in a few steps. When this flag is specified, each reading returns only a part of the data.

❏   `pOverlapped` and `pCompletionRoutine` — are specified when an overlapped I/O is used. This is one of the asynchronous models supported by WinSock.

I should mention that if you use a message-oriented protocol (such as UDP) and specify an insufficient buffer length, any of the data-receiving functions will return the `WSAEMSGSIZE` error. If the protocol is stream-oriented (such as TCP), this error won't occur because received data are cached by the system, and the application receives them completely. If the buffer length is insufficient, the remaining data can be obtained by repeatedly reading.

There is an interesting network function that appeared in WinSock2. While the functions discussed in this chapter (that miss the WSA prefix) exist both in Windows and in Unix, the `TransmitFile` function is a Microsoft extension and works only in Windows.

The `TransmitFile` function sends an entire file via the network. This is done very quickly because sending is performed by the library's kernel. You don't need to worry about sequential reading and check the number of the sent bytes. WinSock2 will do everything.

The function is:

```
BOOL TransmitFile(
    SOCKET hSocket,
    HANDLE hFile,
    DWORD nNumberOfBytesToWrite,
    DWORD nNumberOfBytesPerSend,
    LPOVERLAPPED lpOverlapped,
    LPTRANSMIT_FILE_BUFFERS lpTransmitBuffers,
    DWORD dwFlags
    );
```

Its parameters are:

❏   `hSocket` — a socket used to send data.

❏   `hFile` — a handle to an opened file to send.

❏   `nNumberOfBytesToWrite` — the number of bytes from the file to send. If you specify a zero, the entire file will be sent.

❏ nNumberOfBytesPerSend — the size of a package to send. If you specify 1024, the data will be sent in packages 1024 bytes long. If you specify zero, the default value will be used.

❏ lpOverlapped — is used in an overlapped I/O.

❏ lpTransmitBuffers — contains auxiliary information sent before and after the file is sent. These data are used by the receiving party to detect the beginning and the end of the transmission.

❏ dwFlags — flags. The following values are valid:

- TF_DISCONNECT — closes the socket when the data transmission is completed
- TF_REUSE_SOCKET — prepares the socket for reuse
- TF_WRITE_BEHIND — stops working without waiting for confirmation from the client that it has received the data

The lpTransmitBuffers parameter is the following structure:

```
typedef struct _TRANSMIT_FILE_BUFFERS {
    PVOID Head;
    DWORD HeadLength;
    PVOID Tail;
    DWORD TailLength;
} TRANSMIT_FILE_BUFFERS;
```

It has the following elements:

❏ Head — a pointer to a buffer that contains data to be sent before the file is sent
❏ HeadLength — the size of the Head buffer
❏ Tail — a pointer to a buffer that contains data to be sent after the file is sent
❏ TailLength — the size of the Tail buffer

4.6.7. Closing the Connection

To complete the session, you should first inform the other party that the data exchange is over. To do this, use the shutdown function:

```
int shutdown (
    SOCKET s,
    int how
);
```

Its first parameter is the socket whose connection should be closed. The second parameter can take one of the following values:

☐ SD_RECEIVE — prohibits all data receiving functions. This parameter has no effect on protocols of lower layers. If a stream protocol is used (such as TCP), and there are data in the queue waiting for the recv function, or the data come later, the connection will be broken. If the UDP protocol is used, messages will be received.

☐ SD_SEND — prohibits all data-sending functions.

☐ SD_BOTH — prohibits both sending and receiving data.

After you inform the other party, you can close the socket. To do this, use the closesocket function:

```
int closesocket (
    SOCKET s
    );
```

The socket specified as a parameter will be closed. If you try to use it in a function, you'll get the WSAENOTSOCK error (the descriptor isn't a socket). All packages waiting to be sent will be interrupted or cancelled.

4.6.8. Working Principles of Protocols without a Connection

Everything I mentioned earlier relates to protocols that set a connection between the client and the server (such as TCP). However, there are protocols (such as UDP) that don't set a connection. They don't need the connect function and carry out data exchange in a different way. I deliberately avoided this topic to keep you from being confused. When working with protocols that don't require a connection, you just need to call the socket and bind functions on the server to bind the socket to the port and address. You shouldn't call the listen and accept functions, because the server receives data from the clients without setting a connection. Rather, you should just wait for the data to come. Use the recvfrom function below:

```
int recvfrom (
    SOCKET s,
    char FAR* buf,
    int len,
    int flags,
    struct sockaddr FAR* from,
```

```
    int FAR* fromlen
  );
```

The first four parameters of this function are the same as in `recv`. The `from` parameter points to a `sockaddr` structure that stores the IP address of the computer that has sent the data. The `fromlen` parameter stores the length of the structure.

The second version of WinSock includes the `WSARecvFrom` function that is similar to `WSARecv` with two parameters added, `recv` and `fromlen`:

```
int WSARecvFrom (
    SOCKET s,
    LPWSABUF lpBuffers,
    DWORD dwBufferCount,
    LPDWORD lpNumberOfBytesRecvd,
    LPDWORD lpFlags,
    struct sockaddr FAR * lpFrom,
    LPINT lpFromlen,
    LPWSAOVERLAPPED lpOverlapped,
    LPWSAOVERLAPPED_COMPLETION_ROUTINE lpCompletionROUTINE
  );
```

On the client side, everything is also very simple. Just create a socket, and you'll be able to send data. To send it via a network, use the `sendto` function:

```
int sendto (
    SOCKET s,
    const char FAR * buf,
    int len,
    int flags,
    const struct sockaddr FAR * to,
    int tolen
  );
```

The first four parameters are similar to those of the `send` function. The `to` parameter is a structure of the `sockaddr` type. It contains the address and port of the computer, to which the data are sent. Since there is no connection between the client and the server, this information should be provided in the data-sending function. The last parameter is the length of the `to` structure.

Starting with the second version, you can use the `WSASendTo`. Its parameters are the same as those of `WSASend`, with two new parameters added: `lpTo` and `iToLen` that store a structure with the receiver's address and length of the structure, respectively.

```
int WSASendTo (
```

```
SOCKET s,
LPWSABUF lpBuffers,
DWORD dwBufferCount,
LPDWORD lpNumberOfBytesSent,
DWORD dwFlags,
const struct sockaddr FAR * lpTo,
int iToLen,
LPWSAOVERLAPPED lpOverlapped,
LPWSAOVERLAPPED_COMPLETION_ROUTINE lpCompletionROUTINE
);
```

As you see, the work with protocols that don't require a connection is even simpler. You don't have to call the functions for listening to a port and connecting to a server. If you understand TCP, you are sure to understand UDP.

4.7. Working with a Network Using the TCP Protocol

It is time to look at how the functions of the Winsock library can be used to work with a network. I'll demonstrate to you a simple program, in which a client sends requests to a server, and the server responds to them. This example will help you understand how hackers create Trojan horses and steal data from remote computers.

4.7.1. An Example of a TCP Server

I'll begin with developing a server. Create a new **Win32 Project** and name it TCPServer. Open the TCPServer.cpp file and insert two procedures from Listing 4.12 after the declarations of global variables, but before the _tWinMain function. Keep the order of the procedures: first ClientThread, then NetThread.

Listing 4.12. Functions for work with the network

```
DWORD WINAPI ClientThread(LPVOID lpParam)
{
    SOCKET    sock = (SOCKET)lpParam;
    char      szRecvBuff[1024],
        szSendBuff[1024];
    int       ret;
```

```
    // Start an infinite loop
    while(1)
    {
       // Receive data
        ret = recv(sock, szRecvBuff, 1024, 0);
       // Check the received data
        if (ret == 0)
            break;
        else if (ret == SOCKET_ERROR)
        {
            MessageBox(0, "Recive data failed", "Error", 0);
            break;
        }
        szRecvBuff[ret] = '\0';

       // Here you can check the received text
       // stored in the szRecvBuffer variable

       // Prepare a string to send to the client
       strcpy(szSendBuff, "Command get OK");

       // Send the contents of the szSendBuff variable to the client
        ret = send(sock, szSendBuff, sizeof(szSendBuff), 0);
        if (ret == SOCKET_ERROR)
        {
           break;
        }
        }
    return 0;
}


DWORD WINAPI NetThread(LPVOID lpParam)
{
    SOCKET   sServerListen,
             sClient;
    struct sockaddr_in localaddr,
                        clientaddr;
    HANDLE   hThread;
    DWORD    dwThreadId;
    int      iSize;
```

```cpp
// Create a socket
sServerListen = socket(AF_INET, SOCK_STREAM, IPPROTO_IP);
if (sServerListen == SOCKET_ERROR)
{
   MessageBox(0, "Can't create socket", "Error", 0);
    return 0;
}
// Fill the localaddr structure of the sockaddr_in type
// that contains information on the server's local address
// and the port number
localaddr.sin_addr.s_addr = htonl(INADDR_ANY);
localaddr.sin_family = AF_INET;
localaddr.sin_port = htons(5050);

// Bind the address to the localaddr variable of the sockaddr_in type
if (bind(sServerListen, (struct sockaddr *)&localaddr,
        sizeof(localaddr)) == SOCKET_ERROR)
{
   MessageBox(0, "Can't bind", "Error", 0);
   return 1;
}

// Output a message that binding was successful
MessageBox(0, "Bind OK", "Error", 0);

// Start listening to the port
listen(sServerListen, 4);

// Output a message that listening started successfully
MessageBox(0, "Listen OK", "Error", 0);

// Start an infinite loop
while (1)
{
    iSize = sizeof(clientaddr);
    // Accept the next connection request from the queue.
    // If there is no connection, wait for a request from the client
    sClient = accept(sServerListen, (struct sockaddr *)&clientaddr,
                 &iSize);
```

```
    // Check the client's socket ID
    if (sClient == INVALID_SOCKET)
    {
        MessageBox(0, "Accept failed", "Error", 0);
        break;
    }

    // Create a new thread for the work with the client
    hThread = CreateThread(NULL, 0, ClientThread,
                (LPVOID)sClient, 0, &dwThreadId);
    if (hThread == NULL)
    {
        MessageBox(0, "Create thread failed", "Error", 0);
        break;
    }
    CloseHandle(hThread);
    }
    // Close the socket after the thread is closed
    closesocket(sServerListen);
    return 0;
}
```

Now, add the following code to the _tWinMain function before the main message loop:

```
WSADATA         wsd;
if (WSAStartup(MAKEWORD(2,2), &wsd) != 0)
{
MessageBox(0, "Can't load WinSock", "Error", 0);
    return 0;
}

HANDLE          hNetThread;
DWORD           dwNetThreadId;
hNetThread = CreateThread(NULL, 0, NetThread,
                    0, 0, &dwNetThreadId);
```

Well, let's look at what we have written. The _tWinMain function loads the WinSock library version 2.2.

Then a new thread is created with the `CreateThread` function. The `accept` server function locks the program. If you call it in the main thread, the window will become inactive and stop responding to messages. This is why a separate thread is created for the server. As a result, the main program is working in its own thread, and another thread with the server listening to the port is running concurrently.

From a programmer's point of view, a thread is a function that works parallel with the other threads in the operating system. In such a way, multitasking is implemented in Windows. For more detailed information on threads, refer to the user manual or books on Visual C++.

The third parameter of the `CreateThread` function is a pointer to a function that should execute in the newly created thread.

The most interesting thing happens in the `NetThread` function. All the functions it calls were discussed earlier, and it just combines them.

First, a socket is created with the `socket` function. Next, the `localaddr` structure of the `sockaddr_in` type is filled with appropriate values. For the suggested server, three elements are filled:

- ❒ `localaddr.sin_addr.s_addr` — the `INADDR_ANY` flag is specified to receive connections from any interface installed in the computer.
- ❒ `localaddr.sin_family` — the `AF_INET` value indicating the Internet protocol family is specified.
- ❒ `localaddr.sin_port` — the port No. 5050 is specified that is unused on mostcomputers.

Then the filled structure is bound to the socket with the `bind` function.

Now, the socket is ready to start listening, which is done with the `listen` function. A four is specified as the second parameter that indicates a queue of four clients. If more than four clients try to connect simultaneously, only the first four of them will be queued. The rest will get an error message.

To receive connections from clients, an infinite loop is started. It will process all connections. Why is the loop infinite? The server should always be in the memory and receive requests to connections at any time.

The `accept` function is called inside the loop to accept a client's connection from the queue. As soon as the connection is accepted, the function will create a socket and return a pointer to the socket that will be stored in the `sClient` variable. Before using the new socket, it should be checked for correctness. If the `sSocket` variable is equal to `INVALID_SOCKET`, you shouldn't use this socket.

If the socket is correct, another thread is created. It will exchange data, that is, read data received from the client and respond to requests. The thread is created with the CreateThread function already familiar to you. Its third parameter is the ClientThread function that will work concurrently to the main program.

As a fourth parameter of the CreateThread function, you can specify any value, which will be passed to the thread function. It would be reasonable to specify the client socket here, so that the ClientThread function knows, which socket is used.

The ClientThread function takes the only parameter whose value is the value of the fourth parameter specified when creating the thread. In this case, it is a handle to the socket, and the first line of the function stores this socket in the sock variable:

```
SOCKET sock = (SOCKET)lpParam;
```

This function also starts an infinite loop in case of receiving many commands from the client and responding to them.

Inside the loop, the recv function receives the text first. Then the received data are checked for correctness.

If the check is successful, you should check the received command. When writing a Trojan horse, a hacker can send requests for sending passwords, rebooting the computer, or starting a prankish program. You should check the request received from the client and perform actions depending on the result of the check.

The requests can have a form of simple text commands such as "restart" or "sendmepassword." Since we are only discussing the working principles of a Trojan horse, rather than creating it, the client will send a text command "get" in this example. The server will respond with the text "Command get OK." The text is stored in a variable whose contents will be sent to the client with the send function:

```
strcpy(szSendBuff, "Command get OK");

ret = send(sock, szSendBuff, sizeof(szSendBuff), 0);
if (ret == SOCKET_ERROR)
    {
        break;
    }
```

Then the loop enters the next iteration, and if the server reads another command, it will execute the command. Otherwise, the loop will be broken.

As aforementioned, all network functions are declared in the winsock2.h file, and you should include it into your project to avoid compiling errors. Locate the following line at the beginning of the source code of your program:

```
#include "stdafx.h"
```

Add the line

```
#include <winsock2.h>
```

after it to include the winsock2.h file.

To build the project without errors, link the ws2_32.lib library to it. To do this, right-click the project name in the **Solution Explorer** window, and select the **Properties** item in the pop-up menu.

A window will open. Move to the **Configuration Properties/Linker/Input** section and enter the ws2_32.lib library name into the **Additional Dependencies** line.

And that's all there is to it! When you start this server application, two messages, "Bind OK" and "Listen OK," should appear. If they do, this indicates the server is working correctly and waiting for requests for connection from the client side.

NOTE

The source code of this example is located in the \Demo\Chapter4\TCPServer directory on the accompanying CD-ROM.

However, to test the example completely, we should write a client program that would connect to the server and send it commands. This is the topic of the next section.

4.7.2. An Example of a TCP Client

The server is ready, and you can start writing the client. Create a new **Win32 Project** and name it TCPClient.

Find the _tWinMain function and add the following code before the main message loop:

```
WSADATA    wsd;
if (WSAStartup(MAKEWORD(2,2), &wsd) != 0)
{
        MessageBox(0, "Can't load WinSock", "Error", 0);
        return 0;
}

HANDLE         hNetThread;
DWORD          dwNetThreadId;
hNetThread = CreateThread(NULL, 0, NetThread,
                0, 0, &dwNetThreadId);
```

This code loads the Winsock library version 2.2. In our example, only functions of the first version will be used, and it would be sufficient to load that version. However, I preferred to use the second version in this section for training purposes, because old mistakes might have been corrected in the latest version.

As is the case with the server, a separate thread will be used to work with the network, and one thread will be enough for the client. The thread is created with the CreateThread function whose third parameter should be NetThread, the name of a function that will run in the separate thread. This function is still missing from the project, so let's write it now. Add the code from Listing 4.13 before the _tWinMain function.

Listing 4.13. A thread to work with the network

```
DWORD WINAPI NetThread(LPVOID lpParam)
{
    SOCKET   sClient;
    char     szBuffer[1024];
    int      ret, i;
    struct sockaddr_in server;
    struct hostent     *host = NULL;
    char   szServerName[1024], szMessage[1024];

    strcpy(szMessage, "get");
    strcpy(szServerName, "127.0.0.1");

    // Create a socket
    sClient = socket(AF_INET, SOCK_STREAM, IPPROTO_TCP);
    if (sClient == INVALID_SOCKET)
    {
        MessageBox(0, "Can't create socket", "Error", 0);
        return 1;
    }
    // Fill the structure with the server address and the port number
    server.sin_family = AF_INET;
    server.sin_port = htons(5050);
    server.sin_addr.s_addr = inet_addr(szServerName);

    // If a name is specified, convert the symbolic server address to an IP address
    if (server.sin_addr.s_addr == INADDR_NONE)
    {
        host = gethostbyname(szServerName);
```

```
    if (host == NULL)
    {
        MessageBox(0, "Unable to resolve server", "Error", 0);
        return 1;
    }
    CopyMemory(&server.sin_addr, host->h_addr_list[0],
        host->h_length);
}
// Connect to the server
if (connect(sClient, (struct sockaddr *)&server,
    sizeof(server)) == SOCKET_ERROR)
{
    MessageBox(0, "connect failed", "Error", 0);
    return 1;
}

// Send the data
ret = send(sClient, szMessage, strlen(szMessage), 0);
if (ret == SOCKET_ERROR)
{
    MessageBox(0, "send failed", "Error", 0);
}

// A delay
Sleep(1000);

// Receive data
char szRecvBuff[1024];
ret = recv(sClient, szRecvBuff, 1024, 0);
if (ret == SOCKET_ERROR)
{
    MessageBox(0, "recv failed", "Error", 0);
}
MessageBox(0, szRecvBuff, "Received data", 0);
closesocket(sClient);
}
```

Let's look at this code more closely. The szMessage variable stores a message to send to the server. In our example, the "get" string is predefined. The szServerName variable stores the address of the server to connect to. In the example, this is the 127.0.0.1 address that indicates the local computer. This means that the client and the server will run on the same computer. Then a socket is created, just like in the previous example.

The next stage involves filling a structure of the `sockaddr_in` type (named `server`) that should store a protocol family, a port (we used 5050 in the server), and the server address.

An IP address is specified in the example. However, an actual program can specify the name of a remote computer that should be converted to an IP address. This is why the address is checked for equality to the `INADDR_NONE` constant:

```
if (server.sin_addr.s_addr == INADDR_NONE)
```

If the condition is true, a symbolic name was specified, and it should be converted to an IP address with the `gethostbyname` function. The result is stored in a variable of the `hostent` type. As I pointed out earlier, a computer can have several addresses. In such a case, the result will be an array of structures of the `hostent` type. To simplify the program, take the first address that can be accessed like this: `host->h_addr_list[0]`.

Now, everything is ready for connection to the server. The `connect` function will be used for this purpose. As parameters, it takes the newly-created socket, the structure containing the address and the length of the structure. If the function returns a value other than `SOCKET_ERROR`, it will indicate a successful connection; otherwise, an error occurred.

Next, data should be sent to the server using the `send` function. After you send the data, you might expect a response from the server. However, don't rush to read the data from the buffer because it takes a certain amount of time for the server to receive and process your message. If you call the `recv` function immediately after sending the data, you are likely to get an error message because the response hasn't come yet. This is why a delay is made after the `send` function.

In an actual program, you don't need to set a delay. Instead, you can start a loop to get a response and wait until the `recv` function returns data rather than an error. This would be the simplest method in order to work with accuracy and efficacy.

As with the server, you should include the winsock2.h file and link the ws2_32.lib library to build the project.

The source code of this example is located in the \Demo\Chapter4\TCPClient directory on the accompanying CD-ROM.

NOTE

4.7.3. An Analysis of the Examples

If you make the server invisible and capable of sending passwords or rebooting the computer in response to external requests, the example will become a Trojan horse. However, I won't demonstrate this because it would violate my principles. In the previous sections, everything was presented for educational purposes, so let's continue in that vein.

I should also mention that after each network operation a check for an error is done. If a failure occurs when creating a socket, the subsequent work will be pointless.

Let's look at how the code of the examples can be made universal. The examples have a flaw. If either of the parties tries to send a large amount of data, the data will neither be sent nor received completely. This is because the data are transferred in small portions (packages), and the capacity of the system buffer is limited.

Suppose the length of the buffer is 64 KB. When you try to send more than 64 KB of information via the network, the client will receive only 64 KB. The rest will be lost. To avoid this, you should check the actual amount of the sent data and adjust your actions.

Listing 4.14 shows an example that can send any amount of data to the client, even if it exceeds the buffer length. The algorithm is quite simple, but I'll discuss it thoroughly.

Listing 4.14. An algorithm for sending large amounts of data

```cpp
char szBuff[4096];
szBuff = "Data to send...";
int nSendSize = sizeof(szBuff);
int iCurrPos = 0;

while(nSendSize > 0)
{
        int ret = send(sock, &szBuff[iCurrPos], nSendSize, 0);
        if (ret == 0)
                break;
        else if (ret == SOCKET_ERROR)
                {
                // An error happened
                MessageBox(0, "Send failed", "Error", 0);
                break;
                }
        nSendSize -= ret;
        iCurrPos += ret;
}
```

This code finds the size of the data being sent and stores it in the nSendSize variable. Then an infinite loop starts. It will run while the variable is greater than zero, i.e., there are data to send. The iCurrPos variable indicates the current position in the buffer, and sending starts from the zero position.

As the second parameter, the send function takes the buffer with the data, and the value in square brackets is the position in the buffer, from which sending should start.

The function returns the actual number of sent bytes. After checking the value returned by the send function, the size of the data waiting for sending in the buffer should be decreased, and the current position in the buffer should be increased.

If not all of the data were sent, the function will try to send the next portion in the next iteration of the loop.

Similarly, it is impossible to receive a large amount of data. This is why you should start a similar loop to receive a large amount of data. However, while you know the size of the data being sent, you don't know how much data will be received. How can you find this out?

It's easy. Before a program sends data, it should tell the receiving party how many bytes will be sent. For this purpose, a protocol should be defined beforehand. For example, a few bytes can be allocated in the get command for the size of the data being sent. A command such as data can be put before the data. This will allow the other party to find out how much data will come, and to receive it completely. Data receiving code can look like that in Listing 4.15.

Listing 4.15. An algorithm for receiving large amounts of data

```
char szBuff[4096];
int nSendSize = 1000000; // The size of the data
int iCurrPos = 0;

while(nSendSize > 0)
{
        int ret = recv(sock, &szBuff[iCurrPos], nSendSize, 0);
        if (ret == 0)
                break;
        else if (ret == SOCKET_ERROR)
                {
                    // An error happened
                    MessageBox(0, "Send failed", "Error", 0);
                    break;
                }
}
```

```
        nSendSize -= ret;
        iCurrPos += ret;
}
```

4.8. Examples Using the UDP Protocol

As you already know, the work with protocols such as UDP differs from what we discussed in the previous section. Since there is no connection between a client and a server, you will be unable to use certain functions.

Functions necessary for work with the UDP protocol were described in *Section 4.6.8.*

Now you're about to see an actual example, and put your knowledge to use.

4.8.1. An Example of a UDP Server

Create a new **Win32 Project** and name it UDPServer. Open the UDPServer.cpp file and add the following code into the `_tWinMain` function before the main message loop:

```
WSADATA        wsd;
if (WSAStartup(MAKEWORD(2, 2), &wsd) != 0)
{
        MessageBox(0, "Can't load WinSock", "Error", 0);
        return 0;
}


HANDLE        hNetThread;
DWORD         dwNetThreadId;
hNetThread = CreateThread(NULL, 0, NetThread, 0, 0, &dwNetThreadId);
```

As with the TCP server, the WinSock library is loaded, and a new thread to work with the network is created. The thread function is shown in Listing 4.16.

Listing 4.16. The thread function for working with the network

```
DWORD WINAPI NetThread(LPVOID lpParam)
{
        SOCKET         sServerListen;
        struct sockaddr_in localaddr,
                       clientaddr;
        int            iSize;
```

```
        sServerListen = socket(AF_INET, SOCK_DGRAM, IPPROTO_UDP);
    if (sServerListen == INVALID_SOCKET)
        {
                MessageBox(0, "Can't create socket", "Error", 0);
                return 0;
        }
        localaddr.sin_addr.s_addr = htonl(INADDR_ANY);
        localaddr.sin_family = AF_INET;
        localaddr.sin_port = htons(5050);

        if (bind(sServerListen, (struct sockaddr *)&localaddr,
            sizeof(localaddr)) == SOCKET_ERROR)
        {
                MessageBox(0, "Can't bind", "Error", 0);
                return 1;
        }

        MessageBox(0, "Bind OK", "Warning", 0);

        char buf[1024];

        while (1)
        {
                iSize = sizeof(clientaddr);
          int ret = recvfrom(sServerListen, buf, 1024, 0,
                        (struct sockaddr *)&clientaddr, &iSize);
                MessageBox(0, buf, "Warning", 0);
        }
        closesocket(sServerListen);
        return 0;
}
```

When creating a socket with the socket function, the SOCK_DGRAM value is passed as the second parameter. It indicates that a message-based protocol should be used. As the last parameter, you should pass a constant that precisely specifies the protocol. In this example, you can explicitly define the UDP protocol with the IPPROTO_UDP constant or just specify a zero.

The rest of the code should be familiar to you. After a socket is created, it is bound to the local address using the `bind` function. This will be enough for a UDP server. After the socket is bound, an infinite loop starts that calls the `recvfrom` function to receive data from the client.

When the data are received, the server displays a window with the received information. The sender's address is stored in the `clientaddr` variable, and it can be used to respond to the client.

NOTE

The source code of this example is located in the \Demo\Chapter4\UDPServer directory on the accompanying CD-ROM.

4.8.2. An Example of a UDP Client

This section describes a client program that sends data to a server. Create a new **Win32 Project** and name it UDPClient. In this case, we can do without additional threads and send data directly from the `_tWinMain` function. This is because sending data using the UDP protocol doesn't make a delay, and the data are sent instantly. Therefore, it is pointless to create a multithread application, and the task is much simpler.

Open the UDPClient.cpp file and copy the code from Listing 4.17 to somewhere before the main message loop.

Listing 4.17. Sending data to an UDP server

```
WSADATA        wsd;
if (WSAStartup(MAKEWORD(2, 2), &wsd) != 0)
{
       MessageBox(0, "Can't load WinSock", "Error", 0);
       return 0;
}

SOCKET         sSocket;
struct sockaddr_in servaddr;
char    szServerName[1024], szMessage[1024];
struct hostent    *host = NULL;

strcpy(szMessage, "This is message from client");
```

```
strcpy(szServerName, "127.0.0.1");

sSocket = socket(AF_INET, SOCK_DGRAM, IPPROTO_UDP);
if (sSocket == INVALID_SOCKET)
{
        MessageBox(0, "Can't create socket", "Error", 0);
        return 0;
}
servaddr.sin_family = AF_INET;
servaddr.sin_port = htons(5050);
servaddr.sin_addr.s_addr = inet_addr(szServerName);

if (servaddr.sin_addr.s_addr == INADDR_NONE)
{
        host = gethostbyname(szServerName);
        if (host == NULL)
        {
            MessageBox(0, "Unable to resolve server", "Error", 0);
            return 1;
        }
        CopyMemory(&servaddr.sin_addr, host->h_addr_list[0],
        host->h_length);
}

sendto(sSocket, szMessage, 30, 0, (struct sockaddr *)&servaddr,
                sizeof(servaddr));
```

As with the server, you should create a socket and specify the SOCK_DGRAM value as the second parameter. The third parameter specifies a protocol, IPPROTO_UDP in our case.

Then the servaddr variable of the sockaddr_in type is filled with the address and port of the computer to send data to. If a symbolic name is specified as the address, it is converted to an IP address like with a TCP client.

Now, you can send data using the sendto function directly, without setting a connection to the server. In this example, the contents of the szMessage are sent to the server.

Remember that you should link the ws2_32.lib library to compile examples that work with the network (see *Section 4.7.1*).

The source code of this example is located in the \Demo\Chapter4\UDPClient directory on the accompanying CD-ROM.

NOTE

4.9. Processing Received Data

You should carefully verify all data received via the network. When it is necessary to control access to certain features by a password, I recommend that you first check the rights of executing the command. Then check the specified command and its parameters for correctness.

Suppose a client requests a certain file from the server. If you first check the path and the file name and send an error message when the file is missing, a hacker will know that there is no such file in the system. Sometimes, this information can make it easy for a hacker to break into the system. This is why you should first check the rights of executing the command and only then parse its parameters and verify them.

You should implement strict checks if you can. For example, you should check the "get filename" command in such a way that the first three letters compose the word "get." You shouldn't look for the "get" string in the entire text because this would allow a hacker to send incorrect data. Most break-ins are successful because the received data are improperly analyzed, and incorrect data are sent to a server.

When you develop a protocol to exchange commands between a client and a server, make sure that the command name is sent first, and the parameters follow it. For example, you have the "get" command. It can work in two modes:

❐ Get a file from a server: GET name FROM address.
❐ Get a file from the client connected to the server: GET name.

The first command is insecure. To find the FROM keyword, you'll have to look for it in the entire string. This is wrong! All keywords should be in strictly defined positions. In this example, it would be best to use the following command:

```
GET FROM name, address
```

In this case, all keywords are at the beginning of the command, and you can check for their presence. If a hacker tries to use incorrect parameters, he or she will fail.

If the sent data are varied, but has a particular template, be sure to check for this template. This will allow you to make an additional check, but won't protect you completely. Programmers often check templates erroneously. The more complicated the check or the template, the more difficult it is to take into account all limitations put on the sent data. Before you use a program in actual practice, you should spend as much time as possible testing this portion of the code. It is desirable that another person test your program because a user or a hacker is likely to enter data, which you are unaware of.

The task becomes more complicated when the data are used to access the file system. This can lead to unauthorized access to your disk with far-reaching consequences. When a path is specified as a parameter, it is easy to check it using a template, but it is also easy to make a mistake. Most programmers just check the beginning of the path, but this is a mistake.

Suppose that only the `interpub` folder on the disk C is shared on your computer. If you check only the beginning of the path, a hacker will be able to write the following path:

```
c:\interpub\..\winnt\system32\cmd.exe\
```

Two dots (..) will allow the hacker to leave the `interpub` folder and access any folder on the disk, including those, which contain system files.

Before you write a check using a template, you should learn all its exceptions. I'd like to reiterate that you should test your program as much as possible and with illogical data. Users, especially inexperienced ones, are unpredictable, and hackers are clever enough to examine the system from all sides, including those you are unaware of.

4.10. Sending and Receiving Data

You have learned the theory and practice of how to exchange data between computers. However, a hacker's art is to correctly use various methods and modes for exchanging data. Sockets have two working modes, and you should learn how to use them correctly, because this will make your programs faster and more effective.

The following modes of network I/O (data exchange) are used:

❑ Locking (synchronous): When a sending function is called, the application stops execution and waits for the operation to complete.

❑ Non-locking (asynchronous): When a sending function is called, the application doesn't stop execution regardless of the completion of the data exchange operation.

I introduced these notions when describing the functions (see *Sections 6.5* and *4.6.6*). Now I'll discuss them comprehensively, because they allow you to speed up your programs and make the most of the system.

By default, locking sockets are created. This is why the synchronous mode was used in all the previous examples as the simplest one. In this case, you have to create threads for network functions so that the program window isn't locked and responds to user events.

However, this is not the most important problem. Simplicity and security are incompatible. Suppose the `recv` function was called, but didn't return data for some reason. In this case, the program will be locked forever, and the server won't respond to the user's actions. To avoid this problem, some programmers check data for accuracy by calling the `recv` function with the `MSG_PEEK` flag before actually reading the data. You already know that this method is insecure, and such data aren't trustworthy. In addition, the method overloads the system with unnecessary checks for the presence of data in the buffer.

Non-locking sockets are more difficult to program, but they don't have these disadvantages. To switch on the asynchronous mode of a socket, use the `ioctlsocket` function:

```
int ioctlsocket (
    SOCKET s,
    long cmd,
    u_long FAR* argp
);
```

This function takes three parameters:

❏ A socket whose mode should be changed
❏ A command to execute
❏ A parameter for the command

Changing the mode is done when the `FIONBIO` constant is specified as a command. If its parameter is a zero, the locking mode will be switched on; otherwise, the non-locking mode will be used.

Let's look at an example of how to create a socket and switch its non-locking mode on:

```
SOCKET s;
unsigned long ulMode;

s = socket(AS_INET, SOCK_STREAM, 0);
ulMode = 1;
ioctlsocket(s, FIONBIO, (unsigned long*)&ulMode);
```

From this moment on, all sending and receiving functions will return errors. This will be normal, and you should take it into account when creating network applications working in non-locking mode. If an I/O function returns the `WSAEWOULDBLOCK` error, this doesn't indicate an incorrect data transfer. Everything is all right; just the non-locking mode is used. In the case of a failure, you'll get an error message other than `WSAEWOULDBLOCK`.

In the non-locking mode, the `recv` function won't wait for data to come but will simply return the `WSAEWOULDBLOCK` error. How can you know that data have come to the port? Some programmers start an infinite loop that calls recv until the function returns data. However, this isn't a good idea, because the application is locked and the processor is overloaded.

Of course, you can perform useful actions between calls to the function, thus using the processor a little more effectively. However, I will refrain from discussing this method because there is a better one.

4.10.1. The select *Function*

Starting with the first version, Winsock has an interesting feature to control non-locking sockets. This is the select function:

```
int select (
    int nfds,
    fd_set FAR * readfds,
    fd_set FAR * writefds,
    fd_set FAR * exceptfds,
    const struct timeval FAR * timeout
);
```

The function returns the number of socket handles that are ready for use.
Below are its parameters:

☐ nfds — is ignored (it is used only for compatibility with the Berkeley socket model)
☐ readfds — an option for reading (a structure of the fd_set type)
☐ writefds — an option for writing (a structure of the fd_set type)
☐ exceptfds — the importance of the message (a structure of the fd_set type)
☐ timeout — the maximum time-out or NULL to lock the work (an infinite time-out)

The fd_set structure is a set of sockets that can send the application permission to perform a certain operation. For example, if you need to wait for data to come to either of two sockets, you can proceed as follows:

1. Add two sockets created beforehand to the fd_set set.
2. Call the select function and specify the set of sockets as the second parameter.

The select function will be waiting for a specified time, after which you can read data. However, the data can be received only at one of the sockets. How can you know, which socket to check? First, call the FD_ISSET function to check whether the socket is contained in the set.

When using a structure of the `fd_set` type, you'll need the following functions:

❏ `FD_ZERO` — cleans up the set. Be sure to call this function before you add new sockets to the set to initialize the set. This function takes only one parameter, a pointer to a variable of the `fd_set` type.

❏ `FD_SET` — adds a socket to a set. This function takes two parameters: a socket to add and a variable of the `fd_set` type to add the socket to.

❏ `FD_CLR` — deletes a socket from a set. This function takes two parameters: a socket to delete and a set to delete the socket from.

❏ `FD_ISSET` — checks whether the socket specified as the first parameter is included in the set specified as the second parameter.

4.10.2. Using the select Function: A Simple Example

Let's put to use the information from the previous section. Open the TCPServer example (*Section 4.7.1*) and add the following code after the piece of code where the socket is created:

```
ULONG ulBlock;
ulBlock = 1;
if (ioctlsocket(sServerListen, FIONBIO, &ulBlock) ==
    SOCKET_ERROR)
{
        return 0;
}
```

This switches on the asynchronous mode of the socket. Try to start the example. You'll see two messages, "Bind OK" and "Listen OK," and then the program will display the "Accept failed" error message. In the asynchronous mode, the `accept` function doesn't lock the application, therefore, it doesn't wait for a connection. If there are no clients waiting for a connection in the queue, the function will return the `WSAEWOULDBLOCK` error.

To solve the problem, change the connection-waiting loop (the infinite `while` loop that follows the call to the `listen` function). The asynchronous version of your application should look like that shown in Listing 4.18.

Listing 4.18. The connection-waiting loop

```
FD_SET ReadSet;
int ReadySock;
```

```
while (1)
{
        FD_ZERO(&ReadSet);
        FD_SET(sServerListen, &ReadSet);

        if ((ReadySock = select(0, &ReadSet, NULL, NULL, NULL)) ==
            SOCKET_ERROR)
        {
                MessageBox(0, "Select failed", "Error", 0);
        }

        if (FD_ISSET(sServerListen, &ReadSet))
        {
            iSize = sizeof(clientaddr);
            sClient = accept(sServerListen,
                (struct sockaddr *)&clientaddr,
                              &iSize);
          if (sClient == INVALID_SOCKET)
          {
                  MessageBox(0, "Accept failed", "Error", 0);
                  break;
          }

          hThread = CreateThread(NULL, 0, ClientThread,
                        (LPVOID)sClient, 0, &dwThreadId);
          if (hThread == NULL)
          {
                  MessageBox(0, " thread failed", "Error", 0);
                  break;
          }
          CloseHandle(hThread);
        }
}
```

Two variables were added before the loop: ReadSet of the FD_SET type to store the set of sockets and ReadySock of the int type to store the number of sockets ready to use. Currently, we only have one socket, so we won't use this variable now.

At the beginning of the loop, the socket set is zeroed with the FD_ZERO function, and the newly-created socket waiting for a connection is added to the set. Then the select function is called. Only its second parameter is set, the others having NULL values. The second parameter indicates that the function should wait until it can read data for the sockets in the socket set. The last parameter is NULL indicating an infinite waiting time.

Well, the server socket is waiting for a connection and is ready for reading. When a request for connection is received from a client, the socket will accept it. However, before you perform any actions, you should check the socket for the presence in the socket set using the FD_ISSET function.

The rest of the code doesn't change. We accept the connection with the accept function, get a new socket to work with the client, and store it in the sClient variable. Then we create a new thread that will exchange data with the client.

Start the example and make sure it works correctly. There are no errors, and the program is waiting for a connection from the client.

You might be wondering, which mode is used by the sClient socket created with the accept function to work with a client's connection. Earlier, I mentioned that the default mode for sockets is the locking mode, and we haven't changed this value. If we remove from the client program the code sending data and disconnecting from the server, start the server, and connect to it with the client, the server will then accept the connection and "fall asleep." This will indicate that the recv function has frozen the thread in the locking mode and will wait for data infinitely. Despite the fact that the socket works in the non-locking mode, sockets created with the accept function will be locking ones.

The select function allows you to abandon the second thread that is used to exchange data between the server and the client. In addition, the current version of the example forces us to create multiple threads for the client. Thanks to the select function, you can abandon the threads and make the program simpler and more effective. I'll return to this issue in *Chapter 6*, which looks at a few interesting algorithms.

NOTE

The source code of this example is located in the \Demo\Chapter4\Select directory on the accompanying CD-ROM.

4.10.3. Working with Sockets Using Windows Messages

The select function was added to the Winsock library for compatibility with similar libraries on other platforms. In Windows, there is a more powerful function WSAAsyncSelect that allows you to monitor sockets using Windows messages. Therefore, you can receive messages in the WndProc function and don't have to lock the application and wait until the sockets are available.

The function looks as follows:

```
int WSAAsyncSelect (
    SOCKET s,
    HWND hWnd,
    unsigned int wMsg,
    long lEvent
    );
```

Below are its parameters:

- ❑ s — a socket whose messages should be monitored.
- ❑ hWnd — a window, to which the messages should be sent. This window (or its parent) should have the WndProc function to receive the messages.
- ❑ wMsg — a message to send to the window. Its type indicates that it is a network event.
- ❑ lEvents — a bit mask for the network event you are interested in. This parameter can be a combination of the following values:
    - ● FD_READ — readiness for reading
    - ● FD_WRITE — readiness for writing
    - ● FD_OOB — receiving urgent data
    - ● FD_ACCEPT — accepting clients
    - ● FD_CONNECT — connecting to the server
    - ● FD_CLOSE — closing the connection
    - ● FD_QOS — changing QoS (Quality of Service)
    - ● FD_GROUP_QOS — changing the QoS group

If the function terminates successfully, it will return a value greater than zero; otherwise, it will return SOCKET_ERROR.

This function automatically switches on the non-locking mode of the socket, and it would be pointless to call the ioctlsocket function.

Here is a simple example of how to use the WSAAsyncSelect function:

```
WSAAsyncSelect(s, hWnd, wMsg, FD_READ|FD_WRITE);
```

After this line is executed, the hWnd window will receive the wMsg message every time the s socket is ready to receive and send data. To cancel this, just call the same function with a zero passed as the fourth parameter:

```
WSAAsyncSelect(s, hWnd, 0, 0);
```

In this case, it is necessary to specify the first two parameters correctly and pass a zero as the last parameter. The value of the third parameter makes no difference because the message won't be sent, so you can specify a zero. If you just need to change the types of events, you can call the function with another value of the fourth parameter. It would be futile to first pass a zero and then to pass an actual value.

You can only use one message for all events on one socket. In other words, you cannot send to the window one message related to the FD_READ event and another message related to the FD_WRITE event.

Before we look at an example, we should make heads or tails of the parameters passed to the WndProc function when an event occurs. Remember this function:

```
LRESULT CALLBACK WndProc(
  HWND hWnd,
  UINT message,
  WPARAM wParam,
  LPARAM lParam)
```

The wParam and lParam parameters contain auxiliary information (depending on the event). For network events, the wParam parameter contains the handle to a socket, in which the event happened. Thus you don't need to have an array of sockets; a required socket is always available in the event.

The lParam parameter consists of two words: The least significant word determines the event, and the most significant one determines an error code. Well, now you are ready to look at an actual example. Create a new **Win32 Application** project and name it WSASel. Open the WSASel.cpp file and make a few changes to the _tWinMain function. As always, the code should be added before the main message loop. The code of the function is shown in Listing 4.19.

Listing 4.19. The _tWinMain function

```
int APIENTRY _tWinMain(HINSTANCE hInstance,
                       HINSTANCE hPrevInstance,
                       LPTSTR    lpCmdLine,
                       int       nCmdShow)
{
     // TODO: Place code here.
     MSG msg;
     HACCEL hAccelTable;

     // Initialize global strings
```

```
LoadString(hInstance, IDS_APP_TITLE, szTitle, MAX_LOADSTRING);
LoadString(hInstance, IDC_WSASEL, szWindowClass, MAX_LOADSTRING);
MyRegisterClass(hInstance);

// Perform application initialization:
if (!InitInstance (hInstance, nCmdShow))
{
      return FALSE;
}

hAccelTable = LoadAccelerators(hInstance, (LPCTSTR)IDC_WSASEL);

WSADATA        wsd;
if (WSAStartup(MAKEWORD(2, 2), &wsd) != 0)
{
      MessageBox(0, "Can't load WinSock", "Error", 0);
      return 0;
}

SOCKET sServerListen, sClient;
struct sockaddr_in localaddr, clientaddr;
HANDLE hThread;
DWORD dwThreadId;
int iSize;

sServerListen = socket(AF_INET, SOCK_STREAM, IPPROTO_IP);
if (sServerListen == SOCKET_ERROR)
{
      MessageBox(0, "Can't load WinSock", "Error", 0);
      return 0;
}

ULONG ulBlock;
ulBlock = 1;
if (ioctlsocket(sServerListen, FIONBIO, &ulBlock) == SOCKET_ERROR)
{
      return 0;
}

localaddr.sin_addr.s_addr = htonl(INADDR_ANY);
```

```
localaddr.sin_family = AF_INET;
localaddr.sin_port = htons(5050);

if (bind(sServerListen, (struct sockaddr *)&localaddr,
    sizeof(localaddr)) == SOCKET_ERROR)
{
    MessageBox(0, "Can't bind", "Error", 0);
    return 1;
}

WSAAsyncSelect(sServerListen, hWnd, WM_USER+1, FD_ACCEPT);
listen(sServerListen, 4);

// Main message loop:
while (GetMessage(&msg, NULL, 0, 0))
{
    if (!TranslateAccelerator(msg.hwnd, hAccelTable, &msg))
    {
        TranslateMessage(&msg);
        DispatchMessage(&msg);
    }
}

closesocket(sServerListen);
WSACleanup();

return (int) msg.wParam;
}
```

Because of the use of the WSAAsyncSelect function, the code (without additional threads) can be put into the _tWinMain function.

The code is almost identical to that in the TCPServer (see *Section 4.7.1*). The only difference is that the WSAAsyncSelect function is called before the listen function to select the socket and switch on its asynchronous mode. The following parameters are passed to it:

❑ sServerListen — a variable pointing to the newly created server socket.
❑ hWnd — a handle to the main window of the application; events will be sent to this window.

❐ WM_USER+1 — all user messages should be greater than the WM_USER constant. Lower values can be used by the system, and this can lead to conflicts. I used this construction to demonstrate that explicitly. I recommend that you use a constant with a self-explanatory name in your programs. For example, #define WM_NETMESSAGE WM_USER+1.

❐ FD_ACCEPT — an event to handle. What can a socket do? Of course, it can accept a connection from a client. This is the event we're interested in.

The most interesting things are in WndProc function. The beginning of this function (where the code should be inserted) is shown in Listing 4.20.

Listing 4.20. Handling network events in the WndProc function

---

```
LRESULT CALLBACK WndProc(HWND hWnd,
UINT message, WPARAM wParam, LPARAM lParam)
{
        int wmId, wmEvent;
    PAINTSTRUCT ps;
    HDC hdc;

    SOCKET ClientSocket;
    int ret;
    char szRecvBuff[1024], szSendBuff[1024];

    switch (message)
    {
    case WM_USER+1:
        switch (WSAGETSELECTEVENT(lParam))
        {
        case FD_ACCEPT:
            ClientSocket = accept(wParam, 0, 0);
            WSAAsyncSelect(ClientSocket, hWnd, WM_USER+1,
                FD_READ | FD_WRITE | FD_CLOSE);
            break;

        case FD_READ:
            ret = recv(wParam, szRecvBuff, 1024, 0);
            if (ret == 0)
                break;
            else if (ret == SOCKET_ERROR)
```

```
          {
            MessageBox(0, "Recive data failed",
                    "Error", 0);
            break;
          }
          szRecvBuff[ret] = '\0';

          strcpy(szSendBuff, "Command get OK");

          ret = send(wParam, szSendBuff,
                sizeof(szSendBuff), 0);
          break;

      case FD_WRITE:
            //Ready to send data
            break;

      case FD_CLOSE:
            closesocket(wParam);
       break;
    }
    case WM_COMMAND:
...
```

A new case statement is added here. It checks whether the caught message is equal to the WM_USER+1 network message we're waiting for. If this is the case, the function starts skimming through network events. The switch statement is used that compares the values in brackets to the coming events:

```
switch (WSAGETSELECTEVENT(lParam))
```

As you know, the lParam parameter stores an error code and an event type. To get an event, the WSAGETSELECTEVENT function is used. Then the events are checked. If a client's request for a connection was received, the following code will be executed:

```
case FD_ACCEPT:
ClientSocket = accept(wParam, 0, 0);
WSAAsyncSelect(ClientSocket, hWnd, WM_USER+1,
FD_READ | FD_WRITE | FD_CLOSE);
break;
```

First, the connection is accepted using the `accept` function. Its result is a socket that can be used to work with the client. Events from this socket should also be caught, therefore, the `WSAAsyncSelect` function is called. To avoid creating too many messages, we use the `WM_USER+1` value for the third parameter. It won't cause conflicts because the server socket handles only the `FD_ACCEPT` event, and the client socket's events include only reading, writing, and closing the socket.

When the server receives data, the `WM_USER+1` message will be caught and the `WSAGETSELECTEVENT(lParam)` function will return the `FD_READ` value. The received data will be read, and the "Command get OK" text will be sent to the client:

```
case FD_READ:
ret = recv(wParam, szRecvBuff, 1024, 0);
        if (ret == 0)
                break;
            else if (ret == SOCKET_ERROR)
            {
                MessageBox(0, "Recive data failed", "Error", 0);
                break;
            }
            szRecvBuff[ret] = '\0';
            strcpy(szSendBuff, "Command get OK");
            ret = send(wParam, szSendBuff, sizeof(szSendBuff), 0);
        break;
```

The same code was used in the TCPServer application to exchange data between the client and server. I deliberately left it as it was so that the server could be tested with the TCPClient program.

Nothing is done in response to the `FD_WRITE` event; there is a comment in the code. The `FD_CLOSE` event closes the socket.

This example using the `select` function can work with only one client. To add the option of handling multiple connections simultaneously, you should create an array of threads to send and receive data. In *Chapter 6*, I'll show you an example that uses the `select` function and doesn't use arrays of threads but, nevertheless, is free of these flaws.

The `WSAAsyncSelect` function is easy to use in a program, and it allows you to work with several clients. Its main advantage is that you don't need additional threads.

To test this example, start the server WSASel first. Then start the client TCPClient.

NOTE

The source code of this example is located in the \Demo\Chapter4\WSASel directory on the accompanying CD-ROM.

I'd like to emphasize that the information exchange is asynchronous. Sending and receiving large amounts of data should be done in portions.

Suppose a client needs to send a server 1 MB of data. Of course, it is impossible to do this in one step. This is why you should stick to the following procedure on the server side:

1. The server gets to know the amount of the data to receive (the client should tell it).
2. The server allocates the required amount of memory or, if there is too much data, creates a temporary file.
3. After the FD_READ event, the server stores the received data in the buffer or the file. The server handles the event until the data are received completely, or the client sends a certain byte sequence indicating the data transfer finished.

The client should act as follows:

1. The client tells the server how much data it is going to send.
2. The client opens the file from which the data will be read.
3. The client sends the first portion of the data. The remaining portions are sent in accordance with the FD_WRITE event.
4. When the data transfer finishes, the client sends to the server a certain sequence of bytes.

Using Windows messages is very convenient, but it deprives you of the compatibility with Unix systems that implement messages in another way and don't have the WSAAsyncSelect function. It would be very difficult to port such a program to another platform because you'd have to rewrite much of its code. However, when I'm not planning to port a program, I always use the WSAAsyncSelect in it, because it allows me to program comfortably and achieve the maximum performance of the program.

4.10.4. Asynchronous Data Exchange Using an Event Object

If your program doesn't use a message handler, you can use event objects. Given this scenario, you should stick to a different procedure:

1. Create an event object with the WSACreateEvent function.
2. Select a socket with the WSAEventSelect function.
3. Wait for the event using the WSAWaitForMultipleEvents function.

Let's look closely at functions necessary to work with event objects.

First, you should call the `WSACreateEvent` function to create an event object. You don't need to pass it any parameters; it will just return a new event of the `WSAEVENT` type:

```
WSAEVENT  WSACreateEvent(void);
```

Now, you should bind a socket to this object and specify events you are interested in. To do this, call the `WSAEventSelect` function:

```
int WSAEventSelect (
    SOCKET s,
    WSAEVENT hEventObject,
    long lNetworkEvents
    )
```

Its first parameter is a socket whose event we want to catch. The second parameter is an event object. The last parameter determines the necessary events. As the last parameter, you can specify the same constants as in the `WSAAsyncSelect` function (all of them begin with the `FD_` prefix).

You already encountered the `WaitForSingleObject` and `WaitForMultipleObjects` functions that wait for an event of the `HANDLE` type. For network events, use a similar function named `WSAWaitForMultipleEvents`:

```
DWORD WSAWaitForMultipleEvents(
    DWORD cEvents,
    const WSAEVENT FAR *lphEvents,
    BOOL fWaitAll,
    DWORD dwTimeOUT,
    BOOL fAlertable
    );
```

Let's look at its parameters:

- ❏ `cEvents` — the number of the event objects whose changes should be monitored. To find out the maximum number, use the `WSA_MAXIMUM_WAIT_EVENTS` constant.
- ❏ `lphEvents` — an array of event objects to wait for.
- ❏ `fWaitAll` — a waiting mode. If `TRUE` is specified, the function will wait until all events happen; otherwise, control will be passed to the application after the first event.
- ❏ `dwTimeOUT` — a time interval in milliseconds, during which the function waits for an event. If there is no event, the function returns `WSA_WAIT_TIMEOUT`. If it should wait infinitely, you can specify the `WSA_INFINITE` constant.

❑ `fAlertable` — is used in overlapping I/O, which is beyond the scope of this book. Therefore, specify `FALSE`.

To find, which events of the event array were triggered, subtract the `WSA_WAIT_EVENT_0` constant from the value returned by the `WSAWaitForMultipleEvents` function.

All events in the array should be empty before the call to the `WSAWaitForMultipleEvents` function. If at least one of them isn't, the function will instantly return control to the application rather than wait. After the function finishes, the triggered events will become non-empty, and they should be reset after handling. To do this, use the `WSAResetEvent` function:

```
BOOL WSAResetEvent(
    WSAEVENT hEvent
    );
```

This function resets an event specified as the parameter.

When you no longer need an event, you should close it. To do this, call the `WSACloseEvent` function. Pass it the event object you want to close:

```
BOOL WSACloseEvent(
    WSAEVENT hEvent
    );
```

If the closure is successful, the function will return `TRUE`; otherwise, it will return `FALSE`.

Chapter 5: Working with Hardware

This chapter looks at issues related to computer hardware. It is important for a hacker to know how to work with hardware and find out its parameters.

Since this book is mainly about working with networks, I'll touch upon this topic in this chapter too. When writing network applications, you often need to know the characteristics of a local computer and sometimes how to change them. I'll show you how to discern the characteristics of a network card and the network settings. In this chapter, you'll learn the answer to a question that beginner programmers often ask, "How can I find out what the IP address of a local computer is?"

In addition, I'll comprehensively discuss operations with COM ports, which are often used when connecting various devices to a computer. During my work with industry automation, I have written quite a few programs that collected data coming to COM ports from devices or monitored the work of instruments.

5.1. Network Parameters

In Windows 9*x*, there was a convenient utility, WinIPConfig, that displayed the network parameters. This utility made it easy to find out the IP or MAC address of any network device.

The MAC address is unique and is stored in the ROM of a network device. This feature of the MAC address has been used to provide security or protect programs. If a computer has a network card, it is quite easy to obtain the card's unique number.

To work with the network parameters, the IPHlpApi.lib library is used. Let's look at an example that introduces its most interesting functions.

Create a new dialog-based **MFC-Application** project. Put five **Edit Control** boxes, one **List Box**, and a button labeled **Get info** onto the main window. Fig. 5.1 shows a window that I created.

For the edit controls, create the following variables: eHostName, DNSServers, eNodeType, eIPRouting, and eWinsProxy. For the list box, create the eAdaptersInfo variable.

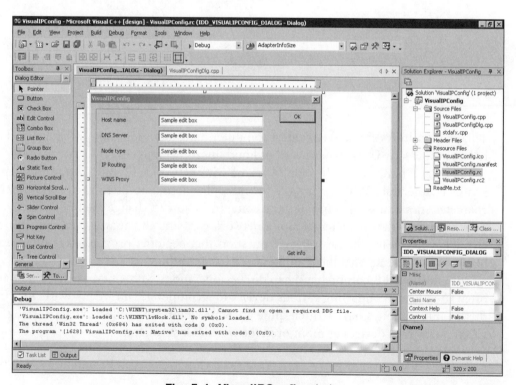

Fig. 5.1. VisualIPConfig window

There can be several network devices in a computer, therefore, information about them will be output to the list box. General information will be displayed in the edit controls.

Create a handler for the BN_CLICKED event of the button (to do this, double-click the button) and add the contents of Listing 5.1 to this handler. I recommend that you type the code manually rather than copy it from the CD.

Listing 5.1. Getting information on the parameters of a network card

```
void CVisualIPConfigDlg::OnBnClickedButton1()
{
    PFIXED_INFO pFixedInfo;
    ULONG iFixedInfo = 0;

    PIP_ADAPTER_INFO pAdapterInfo, pAdapter;
    ULONG iAdapterInfo;
    PIP_ADDR_STRING chAddr;

    CString Str;
    TCHAR lpszText[1024];
    int iErr;

    if ((iErr = GetNetworkParams(NULL, &iFixedInfo)) != 0)
    {
        if (iErr != ERROR_BUFFER_OVERFLOW)
        {
            AfxMessageBox("GetNetworkParams failed");
            return;
        }
    }

    if ((pFixedInfo=(PFIXED_INFO)GlobalAlloc(GPTR, iFixedInfo)) != NULL)
    {
        AfxMessageBox("Memory allocation error");
        return;
    }

    if (GetNetworkParams(pFixedInfo, &iFixedInfo) != 0)
    {
        AfxMessageBox("GetNetworkParams failed");
```

```cpp
        return;
    }

    eHostName.SetWindowText(pFixedInfo->HostName);

    CString s = pFixedInfo->DnsServerList.IpAddress.String;
    chAddr = pFixedInfo->DnsServerList.Next;
    while(chAddr)
    {
        s = s+" "+chAddr->IpAddress.String;
        chAddr = chAddr->Next;
    }
    DNSServers.SetWindowText(s);

    switch (pFixedInfo->NodeType)
    {
        case 1:
            eNodeType.SetWindowText("Broadcast");
            break;
        case 2:
            eNodeType.SetWindowText("Peer to peer");
            break;
        case 4:
            eNodeType.SetWindowText("Mixed");
            break;
        case 8:
            eNodeType.SetWindowText("Hybrid");
            break;
        default:
            eNodeType.SetWindowText("Don't know");
    }

    eIPRouting.SetWindowText(pFixedInfo->EnableRouting ? "Enabled" : "Disabled");
    eWinsProxy.SetWindowText(pFixedInfo->EnableProxy ? "Enabled" : "Disabled");

    iAdapterInfo = 0;
    iErr=GetAdaptersInfo(NULL, &iAdapterInfo);
    if ((iErr!= 0) && (iErr != ERROR_BUFFER_OVERFLOW))
    {
        AfxMessageBox("GetAdaptersInfo failed");
```

```
    return;
}

if ((pAdapterInfo = (PIP_ADAPTER_INFO) GlobalAlloc(GPTR, iAdapterInfo)) == NULL)
{
    AfxMessageBox("Memory allocation error\n");
    return;
}

if (GetAdaptersInfo(pAdapterInfo, &iAdapterInfo) != 0)
{
    AfxMessageBox("GetAdaptersInfo failed");
    return;
}

pAdapter = pAdapterInfo;

eAdaptersInfo.AddString("=============================");

while (pAdapter)
{
    switch (pAdapter->Type)
    {
        case MIB_IF_TYPE_ETHERNET:
                    Str = "Ethernet adapter: "; break;
        case MIB_IF_TYPE_PPP:
                    Str = "PPP adapter: "; break;
        case MIB_IF_TYPE_LOOPBACK:
                    Str = "Loopback adapter: "; break;
        case MIB_IF_TYPE_TOKENRING:
                    Str = "Token Ring adapter: "; break;
        case MIB_IF_TYPE_FDDI:
                    Str = "FDDI adapter: "; break;
        case MIB_IF_TYPE_SLIP:
                    Str = "Slip adapter: "; break;
        case MIB_IF_TYPE_OTHER:
        default: Str = "Other adapter: ";
    }
```

```
eAdaptersInfo.AddString(Str+pAdapter->AdapterName);

Str = "Description: ";
eAdaptersInfo.AddString(Str+pAdapter->Description);

Str = "Physical Address: ";
for (UINT i = 0; i<pAdapter->AddressLength; i++)
{
    if (i == (pAdapter->AddressLength - 1))
        sprintf(lpszText, "%.2X", (int)pAdapter->Address[i]);
    else
        sprintf(lpszText, "%.2X", (int)pAdapter->Address[i]);
    Str = Str + lpszText;
}
eAdaptersInfo.AddString(Str);

sprintf(lpszText, "DHCP Enabled: %s", (pAdapter->DhcpEnabled ? "yes" : "no"));
eAdaptersInfo.AddString(lpszText);

chAddr = &(pAdapter->IpAddressList);
while(chAddr)
{
        Str = "IP Address: ";
        eAdaptersInfo.AddString(Str+chAddr->IpAddress.String);

        Str = "Subnet Mask: ";
        eAdaptersInfo.AddString(Str+chAddr->IpMask.String);

        chAddr = chAddr->Next;
}

Str = "Default Gateway: ";
eAdaptersInfo.AddString(Str+pAdapter->GatewayList.IpAddress.String);

chAddr = pAdapter->GatewayList.Next;
while(chAddr)
{
// Print next Gateway
        chAddr = chAddr->Next;
```

```
        }

        Str = "DHCP Server: ";
        eAdaptersInfo.AddString(Str+pAdapter->DhcpServer.IpAddress.String);

        Str = "Primary WINS Server: ";
        eAdaptersInfo.AddString(Str+pAdapter->PrimaryWinsServer.IpAddress.String);

        Str = "Secondary WINS Server: ";
        eAdaptersInfo.AddString(Str+pAdapter->SecondaryWinsServer.IpAddress.String);

        eAdaptersInfo.AddString("============================");
        pAdapter = pAdapter->Next;
    }
}
```

General information on a network can be obtained with the `GetNetworkParams` function. It takes two parameters: a structure of the `PFIXED_INFO` type and the size of this structure.

If you pass `NULL` as the first parameter and a numeric variable as the second parameter, the size of the memory necessary for the structure will be written into the variable. This is done when the function is called for the first time. The memory should be allocated in the global area with the `GlobalAlloc` function; otherwise, the function can return incorrect data.

After that, the `GetNetworkParams` function is called once more with two actual parameters. If it returns a zero, this will mean that the data was received successfully.

Below are the elements of the `PFIXED_INFO` structure:

- ❏ `HostName` — the name of a computer
- ❏ `DnsServerList.IpAddress` — a list of the IP addresses of the DNS servers
- ❏ `NodeType` — the type of network device
- ❏ `EnableRouting` — when `TRUE`, routing is enabled
- ❏ `EnableProxy` — when `TRUE`, caching is enabled

After you obtain general information, you can get information on all installed adapters with the `GetAdaptersInfo` function. It also takes two parameters: a variable of the `PIP_ADAPTER_INFO` type and its size. If a zero is specified as the first parameter, the function will use the second parameter to return an amount of memory necessary for the `PIP_ADAPTER_INFO` structure.

Below are the elements of the `PIP_ADAPTER_INFO` structure:

❑ `Type` — the type of an adapter. It can take one of the following values that are quite self-explanatory:
  - `MIB_IF_TYPE_ETHERNET`
  - `MIB_IF_TYPE_TOKENRING`
  - `MIB_IF_TYPE_FDDI`
  - `MIB_IF_TYPE_PPP`
  - `MIB_IF_TYPE_LOOPBACK`
  - `MIB_IF_TYPE_SLIP`
  - `MIB_IF_TYPE_OTHER`

❑ `AdapterName` — self-explanatory
❑ `Description` — a description that can contain the manufacturer's name or a purpose
❑ `AddressLength` — the length of the MAC address
❑ `Address` — the MAC address
❑ `DhcpEnabled` — is `TRUE` when DHCP is enabled
❑ `IpAddressList` — a list of IP addresses and network masks (each adapter can have several addresses)
❑ `GatewayList` — self-explanatory
❑ `DhcpServer` — DHCP server addresses
❑ `PrimaryWinsServer` — the address of the primary WINS server
❑ `SecondaryWinsServer` — the address of the secondary WINS server

To compile the example without errors, you should open the project properties and in the **Linker/Input** section, add the IPHlpApi.lib library to the **Additional Dependencies** property. In addition, put the description of the iphlpapi.h header file at the beginning of the module.

Start the VisualIPConfig.exe file. Click the **Get Info** button. All information on the network card obtained using this program is shown in Fig. 5.2.

NOTE

The source code of this example is located in the \Demo\Chapter5\VisualIPConfig directory on the accompanying CD-ROM.

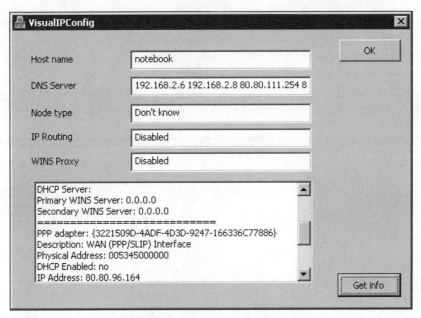

Fig. 5.2. Result of VisualIPConfig

5.2. Changing the IP Address

In this section, I'll try to answer a frequently asked question and explain how to change the IP address programmatically. This will allow you to write a program that will periodically change the address of your computer. It will increase the security of the computer and protect it against many types of attacks.

A network card can have several addresses, therefore, there are functions that add or delete addresses. To add an address, use the AddIPAddress function that takes the following parameters:

❑ The IP address.
❑ A network mask for the address.
❑ The ID of an adapter the address is being added for.
❑ The address context. As my experience shows, it is best to specify zero. The context will be set by the system.
❑ An instance that is usually set to zero.

Each IP address is associated with a certain adapter. For example, if there are two network cards in the system, two different records for addresses will be created.

The context unambiguously identifies the address record in the system. There cannot be two records with the same context for one or more network adapters.

By knowing the context of an address, you can easily delete the address using the `DeleteIPAddress` function whose one and only parameter is that context.

I'll illustrate this with an example. Create a new dialog-based **MFC Application** project and name it ChangeIPAddress. Fig. 5.3 shows a window of such an application.

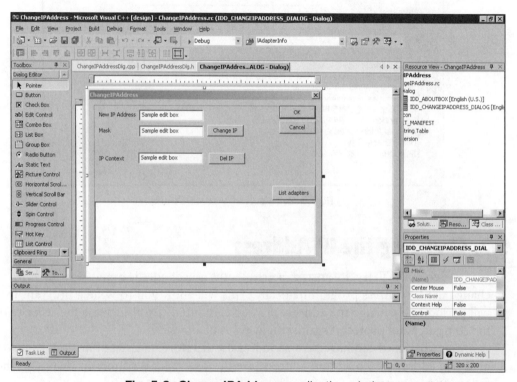

Fig. 5.3. ChangeIPAddress application window

Upon clicking the **List adapters** button, information on network addresses will be obtained and output to the **List Box** control that is stretched along the bottom of the window. Listing 5.2 shows the code that is executed when the button is clicked.

Listing 5.2. Displaying information on the addresses

```
void CChangeIPAddressDlg::OnBnClickedButton3()
{
    PIP_ADAPTER_INFO pAdapterInfo, pAdapter;
```

```
    ULONG iAdapterInfo;
    int iErr;
    CString Str;

    iAdapterInfo = 0;
    iErr = GetAdaptersInfo(NULL, &iAdapterInfo);
if ((iErr != 0) && (iErr != ERROR_BUFFER_OVERFLOW))
{
    AfxMessageBox("GetAdaptersInfo failed");
    return;
}

if ((pAdapterInfo = (PIP_ADAPTER_INFO)
    GlobalAlloc(GPTR, iAdapterInfo)) == NULL)
{
    AfxMessageBox("Memory allocation error\n");
    return;
}

if (GetAdaptersInfo(pAdapterInfo, &iAdapterInfo) != 0)
{
    AfxMessageBox("GetAdaptersInfo failed");
    return;
}

pAdapter = pAdapterInfo;
lAdapters.AddString("=====================");
    while (pAdapter)
    {
            Str = "Adapter: ";
        lAdapters.AddString(Str+pAdapter->AdapterName);

            char s[20];
            Str = itoa(pAdapter->Index, s, 10);
            Str = "Index: "+Str;
            lAdapters.AddString(Str);

            PIP_ADDR_STRING chAddr = &(pAdapter->IpAddressList);
            while(chAddr)
        {
```

```
        lAdapters.AddString("------------------------------");

                Str = itoa(chAddr->Context, s, 10);
                Str = "Context: "+Str;
                lAdapters.AddString(Str);

                Str = "IP Address: ";
                lAdapters.AddString(Str+chAddr->IpAddress.String);

                Str = "Subnet Mask: ";
                lAdapters.AddString(Str+chAddr->IpMask.String);

                chAddr = chAddr->Next;
        }
    pAdapter = pAdapter->Next;
    }

}
```

As was the case in *Section 5.1*, all information on addresses is obtained with the GetAdaptersInfo function. Remember that its first parameter should be a structure of the PIP_ADAPTER_INFO type. In this structure, the Index element stores the index of the network device that should be specified as the third parameter of the AddIPAddress function when adding a new IP address. The IpAddressList parameter is an array of structures of the PIP_ADDR_STRING type. In such a structure, we need the Context field that stores an IP-address context.

The IpAddress parameter is the address, and the IpMask parameter is the network mask.

Upon clicking the **Change IP** button, the new address for the network adapter is added to the address list. Before adding it, you can find and delete all existing addresses. In Listing 5.3, you can see the code that is executed when the button is clicked.

Listing 5.3. Adding a new address for the first network adapter in the system

```
void CChangeIPAddressDlg::OnBnClickedButton1()
{
    PIP_ADAPTER_INFO pAdapterInfo, pAdapter;
        ULONG iAdapterInfo;
        int iErr;
```

```
    ULONG iInst, iContext;
    iInst = iContext = 0;

    iAdapterInfo = 0;
    iErr = GetAdaptersInfo(NULL, &iAdapterInfo);
if ((iErr != 0) && (iErr != ERROR_BUFFER_OVERFLOW))
{
    AfxMessageBox("GetAdaptersInfo failed");
    return;
}

if ((pAdapterInfo = (PIP_ADAPTER_INFO)
GlobalAlloc(GPTR, iAdapterInfo)) == NULL)
{
    AfxMessageBox("Memory allocation error\n");
    return;
}

if (GetAdaptersInfo(pAdapterInfo, &iAdapterInfo) != 0)
{
    AfxMessageBox("GetAdaptersInfo failed");
    return;
}

pAdapter = pAdapterInfo;

    char sNewAddr[20], sNewMask[20];

    eIPEdit.GetWindowText(sNewAddr, 20);
    eMaskEdit.GetWindowText(sNewMask, 20);

    iErr = AddIPAddress(inet_addr(sNewAddr), inet_addr(sNewMask),
        pAdapter->Index, &iContext, &iInst);
    if (iErr != 0)
        AfxMessageBox("Can't change address");
}
```

To add a new address, you should know the index of the network adapter. To find it, use the GetAdaptersInfo function. Then you can call the AddIPAddress function. After the user clicks the **Del IP** button, the address with the context specified in the IP Context control will be deleted. Listing 5.4 shows the code that is executed when the button is clicked.

Listing 5.4. Deleting an IP address

```
void CChangeIPAddressDlg::OnBnClickedButton2()
{
    char sContext[20];
    eContext.GetWindowText(sContext, 20);

    int Context = atoi(sContext);
    if (DeleteIPAddress(Context) != 0)
    {
        AfxMessageBox("Can't delete address");
    }
}
```

You can obtain an interesting effect if you delete all the addresses. When you do this, the computer "disappears" from the network and is not able to work with it. However, this concerns prankish programs.

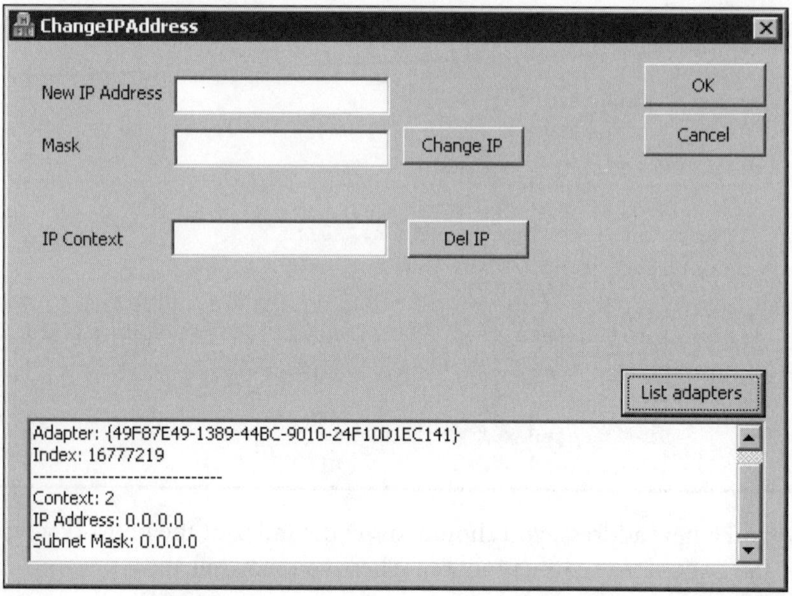

Fig. 5.4. Result of ChangeIPAddress when the network cable is disconnected

To conclude this section, I'd like to warn you that these functions will only work correctly if you properly adjust the network. Even if you just disconnect the network cable, the functions won't work. Fig. 5.4 shows the result of the program on my notebook. Before clicking the **List adapters** button, I disconnected the network cable. The IP address and the network mask became zeroes (0.0.0.0).

The source code of this example is located in the \Demo\Chapter5\ChangeIPAddress directory on the accompanying CD-ROM.

NOTE

5.3. Working with a COM Port

In my work, I often have to use the RS-232 interface. This is the official name of the COM port. Contemporary hardware (such as controllers, information collecting devices, etc.) works via this port. Any modem, even an internal one, is accessed via this port. It is impossible to count external devices connected to this interface.

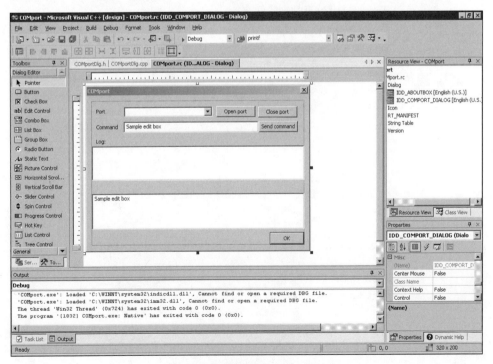

Fig. 5.5. COMport window

Working with ports is similar to working with files. Let's look at a simple example. Create a new dialog-based **MFC Application** and name it COMport. A window of such an application is shown in Fig. 5.5.

The top part of the window contains a drop-down list **Combo Box**, in which you can select a port name. There are two buttons next to the list to open and close the port. A text box for a command and a button to send the command are located below. In the middle of the window, there are **List Box** controls to display the progress of working with the port and a multiline edit control to display the data being received.

Create a similar interface. After you click the **Open port** button, the code from Listing 5.5 should be executed.

Listing 5.5. Opening a port

```
void CCOMportDlg::OnBnClickedOpenportButton()
{
        if (hCom != INVALID_HANDLE_VALUE)
        {
                OnBnClickedButton1();
                Sleep(300);
        }

        char sPortName[10];
        cbPorts.GetWindowText(sPortName, 10);

        hCom = CreateFile(sPortName, GENERIC_READ | GENERIC_WRITE,
                             0, NULL, OPEN_EXISTING, 0, NULL);

        if (hCom == INVALID_HANDLE_VALUE)
                lLogList.AddString("Error opening port");
        else
        {
                lLogList.AddString("Port successfully opened.");

                DCB dcb;
                GetCommState(hCom, &dcb);
                dcb.BaudRate = CBR_57600;
                dcb.ByteSize = 8;
                dcb.Parity = NOPARITY;
                dcb.StopBits = ONESTOPBIT;
```

```
        if (SetCommState(hCom, &dcb))
                lLogList.AddString("Configuring OK");
        else
                lLogList.AddString("Configuring Error");

        hThread = CreateThread(0, 0, ReadThread, (LPVOID)this, 0, 0);
}
}
```

If you try to open a port a second time, you'll get an error message. This is why an appropriate check should be done first. If the port is open, it should be closed. The check is done in the OnBnClickedButton1 function whose code will be shown later. This function is called after the user clicks the **Close Port** button.

Now get the name of the selected port and open the port. To do this, use the CreateFile function that works with common files and pass it the port name rather than a file name.

If the port opens successfully, an appropriate message will be displayed, and you can configure the parameters of the connection. To do this, first obtain the current system settings using the GetCommState function. Pass it two parameters: a handle to the open port and a pointer to a structure of the DCB type. This structure contains complete information on the connection and looks as follows:

```
typedef struct _DCB {
    DWORD DCBlength;            // The length of the DCB structure
DWORD BaudRate;                 // The baud rate
    DWORD fBinary: 1;           // The binary mode; the end of the
                                // line isn't checked
    DWORD fParity: 1;           // The parity click is on
    DWORD fOutxCtsFlow:1;       // CTS control on the output flow
    DWORD fOutxDsrFlow:1;       // DSR control on the output flow
    DWORD fDtrControl:2;        // DTR control on the data transmission
                                // speed
    DWORD fDsrSensitivity:1;    // DSR sensitivity

    DWORD fTXContinueOnXoff:1;  // A stop bit; transmission continues
    DWORD fOutX: 1;             // A start/stop bit to control the
                                // output flow
    DWORD fInX: 1;              // A start/stop bit to control the
                                // input flow
```

```
    DWORD fErrorChar: 1;          // The error check is on
    DWORD fNull: 1;               // Reject an empty flow
    DWORD fRtsControl: 2;         // RTS control on the data flow
    DWORD fAbortOnError: 1;       // Check read/write operations
    DWORD fDummy2: 17;            // Reserved
    WORD wReserved;               // Reserved
    WORD XonLim;                  // The start signal threshold
    WORD XoffLim;                 // The stop signal threshold

    BYTE ByteSize;                // The bit size (usually seven or eight)
    BYTE Parity;                  // Byte parity
    BYTE StopBits;                // Stop bits
    char XonChar;                 // The start signal in a flow
    char XoffChar;                // The stop signal in a flow
    char ErrorChar;               // The error signal

    char EofChar;                 // The end-of-flow signal
    char EvtChar;                 // Reserved
    WORD wReserved1;              // Reserved
} DCB;
```

If these elements are filled incorrectly, the data will neither be sent nor received. It is very important to fill the following elements:

❏ BaudRate — data transmission speed (bits per second). Specify a constant with the CBR_speed syntax, where speed is the speed supported by the device used, for example, CBR_56000.

❏ ByteSize — the byte size used in the transmission (seven or eight).

❏ Parity — the parity flag.

❏ StopBits — one of the following values: ONESTOPBIT, ONE5STOPBITS ("one and a half"), or TWOSTOPBITS.

You may leave the default values (i.e., those returned by the system) for the other elements. Before you specify any values for the elements of the structure, be sure to read the user manual for the device you want to connect to. I have never seen a device that could support all working modes. For example, a ZyXel Omni 56K modem supports a baud rate from 24,000 to 56,000. Therefore, for this modem type you can specify only values from this range.

In addition, both devices (the transmitter and the receiver) should have the same settings (such as the baud rate, the byte size, etc.), otherwise, you will neither be able to send nor receive the data.

After the port is configured, a thread is created. Within the thread, the program infinitely tries to read data from the port. Of course, this isn't an effective solution because it would be more convenient to use Windows messages. However, this isn't very important since it is a training example. The `ReadThread` function looks as follows:

```
DWORD __stdcall ReadThread(LPVOID hwnd)
{
        DWORD iSize;
        char sReceivedChar;
        while(TRUE)
        {
                ReadFile(hCom, &sReceivedChar, 1, &iSize, 0);
                SendDlgItemMessage((HWND)hwnd, IDC_EDIT2, WM_CHAR,
                sReceivedChar, 0);
        }
}
```

It contains an infinite loop to read data using a standard file-reading function `ReadFile`.

Now, look at the port-closing function called when the **Close Port** button is clicked:

```
void CCOMportDlg::OnBnClickedButton1()
{
        if (hCom == INVALID_HANDLE_VALUE)
                return;

        if (MessageBox("Close port?", "Warning", MB_YESNO) == IDYES)
        {
                TerminateThread(hThread, 0);
                CloseHandle(hCom);
                hCom = INVALID_HANDLE_VALUE;
        }
}
```

Before closing the port, it checks the `hCom` variable. It is quite likely that the port is already closed or has never been opened. If the variable contains an invalid handle value, the function simply returns.

If the port is open, a request for confirmation of the operation is displayed. If the user confirms that he or she wishes to close the port, the thread is terminated, the port handle is closed, and the `INVALID_HANDLE_VALUE` value is assigned to the `hCom` variable.

The last thing you should add to the program is an option for sending messages. The code shown in Listing 5.6 should be executed when the **Send command** button is clicked.

Listing 5.6. A function to send data to a port

```
void CCOMportDlg::OnBnClickedSendcommandButton()
{
        if (hCom == INVALID_HANDLE_VALUE)
        {
                AfxMessageBox("Open port before send command");
                return;
        }

        char sSend[10224];
        eSendCommand.GetWindowText(sSend, 1024);

        if (strlen(sSend)>0)
        {
                lLogList.AddString(sSend);

                sSend[strlen(sSend)] = '\r';
                sSend[strlen(sSend)] = '\0';

                TerminateThread(hThread,0);
                DWORD iSize;
                WriteFile(hCom, sSend, strlen(sSend), &iSize,0);
                hThread = CreateThread(0, 0, ReadThread,
                        (LPVOID)this, 0, 0);
        }
}
```

First, it checks whether the port is open. If it isn't, there is no point in writing data to it. Then the length of the data being sent is checked. If the length is greater than zero, the code adds a string-terminating character (a null character) to the end of the string. I have worked with various devices, and most of them have required line feed and carriage return characters at the end of a command. Sometimes, a line-feed character is enough.

Then the data-reading thread is terminated, and the data are written to the port using a standard file-writing function `WriteFile`. After that, the reading thread can be started again.

If you have a modem, you can start the program and open the port, to which the modem is connected. Send the `ATDTxxxxxxx` command, where xxxxxxx is a telephone number. The modem will dial the number.

NOTE

The source code of this example is located in the \Demo\Chapter5\COMport directory on the accompanying CD-ROM.

5.4. "Frozen" Files

You already know how to work with files. In *Section 4.2*, you tried to create a file on a remote computer and write some data to it. Let's look at a prank with files.

Remember that a network path has the following form:

```
\\computer-name\disk\path
```

If you need to access a local disk as a network one but the disk isn't shared, you should put the `$` character after the disk name. For example, to access the myfile.txt file on the disk C:, you should specify the following path:

```
\\MyComputer\C$\myfile.txt
```

Now, the most interesting things are to come. In Windows, you cannot create files whose names contain the `?` character, and the operating system checks file names for this character. However, when the file is accessed via a network, this check isn't done. If your computer is connected to a network, open any network disk of another computer. Suppose its name is `e:`. If you execute the code from Listing 5.7, the program will be frozen and it will be impossible to abort it.

☺ **Listing 5.7. Creating a wrong file in a network**

```
if ((FileHandle = CreateFile("\\\\notebook\\e$\\?myfile.txt",
          GENERIC_WRITE | GENERIC_READ,
          FILE_SHARE_READ | FILE_SHARE_WRITE, NULL,
          CREATE_ALWAYS, FILE_ATTRIBUTE_NORMAL, NULL
          )) == INVALID_HANDLE_VALUE)
```

```
{
        MessageBox(0, "Create file error", "Error", 0);
        return;
}

// Write to file 9 symbols
if (WriteFile(FileHandle, "Test line", 9, &BWritten, NULL)== 0)
{
        MessageBox(0, "Write to file error", "Error", 0);
        return;
}

// Close file
CloseHandle(FileHandle);
```

In this code, I try to create a file and write nine characters to it, like in *Section 4.2*. However, the name of the file is incorrect (it contains the ? character), and it is impossible to create the file. On the other hand, the check hasn't been done and the program will be waiting for a response from the operating system, which will never come.

The source code of this example is located in the \Demo\Chapter5\TestFile directory on the accompanying CD-ROM.

NOTE

Chapter 6: Tips, Tricks, and Other Useful Information

In previous chapters, I covered many prankish programs and discussed theoretical aspects of network programming. In this chapter, I'll demonstrate a few useful algorithms for you with examples. You'll learn many interesting methods used by hackers. In addition, you'll consolidate your theoretical knowledge.

When discussing network functions in *Chapters 4* and *5*, we looked at some interesting examples. However, they had flaws. For example, the port scanner was slow, and it took too much time to check a thousand ports (*Section 4.4*). I already told you what was necessary to do to speed up the process. In this chapter, I'll show you the quickest port scanner that can be made flexible and universal.

In addition, I'll teach you how to improve the sending and receiving of data. This is often a "bottleneck" when the maximum performance of an application and the minimum load on the processor are required.

There are many nuances in programming, and you can act differently in different situations to achieve your goal. I won't be able to look at each situation because it would take several thousand pages and require you to have a deep knowledge of mathematics. Therefore, I'll confine myself to network issues.

6.1. Data Sending/Receiving Algorithm

In *Section 4.10.2*, we looked at an example, in which a server asynchronously waited for a connection using the `select` function. As soon as the connection took place, a new thread was created that exchanged data with a client.

I already told you that the asynchronous work of network functions allowed you to work with several clients simultaneously. In such a case, a separate thread for exchanging messages would be excessive. Listing 6.1 contains an example, in which a server waits for a connection and works with a client within one function. Nevertheless, it can serve multiple clients simultaneously.

Listing 6.1. An algorithm for simultaneous work with clients

```
DWORD WINAPI NetThread(LPVOID lpParam)
{
      SOCKET sServerListen;
      SOCKET ClientSockets[50];
      int TotalSocket=0;

  struct sockaddr_in localaddr,
                     clientaddr;
  int  iSize;

      sServerListen = socket(AF_INET, SOCK_STREAM, IPPROTO_IP);
  if (sServerListen == SOCKET_ERROR)
  {
             MessageBox(0, "Can't load WinSock", "Error", 0);
             return 0;
  }

      ULONG ulBlock;
      ulBlock = 1;
      if (ioctlsocket(sServerListen, FIONBIO, &ulBlock) == SOCKET_ERROR)
      {
             return 0;
      }

  localaddr.sin_addr.s_addr = htonl(INADDR_ANY);
  localaddr.sin_family = AF_INET;
  localaddr.sin_port = htons(5050);
```

```
if (bind(sServerListen, (struct sockaddr *)&localaddr,
        sizeof(localaddr)) == SOCKET_ERROR)
{
    MessageBox(0, "Can't bind", "Error", 0);
    return 1;
}

MessageBox(0, "Bind OK", "Error", 0);

listen(sServerListen, 4);

MessageBox(0, "Listen OK", "Error", 0);

    FD_SET ReadSet;
    int ReadySock;

while (1)
{
        FD_ZERO(&ReadSet);
        FD_SET(sServerListen, &ReadSet);

        for (int i=0; i<TotalSocket; i++)
            if (ClientSockets[i] != INVALID_SOCKET)
                    FD_SET(ClientSockets[i], &ReadSet);


        if ((ReadySock = select(0, &ReadSet, NULL, NULL, NULL)) ==
            SOCKET_ERROR)
        {
            MessageBox(0, "Select failed", "Error", 0);
        }

        // We have new connection
        if (FD_ISSET(sServerListen, &ReadSet))
        {
            iSize = sizeof(clientaddr);
            ClientSockets[TotalSocket] = accept(sServerListen,
                    (struct sockaddr *)&clientaddr, &iSize);
            if (ClientSockets[TotalSocket] == INVALID_SOCKET)
            {
                MessageBox(0, "Accept failed", "Error", 0);
```

```
                break;
            }
            TotalSocket++;
        }
        // We have data from client
        for (int i=0; i<TotalSocket; i++)
        {
                if (ClientSockets[i] == INVALID_SOCKET)
                    continue;
                if (FD_ISSET(ClientSockets[i], &ReadSet))
                {
                    char szRecvBuff[1024],
                        szSendBuff[1024];

int ret = recv(ClientSockets[i], szRecvBuff, 1024, 0);
if (ret == 0)
    {
            closesocket(ClientSockets[i]);
            ClientSockets[i] = INVALID_SOCKET;
            break;
    }
else if (ret == SOCKET_ERROR)
{
    MessageBox(0, "Receive data failed", "Error", 0);
    break;
}
szRecvBuff[ret] = '\0';

strcpy(szSendBuff, "Command get OK");

ret = send(ClientSockets[i], szSendBuff, sizeof(szSendBuff), 0);
if (ret == SOCKET_ERROR)
{
    break;
}
                }
            }
    }
    closesocket(sServerListen);
    return 0;
}
```

Let's look at how it works. The idea is that two variables are declared:

- ☐ sServerListen — a variable of the SOCKET type to listen to the port and wait for a request for a connection from the client side.
- ☐ ClientSockets — an array of 50 elements of the ClientSockets type. It will be used to work with clients, and 50 clients will be served simultaneously. Every connection will get its own socket, and the 51st client will get an error message. In an actual program, you should use a dynamic array to delete an appropriate socket from the array when a client disconnects.

Then the sServerListen socket is created, moved to the asynchronous mode, bound to the local address using the bind function, and it starts listening. This piece of code should be familiar to you.

The most interesting things happen in the infinite loop that waited for a connection in the previous examples. Not only is the server socket added to the socket set, but active client sockets are as well. Then the select function waits for any of these sockets to be ready to read data.

The deeper we go, the more interesting things we come across. First, the server socket is checked. If it is ready to read, a client has connected to it. The connection is accepted using the accept function, and the result (a socket to work with the client) is stored in the last available element of the ClientSockets array. Then the select function will wait for events from this client.

Then all the sockets from the array are checked for the possibility to read their data. If a client is ready, its data are read and a response is sent. If no data was obtained, i.e., the recv function returned a zero, the client is disconnected from the server.

This algorithm is fast and flexible. Most importantly, it allows you to handle the server and client sockets with one loop. This is both convenient and effective. If your program should exchange small messages, you can already use it. If you wish to exchange large amounts of data, you should add an option for the reading and sending of all the data.

Don't forget to use a dynamic array for client sockets. If you don't want to use dynamic arrays, you can use a simpler method: Before you fill the FD_SET structure, reorder its elements to remove those equal to INVALID_SOCKET. Then set the TotalSocket variable so that it points to the array element next to the last element that is actually used.

The source code of this example is located in the \Demo\Chapter6\AdvancedTCPServer directory on the accompanying CD-ROM.

NOTE

6.2. The Fastest Port Scanner

Threads are a powerful and convenient tool that allow you to multitask within one application. However, they have a disadvantage. Programmers who have become familiar with threads tend to start using them needlessly.

I have seen many port scanners using from 20 to 50 threads to scan many ports simultaneously. I am aware that the example from *Chapter 4* is very slow and should be speeded up. However, it would be wrong to use that method. You can try to scan with multiple threads if you wish. You'll see that this isn't easy. In addition, threads overload the operating system.

Now, you're about to see how a fast port scanner can be put into place without using threads. As you might have guessed, this is done with asynchronously working with a network. You can create a few asynchronous sockets and start waiting for a connection. Then collect all these sockets in the `fd_set` set and call the `select` function to wait for a connection with the server. When it finishes, check all the sockets for successful connections and display the result.

Let's try this out. Create a new dialog-based **MFC Application**. Don't check the checkbox for WinSock support in the **Advanced Features** section. This example will use a few functions from the Winsock2 library, so include the winsock2.h header file manually and specify the need to use the ws2_32.lib library in the project properties. You've done this many times, so rest assured that no problems should arise.

Now, open the main application window in the resource editor. Edit it as shown in Fig. 6.1. Add three **Edit Box** controls, a **List Box**, and a button that will start scanning when a user clicks it. Create the following variables for the edit boxes:

- `chHostName` — the name or IP address of the computer being scanned
- `chStartPort` — the starting port to scan
- `chEndPort` — the end port to scan

There are so many ports that even our fast scanner will need quite a long time to scan them.

Now, let's proceed with the programming. Create a `BN_CLICKED` event handler for the button that starts scanning. The handler's code is quite long (see Listing 6.2), but I recommend that you type it manually rather than copy it from the CD-ROM. This will allow you to understand the purpose of each line. I'll give you all the necessary information.

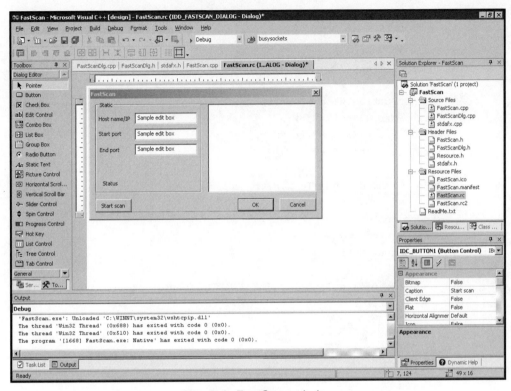

Fig. 6.1. FastScan window

Listing 6.2. A fast port scanner

```
void CFastScanDlg::OnBnClickedButton1()
{
        char tStr[255];
        SOCKET sock[MAX_SOCKETS];
        int busy[MAX_SOCKETS], port[MAX_SOCKETS];
        int iStartPort, iEndPort, iBusySocks = 0;
        struct sockaddr_in addr;
        fd_set fdWaitSet;

        WSADATA wsd;
        if (WSAStartup(MAKEWORD(2, 2), &wsd) != 0)
        {
                SetDlgItemText(IDC_STATUSTEXT, "Can't load WinSock");
```

```
        return;
}

SetDlgItemText(IDC_STATUSTEXT, "Resolving host");

chStartPort.GetWindowText(tStr, 255);
iStartPort = atoi(tStr);
chEndPort.GetWindowText(tStr, 255);
iEndPort = atoi(tStr);

chHostName.GetWindowText(tStr, 255);

struct hostent *host = NULL;
host = gethostbyname(tStr);
if (host == NULL)
{
        SetDlgItemText(IDC_STATUSTEXT, "Unable to resolve host");
        return;
}

for (int i = 0; i < MAX_SOCKETS; i++)
    busy[i] = 0;

SetDlgItemText(IDC_STATUSTEXT, "Scanning");

while (((iBusySocks) || (iStartPort <= iEndPort)))
{
    for (int i = 0; i < MAX_SOCKETS; i++)
      {
            if (busy[i] == 0 && iStartPort <= iEndPort)
            {
                    sock[i] = socket (AF_INET, SOCK_STREAM,
                        IPPROTO_TCP);
                    if (sock[i] < 0)
                    {
                            SetDlgItemText(IDC_STATUSTEXT,
                                "Socket failed");
                            return;
                    }
                    iBusySocks++;
```

```
            addr.sin_family = AF_INET;
            addr.sin_port = htons(iStartPort);
            CopyMemory(&addr.sin_addr,
                    host->h_addr_list[0],
                    host->h_length);

            ULONG ulBlock;
            ulBlock = 1;
            if (ioctlsocket(sock[i], FIONBIO,
                    &ulBlock) == SOCKET_ERROR)
            {
                    return;
            }

            connect (sock[i], (struct sockaddr *)
                    &addr, sizeof (addr));
            if (WSAGetLastError() == WSAEINPROGRESS)
            {
                    closesocket (sock[i]);
                    iBusySocks--;
            }
            else
            {
                    busy[i] = 1;
                    port[i] = iStartPort;
            }
            iStartPort++;
        }
}
FD_ZERO (&fdWaitSet);
for (int i = 0; i < MAX_SOCKETS; i++)
{
        if (busy[i] == 1)
                FD_SET (sock[i], &fdWaitSet);
}

struct timeval tv;
tv.tv_sec = 1;
tv.tv_usec = 0;
if (select (1, NULL, &fdWaitSet, NULL, &tv) ==
```

```
        SOCKET_ERROR)
{

    SetDlgItemText(IDC_STATUSTEXT, "Select error");
    return;

}

for (int i = 0; i < MAX_SOCKETS; i++)
{
    if (busy[i] == 1)
    {
        if (FD_ISSET (sock[i], &fdWaitSet))
        {
            int opt;
            int Len = sizeof(opt);
            if (getsockopt(sock[i], SOL_SOCKET,
                SO_ERROR, (char*)&opt, &Len) ==
                SOCKET_ERROR)
            SetDlgItemText(IDC_STATUSTEXT,
                "getsockopt error");

            if (opt == 0)
            {
                struct servent *tec;
                itoa(port[i], tStr, 10);
                strcat(tStr, " (");
                tec = getservbyport(htons
                        (port[i]), "tcp");
                if (tec == NULL)
                    strcat(tStr, "Unknown");
                else
                    strcat(tStr, tec->s_name);

                strcat(tStr, ") - open");
                m_PortList.AddString(tStr);
                busy[i] = 0;
                shutdown(sock[i], SD_BOTH);
                closesocket(sock[i]);
            }
            busy[i] = 0;
            shutdown (sock[i], SD_BOTH);
```

```
                              closesocket (sock[i]);
                              iBusySocks--;


                    }
                 else
                 {
                              busy[i] = 0;
                              closesocket(sock[i]);
                              iBusySocks--;
                    }
              }
          }
      }
    WSACleanup();
    SetDlgItemText(IDC_STATUSTEXT, "Scanning complete");
    return;
}
```

This example uses three arrays while scanning:

☐ sock — an array of handles to sockets waiting for a connection.

☐ busy — states of the ports being scanned. Any of them can be busy and cause an error. It is explicitly stated in Winsock help file that not all of the ports can be used. This is why the array element whose number corresponds to a busy (reserved) port is set to 1; otherwise, it is reset to 0.

☐ port — an array of the ports being scanned. I could do without this array, but I introduced it for simplicity's sake.

This example has a function that has never been discussed in this book: getservbyport. It is as follows:

```
struct servent FAR * getservbyport (
    int port,
    const char FAR* proto
    );
```

This function returns information on a service available on the port specified as the first parameter. The second parameter determines a protocol. The returned value is a structure of the servent type whose s_name element contains a text description of the service. If the function returns a zero value, it is impossible to determine the parameters of the service from the port number.

It is easy to cheat the `getservbyport` function, and the data it returns lack complete reliability. For example, the function always returns information on FTP protocol for port No. 21. However, nothing can prevent you from starting a Web server on this port, and the `getservbyport` function won't detect it.

The remaining steps should be familiar to you, but I'd like to summarize the algorithm:

1. Load the network library.

2. Determine the address of the computer to scan before starting a loop. This address will be used inside the loop that scrolls through the ports in the `sockaddr_in` structure. The structure is filled inside the loop because a new port will be checked in each iteration, and the address won't change. This is why the address is determined outside the loop. It would be pointless to repeat the same operation in each iteration, especially since finding an IP address can take long if the symbolic name of the computer is specified.

3. Start the loop that will execute until the start port number becomes greater than the end port number. Inside this large loop, do the following:

   - Start a loop from zero to `MAX_SOCKETS`. In the loop, create a socket, move it to the asynchronous mode, and start the `connect` function. Since the sockets are in the asynchronous mode, the program won't wait for a connection and therefore be locked. However, you will not know whether a connection has taken place or not.

   - Reset (to zero) the `fdWaitSet` variable of the `fd_set` type.

   - Start a loop from zero to `MAX_SOCKETS`. In the loop, all the sockets should be put to the `fd_set` socket set.

   - Wait for an event from the current socket using the `select` function.

   - Start a loop from zero to `MAX_SOCKETS`. In the loop, check which sockets have successfully connected to the server. If a connection is successful, get the symbolic name of the port using the `getsockopt` function. Then close the socket to disconnect from the server.

4. Unload the network library.

What is `MAX_SOCKETS`? It is a constant that determines the number of ports to scan. In this example, it is equal to 40. This is an optimum value for various environments. The greater the number of sockets scanned during one pass, the faster the scanning.

The program has a flaw. Scanning locks it, and you'll be able to see open ports only after scanning stops and the program becomes unlocked and updates its window. To remedy this, you can write the following function:

```
void ProcessMessages()
{
      MSG msg;
      while (PeekMessage(&msg, NULL, 0, 0, PM_NOREMOVE))
      {
            if (GetMessage(&msg, NULL, 0, 0))
            {
                  TranslateMessage(&msg);
                  DispatchMessage(&msg);
            }
            else
                  return;
      }
}
```

This function contains a simple loop that handles messages. You've seen such handlers in Win32 applications many times. The loop isn't infinite, and it handles all messages in the queue. When the queue is exhausted, the loop will terminate and the program will continue to scan.

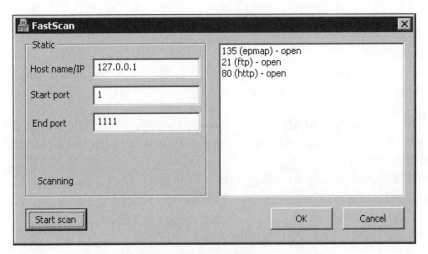

Fig. 6.2. Result of scanning my computer

Put the function somewhere near the beginning of the module and call the `ProcessMessages()` function at the end of the port-searching loop. Thus you'll avoid "freezing" your program and see the open ports instantly.

I'd like to mention that I used a protocol that displays open TCP ports. It has no relation to UDP ports. To scan UDP ports, you should create message-oriented sockets (using the `socket` function).

NOTE

The source code of this example is located in the \Demo\Chapter6\FastScan directory on the accompanying CD-ROM.

6.3. Port Status on a Local Computer

If you need to know the port status on a local computer, you don't have to scan its ports. There is a better method: Get the status of all the ports using the `GetTcpTable` function. You'll obtain comprehensive information that can be arranged in a table with the following columns:

- ❏ A local address — an interface, on which a port is opened
- ❏ A local port — the open port
- ❏ A remote address — the address of a client currently connected to the port
- ❏ A remote port — a port on the remote client computer that is accessing the local computer
- ❏ A status — can take various values such as listening, closing, accepting a connection, etc.

The most important advantage of using the local TCP table is that this method works instantly. Finding information on the ports takes a few milliseconds, regardless of the number of ports.

To look at an example working with a TCP port, create a dialog-based MFC application and name it IPState. Put one **List Box** component and a button with the **TCP Table** label onto the main window. Fig. 6.3 shows such a window.

Upon clicking the **TCP Table** button, the code from Listing 6.3 should be executed.

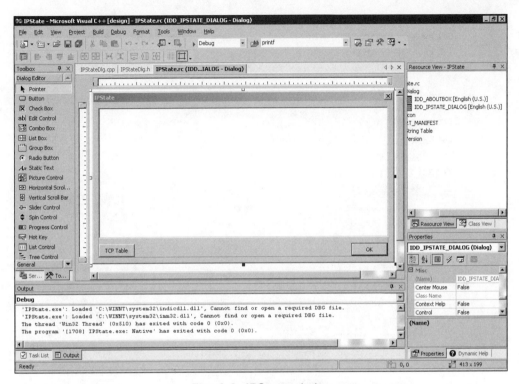

Fig. 6.3. IPState window

Listing 6.3. Getting information on TCP ports

```
void CIPStateDlg::OnBnClickedButton1()
{
    DWORD dwStatus = NO_ERROR;
    PMIB_TCPTABLE pTcpTable = NULL;
    DWORD dwActualSize = 0;

    dwStatus = GetTcpTable(pTcpTable, &dwActualSize, TRUE);

    pTcpTable = (PMIB_TCPTABLE) malloc(dwActualSize);
    assert(pTcpTable);

    dwStatus = GetTcpTable(pTcpTable, &dwActualSize, TRUE);
    if (dwStatus != NO_ERROR)
```

```
    {
        AfxMessageBox("Couldn't get Tcp connection table.");
        free(pTcpTable);
        return;
    }

    CString strState;
    struct in_addr inadLocal, inadRemote;
    DWORD dwRemotePort = 0;
    char szLocalIp[1000];
    char szRemIp[1000];

    if (pTcpTable != NULL)
    {

        lList.AddString("=================================================");
        lList.AddString("TCP table:");
        for (int i = 0; i < pTcpTable->dwNumEntries; i++)
        {
            dwRemotePort = 0;
            switch (pTcpTable->table[i].dwState)
            {
            case MIB_TCP_STATE_LISTEN:
                strState = "Listen";
                dwRemotePort = pTcpTable->table[i].dwRemotePort;
                break;
            case MIB_TCP_STATE_CLOSED:
                strState = "Closed"; break;
            case MIB_TCP_STATE_TIME_WAIT:
                strState = "Time wait"; break;
            case MIB_TCP_STATE_LAST_ACK:
                strState = "Last ACK"; break;
            case MIB_TCP_STATE_CLOSING:
                strState = "Closing"; break;
            case MIB_TCP_STATE_CLOSE_WAIT:
                strState = "Close Wait"; break;
            case MIB_TCP_STATE_FIN_WAIT1:
                strState = "FIN wait"; break;
            case MIB_TCP_STATE_ESTAB:
                strState = "EStab"; break;
```

```
case MIB_TCP_STATE_SYN_RCVD:
    strState = "SYN Received"; break;
case MIB_TCP_STATE_SYN_SENT:
    strState = "SYN Sent"; break;
case MIB_TCP_STATE_DELETE_TCB:
    strState = "Delete"; break;
}
inadLocal.s_addr = pTcpTable->table[i].dwLocalAddr;
inadRemote.s_addr = pTcpTable->table[i].dwRemoteAddr;
strcpy(szLocalIp, inet_ntoa(inadLocal));
strcpy(szRemIp, inet_ntoa(inadRemote));

char prtStr[1000];
sprintf(prtStr, "Loc Addr %1s; Loc Port %1u; Rem Addr %1s;
                Rem Port %1u; State %s;",
                szLocalIp, ntohs((unsigned short)(0x0000FFFF &
                pTcpTable->table[i].dwLocalPort)), szRemIp,
                ntohs((unsigned short)(0x0000FFFF &
                dwRemotePort)), strState);
        lList.AddString(prtStr);
    }
}
free(pTcpTable);
}
```

The GetTcpTable function takes three parameters:

☐ A structure of the PMIB_TCPTABLE type.
☐ The length of the structure specified as the first parameter.
☐ A sort flag: If TRUE is specified, the table will be sorted by port name; otherwise, the information will be displayed unsorted.

If zeroes are specified as the first two parameters, the amount of memory necessary to store the PMIB_TCPTABLE structure will be returned via the second parameter. This technique was used in *Chapter 5*.

The necessary memory should be allocated using the malloc function. In this case, it is unnecessary to allocate global memory.

Another call to the GetTcpTable function allows you to get the status of all TCP ports from the first parameter (the pTcpTable variable of the PMIB_TCPTABLE type).

The number of the ports will be stored in the dwNumEntries element of the pTcpTable structure. Information on a particular port can be taken from the table[i] element, where i is the port number. This element is also a structure, and we're interested in its following elements (whose names are self-explanatory):

❐ dwState — this parameter can take various values (such as MIB_TCP_STATE_LISTEN, MIB_TCP_STATE_CLOSED, etc.) A list of the constants can be found in the code or the online help. You can easily understand their purpose if you look at the code in Listing 6.3.

❐ dwLocalPort

❐ dwRemotePort

❐ dwLocalAddr

❐ dwRemoteAddr

The example starts an infinite loop that scrolls through all records of the table element, and the information is added to the **List Box** control.

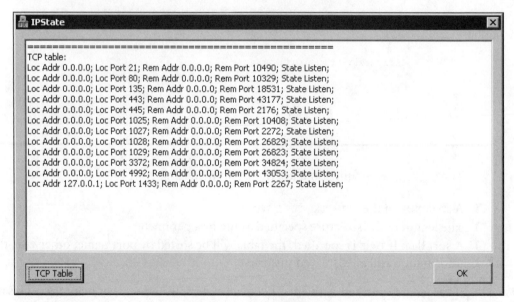

Fig. 6.4. Result of IPState's work

To avoid compiling errors, specify three header files at the beginning of the module:

```
#include <iphlpapi.h>
#include <assert.h>
#include <winsock2.h>
```

In the project properties of the **Linker/Input** section, add two libraries to **Additional Dependencies:** IPHlpApi.lib and ws2_32.lib (Fig. 6.5).

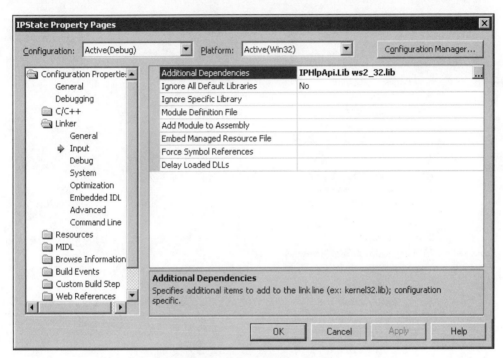

Fig. 6.5. Linking libraries

To get a table of UDP ports, use the GetUdpTable function. It is similar to the GetTcpTable function, but it only lets you know local addresses and local ports. Recall that UDP doesn't set a connection and has no information on the remote computer.

Add the **UDP Table** button to the program so that when you click the button, the code from Listing 6.4 will be executed.

Listing 6.3. Getting information on UDP ports

```
void CIPStateDlg::OnBnClickedButton2()
{
    DWORD dwStatus = NO_ERROR;
    PMIB_UDPTABLE pUdpTable = NULL;
    DWORD dwActualSize = 0;

    dwStatus = GetUdpTable(pUdpTable, &dwActualSize, TRUE);
```

```
pUdpTable = (PMIB_UDPTABLE) malloc(dwActualSize);
assert(pUdpTable);

dwStatus = GetUdpTable(pUdpTable, &dwActualSize, TRUE);

if (dwStatus != NO_ERROR)
{
    AfxMessageBox("Couldn't get UDP connection table.");
    free(pUdpTable);
    return;
}

struct in_addr inadLocal;
if (pUdpTable != NULL)
{
    lList.AddString("===============================================");
    lList.AddString("UDP table:");
    for (UINT i = 0; i < pUdpTable->dwNumEntries; ++i)
    {
        inadLocal.s_addr = pUdpTable->table[i].dwLocalAddr;

        char prtStr[1000];
        sprintf(prtStr, "Loc Addr %1s; Loc Port %1u",
            inet_ntoa(inadLocal),
            ntohs((unsigned short)(0x0000FFFF &
                    pUdpTable->table[i].dwLocalPort)));
        lList.AddString(prtStr);
    }
}
free(pUdpTable);
}
```

The code for obtaining information on UDP ports is similar to that used for TCP protocol, and you'll easily understand it.

The source code of this example is located in the \Demo\Chapter6\IPState directory on the accompanying CD-ROM.

6.4. A DHCP Server

If a DHCP server is used in your network, you cannot delete and add IP addresses as demonstrated in *Chapter 5*. In this case, addresses are allotted and released by the DHCP server, and you should avoid doing this manually to prevent conflicts with other computers.

After a DHCP address is used, it isn't deleted from the system. It is just released, and the server can give an unused address to any other computer not bound to a certain network interface. To release an address, the `IpReleaseAddress` function is used that takes an adapter index as a parameter. To give an adapter an address, the `IpRenewAddress` function is used. Its parameter is also an adapter index.

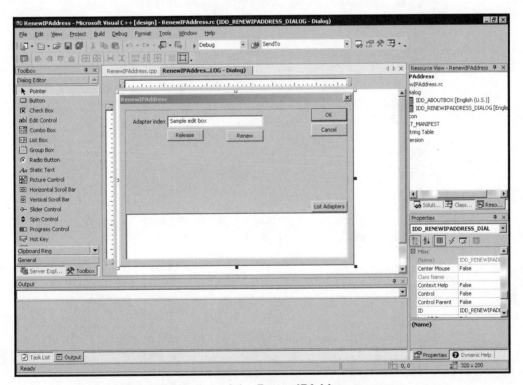

Fig. 6.6. Window of the **RenewIPAddress** program

I'd like to illustrate now the use of these functions. Create a new MFC application. Its main window is shown in Fig. 6.6. To specify an adapter whose address should be released, you should know its index. For this purpose, the **List Box** control located at the bottom of the window will be used. It will display a list of installed interfaces upon clicking the **List Adapters** button. The code that should be executed here is similar to the code from Listing 5.2 that also displayed information on adapters.

The IP address should be released after you click the **Release** button. The necessary code is shown in Listing 6.5.

Listing 6.5. Releasing an IP address

```
void CRenewIPAddressDlg::OnBnClickedButton2()
{
        char sAdaptIndex[20];
        int iIndex;
        sAdapterIndex.GetWindowText(sAdaptIndex, 20);
        iIndex = atoi(sAdaptIndex);

    DWORD InterfaceInfoSize = 0;
    PIP_INTERFACE_INFO pInterfaceInfo;

    if (GetInterfaceInfo(NULL, &InterfaceInfoSize) !=
            ERROR_INSUFFICIENT_BUFFER)
    {
        AfxMessageBox("Error sizing buffer");
        return;
    }

    if ((pInterfaceInfo = (PIP_INTERFACE_INFO) GlobalAlloc(GPTR,
        InterfaceInfoSize)) == NULL)
    {
        AfxMessageBox("Can't allocate memory");
        return;
    }

    if (GetInterfaceInfo(pInterfaceInfo, &InterfaceInfoSize) != 0)
    {
        AfxMessageBox("GetInterfaceInfo failed");
        return;
    }


    for (int i = 0; i < pInterfaceInfo->NumAdapters; i++)
```

```
    if (iIndex == pInterfaceInfo->Adapter[i].Index)
    {
        if (IpReleaseAddress(&pInterfaceInfo->Adapter[i]) != 0)
        {
            AfxMessageBox("IpReleaseAddress failed");
            return;
        }
        break;
    }
}
```

The user selects an adapter index in the list on the main window, and the program scrolls through all the interfaces. If one of them belongs to the adapter, the IpReleaseAddress function is called for it.

Getting an interface list is done with the GetInterfaceInfo function that is similar to the GetAdaptersInfo function already familiar to you. When the function is called for the first time, it determines the amount of memory necessary to store the information. Then the memory is allocated, and the function is called again.

Then a loop is started to scroll through all the obtained interfaces. If the interface of the specified adapter is found, the address is released.

Renewing an IP address is done in a similar way. Listing 6.6 shows code that should be executed when the **Renew** button is clicked.

Listing 6.6. Renewing an IP address

```
void CRenewIPAddressDlg::OnBnClickedButton3()
{
    char sAdaptIndex[20];
    int iIndex;
    sAdapterIndex.GetWindowText(sAdaptIndex, 20);
    iIndex = atoi(sAdaptIndex);

    DWORD InterfaceInfoSize = 0;
    PIP_INTERFACE_INFO pInterfaceInfo;

    if (GetInterfaceInfo(NULL, &InterfaceInfoSize) !=
            ERROR_INSUFFICIENT_BUFFER)
    {
        AfxMessageBox("Error sizing buffer");
```

```
        return;
    }

if ((pInterfaceInfo = (PIP_INTERFACE_INFO) GlobalAlloc(GPTR,
        InterfaceInfoSize)) == NULL)
{
    AfxMessageBox("Can't allocate memory");
    return;
}

if (GetInterfaceInfo(pInterfaceInfo, &InterfaceInfoSize) != 0)
{
    AfxMessageBox("GetInterfaceInfo failed");
    return;
}


for (int i = 0; i < pInterfaceInfo->NumAdapters; i++)
    if (iIndex == pInterfaceInfo->Adapter[i].Index)
    {
        if (IpRenewAddress(&pInterfaceInfo->Adapter[i]) != 0)
        {
            AfxMessageBox("IpRenewAddress failed");
            return;
        }
        break;
    }
}
```

The code that renews an address is similar to the address-releasing code (Listing 6.5). The only difference is that the IpRenewAddress function is called.

NOTE

The source code of this example is located in the \Demo\Chapter6\RenewIPAddress directory on the accompanying CD-ROM.

6.5. The ICMP Protocol

As I have already mentioned, the IP protocol doesn't ensure a reliable data transmission; therefore, it is impossible to check the integrity of the received data. However, by using the Internet Control Message Protocol (ICMP), you can find out whether a package has reached the addressee. ICMP packages are sent in situations where an addressee is inaccessible, the gateway buffer is overflowed or too small for the message, or an addressee requires that the message should be sent via a shorter route.

The ICMP protocol was developed to inform the parties about problems during data sending or receiving and to increase the reliability of data transmission using the IP protocol, which is not reliable by nature. However, you shouldn't rely on ICMP because the data can be lost in the network (and not reach the addressee), but you won't receive any messages about this. This is why protocols of higher layers (such as TCP) that have methods for providing security are used.

If you want to create your own protocol based on IP, you can use ICMP messages to provide a certain level of reliability. However, you should be aware that it is not enough. ICMP messages are sent when a gateway or a computer cannot process the package. However, if the package fails to reach the receiver because the cable is broken or for some other reason, no indication will be given because IP doesn't use acknowledgements.

Because the ICMP protocol has a weak level of reliability, programmers rarely use it for its direct purpose (i.e., to check the data delivery). However, it is widely used for another purpose. If an ICMP package is sent and it reaches the addressee, the latter should respond. Thus you can check the connection to a remote computer. This is how ping programs are implemented.

To test a connection, you should know of an open port on the remote computer to try to connect to it. If the connection is successful, the computer is accessible. When you don't know the port, you can scan the entire range, but this would take too much time. The ICMP protocol allows you to avoid this procedure.

In some networks, all computers have firewalls that prohibit the ICMP protocol. In such cases, the administrators open an echo server on one of the ports (such a server receives data and responds with a package with the same data) and use it to test connection. This is a good method, but it can happen that the echo server is "frozen" or cancelled while the connection is still available. In such a situation, an administrator might get the impression that the connection is broken. However, ICMP packages are usually allowed and work correctly.

Everything is fine theoretically, but there is one problem in practice. The ICMP protocol uses packages that differ from TCP or UDP supported by Winsock. How can you send a package with a control message? Create a package of the required format on your own.

The first WinSock version didn't allow a programmer to access the package data directly. The second parameter of the `select` function could take only two values: `SOCK_STREAM` for the TCP protocol or `SOCK_DGRAM` for the UDP protocol. Winsock2 supports RAW sockets that provide a low-level access to packages. To create such a socket, call the `socket` function and pass it `SOCK_RAW` as the second parameter.

Let's look at how a ping program can be implemented. This will help you understand how to use RAW sockets and check a connection with the ICMP protocol. Create a new MFC application. Its possible window is shown in Fig. 6.7.

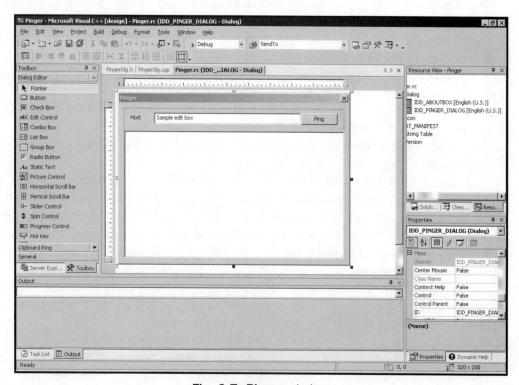

Fig. 6.7. Pinger window

The **Host** line will display the name or IP address of a computer, to which you want to connect. After clicking the button, ICMP packages will be sent and received, and the results will be output to the **List Box** that is stretched along the bottom of the window.

When the **Ping** button is clicked, the code from Listing 6.7 will be executed.

Listing 6.7. Using ICMP packages

```
void CPingerDlg::OnBnClickedButton1()
{
    SOCKET          rawSocket;
    LPHOSTENT lpHost;
    struct    sockaddr_in sDest;
    struct    sockaddr_in sSrc;
    DWORD     dwElapsed;
    int       iRet;
    CString str;

WSADATA        wsd;
if (WSAStartup(MAKEWORD(2, 2), &wsd) != 0)
    {
        AfxMessageBox("Can't load WinSock");
        return;
    }


    // Creation socket
    rawSocket = socket(AF_INET, SOCK_RAW, IPPROTO_ICMP);
    if (rawSocket == SOCKET_ERROR)
    {
        AfxMessageBox("Socket error");
        return;
    }

    // Lookup host
    char strHost[255];
    edHost.GetWindowText(strHost, 255);
    lpHost = gethostbyname(strHost);
    if (lpHost == NULL)
    {
        AfxMessageBox("Host not found");
        return;
    }

    // Socket's address
    sDest.sin_addr.s_addr = *((u_long FAR *) (lpHost->h_addr));
    sDest.sin_family = AF_INET;
```

```
sDest.sin_port = 0;

str.Format("Pinging %s [%s]",
                    strHost, inet_ntoa(sDest.sin_addr));

lMessages.AddString(str);

// Send ICMP echo request
static ECHOREQUEST echoReq;

echoReq.icmpHdr.Type    = ICMP_ECHOREQ;
echoReq.icmpHdr.Code    = 0;
echoReq.icmpHdr.ID      = 0;
echoReq.icmpHdr.Seq     = 0;
echoReq.dwTime = GetTickCount();
FillMemory(echoReq.cData, 64, 80);
echoReq.icmpHdr.Checksum = CheckSum((u_short *)&echoReq,
    sizeof(ECHOREQUEST));

// Send the echo request
sendto(rawSocket, (LPSTR)&echoReq, sizeof(ECHOREQUEST),
            0, (LPSOCKADDR)&sDest, sizeof(SOCKADDR_IN));

struct timeval tOut;
fd_set readfds;
readfds.fd_count = 1;
readfds.fd_array[0] = rawSocket;
tOut.tv_sec = 1;
tOut.tv_usec = 0;

iRet = select(1, &readfds, NULL, NULL, & tOut);

if (!iRet)
{
      lMessages.AddString("Request Timed Out");
}
else
{
      // Receive reply
      ECHOREPLY echoReply;
```

```
        int nRet;
        int nAddrLen = sizeof(struct sockaddr_in);

        iRet = recvfrom(rawSocket, (LPSTR)&echoReply,
                sizeof(ECHOREPLY), 0, (LPSOCKADDR)&sSrc, &nAddrLen);

        if (iRet == SOCKET_ERROR)
                AfxMessageBox("Recvfrom Error");

        // Calculate time
        dwElapsed = GetTickCount() - echoReply.echoRequest.dwTime;
        str.Format("Reply from: %s: bytes=%d time=%ldms TTL=%d",
                        inet_ntoa(sSrc.sin_addr), 64, dwElapsed,
                    echoReply.ipHdr.TTL);
        lMessages.AddString(str);
    }

    iRet = closesocket(rawSocket);
    if (iRet == SOCKET_ERROR)
            AfxMessageBox("Closesocket error");

    WSACleanup();
}
```

Before using a network, you should load the Winsock library with the WSAStartup function. Working with RAW sockets also requires this, but be sure to load WinSocket2 library because the first version misses the required features.

When the library is loaded, you can create a socket by calling the socket function with the following parameters:

- The protocol family: AF_INET (as always)
- The specification: SOCK_RAW so that RAW sockets can be used
- The protocol: IPPROTO_ICMP

To send a package to a computer, you must know the computer's address. If the user entered a symbolic name, you should find the IP address using the gethostbyname function.

After that (like with other protocols), a structure of the sockaddr_in type that contains the computer's address should be filled. An ICMP request doesn't use ports; therefore, the Port element is set to zero.

Then a structure of the ECHOREQUEST type should be filled. This structure is a package that will be sent to the network. Whereas the TCP and UDP protocols allow you to specify only data to send, the ICMP protocol requires that you create a complete package that will be sent using the IP protocol. The ECHOREQUEST structure looks as follows:

```
typedef struct tagECHOREQUEST
{
        ICMPHDR icmpHdr;
        DWORD   dwTime;
        char    cData[64];
} ECHOREQUEST, *PECHOREQUEST;
```

The icmpHdr element is the package header that you need to fill on your own, and the cData element contains the data being sent. In our example, packages 64 bytes long will be sent, so an array of 64 characters is declared. The array is entirely filled with characters with the code 80 using the FillChar function. A ping program doesn't care what data are sent because its purpose is to check whether it is possible to communicate with the remote computer.

The dwTime field is time. You can use this field as you like. Most of programmers use it to determine the time it takes for a package to reach the addressee.

The header depends on the message being sent or received. Since I'm showing you a ping program, I'll discuss what data it needs. For a comprehensive description of the ICMP protocol, see RFC792 document located at **http://info.internet.isi.edu/ in-notes/rfc/files/rfc792.txt**. The header (the icmpHdr field) is a structure with the following elements:

```
typedef struct tagICMPHDR
{
        u_char Type;
        u_char Code;
        u_short Checksum;
        u_short ID;
        u_short Seq;
        char Data;
} ICMPHDR, *PICMPHDR;
```

Let's look at them:

❑ Type — a package type. In our example, it is ICMP_ECHOREQ, meaning that the server has to return the same data that it received. In the response header, this element should be zero.

❑ Code — isn't used in echo requests and should be equal to zero.

❑ Checksum — a checksum. RFC doesn't set strict specifications on the checksum algorithm, and it can be altered. In this program, I use a simplified algorithm shown in Listing 6.8.

❑ ID — should be zero for an echo request, but can have another value.

❑ Seq — the queue number. It should be zero if the code is zero.

Listing 6.8. A function for computing a checksum

```
u_short CheckSum(u_short *addr, int len)
{
        register int nleft = len;
        register u_short answer;
        register int sum = 0;

        while( nleft > 1 )
        {
                sum += *addr++;
                nleft -= 1;
        }
        sum += (sum >> 16);
        answer = ~sum;
        return (answer);
}
```

After the package is arranged, it is sent using the sendto function because IP is used as a transport protocol; IP doesn't support connection (unlike TCP), and is similar to UDP.

To wait for a response, use the select function. If you do not receive a response during the first second, the remote computer is considered inaccessible. Otherwise, the data package is read. In this example, it isn't necessary to read the package because it is obvious that the connection between the two computers has been achieved. However, I have done so to show you the complete procedure of sending and receiving data via RAW sockets. In an actual application, you should read the package to be certain that it came from the computer, to which you had sent the data (it is quite likely that another computer sent you the package). Reading the package is also necessary when several computers are checked asynchronously.

To read the package, use the `recvfrom` function, just like with the UDP protocol. Whereas the data package is sent as an ECHOREQUEST structure, it is received as an ECHOREPLY structure, which is shown below:

```
typedef struct tagECHOREPLY
{
        IPHDR     ipHdr;
        ECHOREQUEST  echoRequest;
        char      cFiller[256];
} ECHOREPLY, *PECHOREPLY;
```

The first element is the header of the received package, and the second is the header of the sent package.

The header of the received package differs from the sent one and looks as follows:

```
typedef struct tagIPHDR
{
        u_char   VIHL;
        u_char   TOS;
        short    TotLen;
        short    ID;
        short    FlagOff;
        u_char   TTL;
        u_char   Protocol;
        u_short  Checksum;
        struct   in_addr iaSrc;
        struct   in_addr iaDst;
} IPHDR, *PIPHDR;
```

This is nothing but a header of the IP protocol.

All the required structures should be declared in a header file. For this example, I declared them in the PingerDlg.h file.

NOTE

The source code of this example is located in the \Demo\Chapter6\Pinger directory on the accompanying CD-ROM.

6.6. Tracing the Route of a Package

How can you trace the route of a package from your computer to an addressee? If you remember the purpose of ICMP messages, it is easy. Each package has a TTL (Time To Live) field. Each router decrements the value in this field. When it becomes equal to zero, the package is considered lost and the router returns an ICMP error message. Using this field makes it easy to trace the route of the package.

Send the server a package whose TTL is 1. The first router it comes to will decrement this value and obtain 0. This will make it to return an ICMP error message, and you will know the first node on the package's route. Then send a package with TTL equal to 2 and find the second router (the first will pass the package, and the second will return an ICMP error message). Thus, you can send several packages until they reach the addressee. Not only can you trace the route, but also the response time of each router. This will allow you to detect a weak link in the package's route. The characteristics of the connection to each device on the route can vary depending on the load; therefore, you should make a few attempts to find an average response time.

Of course, it is likely that one package will follow one route, and the second follows another. However, packages most often follow the same route.

I'll present you with a simple example that traces a package's route. However, I'll send ICMP packages using icmp.dll library rather than RAW sockets. This library includes all the necessary functions for creating a socket and sending a package. You only need to specify an address and the contents and parameters of a package, and the rest will be done for you. Thus, the example will teach you how to use the icmp.dll library and trace the routes of packages.

Create a new MFC application and name it TraceRoute. Its main window should contain one edit control for a computer address, one **List Box** to display the results, and a button (labeled **Trace**) to start pinging the remote computer. When you click the button, the code from Listing 6.9 should be executed.

Listing 6.9. Tracing the route of a package

```
void CTraceRouteDlg::OnBnClickedButton1()
{
        WSADATA wsa;
        if (WSAStartup(MAKEWORD(1, 1), &wsa) != 0)
        {
                AfxMessageBox("Can't load a correct version of WinSock");
                return;
```

```
       }

       hIcmp = LoadLibrary("ICMP.DLL");
       if (hIcmp == NULL)
       {
              AfxMessageBox("Can't load ICMP DLL");
              return;
       }

       pIcmpCreateFile = (lpIcmpCreateFile)GetProcAddress(hIcmp,"IcmpCreateFile");
       pIcmpSendEcho = (lpIcmpSendEcho)GetProcAddress(hIcmp,"IcmpSendEcho");
       pIcmpCloseHandle = (lpIcmpCloseHandle)GetProcAddress(hIcmp,"IcmpCloseHandle");

       in_addr        Address;
       if (pIcmpCreateFile == NULL)
       {
              AfxMessageBox("ICMP library error");
              return;
       }

       char chHostName[255];
       edHostName.GetWindowText(chHostName, 255);
       LPHOSTENT hp = gethostbyname(chHostName);
       if (hp == NULL)
       {
              AfxMessageBox("Host not found");
              return;
       }
       unsigned long        addr;
       memcpy(&addr, hp->h_addr, hp->h_length);

       BOOL bReachedHost = FALSE;
       for (UCHAR i=1; i<=50 && !bReachedHost; i++)
       {
              Address.S_un.S_addr = 0;

              int iPacketSize = 32;
              int iRTT;

              HANDLE hIP = pIcmpCreateFile();
```

```
if (hIP == INVALID_HANDLE_VALUE)
{
        AfxMessageBox("Could not get a valid ICMP handle");
        return;
}

unsigned char* pBuf = new unsigned char[iPacketSize];
FillMemory(pBuf, iPacketSize, 80);

int iReplySize = sizeof(ICMP_ECHO_REPLY) + iPacketSize;
unsigned char* pReplyBuf = new unsigned char[iReplySize];
ICMP_ECHO_REPLY* pEchoReply = (ICMP_ECHO_REPLY*) pReplyBuf;

IP_OPTION_INFORMATION ipOptionInfo;
ZeroMemory(&ipOptionInfo, sizeof(IP_OPTION_INFORMATION));
ipOptionInfo.Ttl = i;

DWORD nRecvPackets = pIcmpSendEcho(hIP, addr, pBuf,
    iPacketSize, &ipOptionInfo, pReplyBuf,
    iReplySize, 30000);

if (nRecvPackets != 1)
{
        AfxMessageBox("Can't ping host");
        return;
}
Address.S_un.S_addr = pEchoReply->Address;
iRTT = pEchoReply->RoundTripTime;

pIcmpCloseHandle(hIP);

delete [] pReplyBuf;
delete [] pBuf;

char lpszText[255];

hostent* phostent = NULL;
phostent = gethostbyaddr((char *)&Address.S_un.S_addr, 4, PF_INET);

if (phostent)
```

```
                        sprintf(lpszText, "%d: %d ms [%s] (%d.%d.%d.%d)",
                                i, iRTT,
                                phostent->h_name, Address.S_un.S_un_b.s_b1,
                                    Address.S_un.S_un_b.s_b2,
                                    Address.S_un.S_un_b.s_b3,
                                    Address.S_un.S_un_b.s_b4);
                else
                        sprintf(lpszText, "%d - %d ms (%d.%d.%d.%d)",
                                i, iRTT,
                                Address.S_un.S_un_b.s_b1,
                                Address.S_un.S_un_b.s_b2,
                                Address.S_un.S_un_b.s_b3,
                                Address.S_un.S_un_b.s_b4);

                lbMessages.AddString(lpszText);

                if (addr == Address.S_un.S_addr)
                        bReachedHost = TRUE;
        }

        if (hIcmp)
        {
                FreeLibrary(hIcmp);
                hIcmp = NULL;
        }

        WSACleanup();
}
```

Although you use the icmp.dll library, you should load the WinSock library. You'll need at least the gethostbyname function to find an IP address if the user specifies a symbolic name of a computer. The first version of the library will suffice because RAW sockets won't be used. Therefore, the program will be able to work in Windows 98 (without Winsock 2.0).

Then you should load the icmp.dll library using the LoadLibrary function. It is located in the windows/system (or windows/system32) folder, therefore, you don't have to specify the full path. Your program will easily find and load the library.

We are interested in the following functions in the library:

❏ IcmpCreateFile — initialization

- ☐ `IcmpSendEcho` — sending an echo package
- ☐ `IcmpCloseHandle` — closing ICMP

Before you send a package, you should initialize it using the `IcmpCreateFile` function. When you complete the work with ICMP, you should close it using the `IcmpCloseHandle` function.

Now, store the addresses of the necessary functions into variables declared beforehand.

```
pIcmpCreateFile = (lpIcmpCreateFile)GetProcAddress(hIcmp,"IcmpCreateFile");
pIcmpSendEcho = (lpIcmpSendEcho)GetProcAddress(hIcmp,"IcmpSendEcho");
pIcmpCloseHandle = (lpIcmpCloseHandle)GetProcAddress(hIcmp,"IcmpCloseHandle");
```

If we want our program to work correctly, we should check each of the obtained addresses for equality to a `NULL`. When at least one function address is a `NULL`, it is pointless to use it because the function hasn't been found. Most often, this happens because of an error in a function name. However, it is likely that the program loads a library with the specified name, but without the specified functions. To detect this, the `pIcmpCreateFile` variable (that should contain the address of the `IcmpCreateFile` function) is checked for `NULL`. If this is the case, the wrong library has been loaded. The program will display an appropriate warning message, and the other two variables will not be checked (we assume the correct function names were specified).

The next step involves getting the computer address and converting it to the IP address. If an error occurs on this step, the computer address is incorrect and it is impossible to execute the code further.

Now you can start pinging the remote computer. Since you are likely to send several packages with various TTLs, a loop from 1 to 50 is started. I don't recommend that you use a `while` loop running until a package reaches the target computer, because it is likely to run infinitely.

Inside the loop, an ICMP package is initialized using the `IcmpCreateFile` function. Its result is a handle to a newly-created object that will be needed when sending an echo package. It is stored into the `hIP` variable of the `HANDLE` type:

```
HANDLE hIP = pIcmpCreateFile();
if (hIP == INVALID_HANDLE_VALUE)
{
        AfxMessageBox("Could not get a valid ICMP handle");
        return;
}
```

If the result is equal to INVALID_HANDLE_VALUE, this will indicate an initialization error and further execution is pointless.

Then a data buffer is allocated. Like with the ping program, it is filled with characters with the code 80. Then a package of the ICMP_ECHO_REPLY type is created. It will be used to return information obtained from a router or the remote computer. Also, create a package of the IP_OPTION_INFORMATION type to store the TTL of the package (the Ttl element).

When everything is ready, you can send the ICMP package with the IcmpSendEcho function that takes the following parameters:

- An ICMP handle (obtained during initialization)
- A computer address
- A buffer with data
- The size of a package (taking into account the amount of data being sent)
- An IP package with a TTL specified (on the first iteration it is one, then two, etc.)
- A buffer to store a structure of the ICMP_ECHO_REPLY type that will contain the resulting package
- The buffer size
- A time-out for the package

The function returns the number of received packages. In our case, it is one. If zero is returned, this means a router (or the computer) hasn't responded with an ICMP package, and it is impossible to determine its parameters.

The response time can be obtained from the RoundTripTime element of the ICMP_ECHO_REPLY structure, and the address of the network device that responded can be obtained from the Address element.

When you finish, don't forget to close the handle to the created ICMP using the IcmpCloseHandle function.

Now, you can display the obtained information. To make it easier for you to understand the example, I converted an IP address to the symbolic name using the gethostbyaddr function. It takes the following parameters:

- The IP address of a computer whose name we need
- The length of the address
- A protocol family (the format of the address depends on this parameter)

Then the code checks whether a response from the remote computer is received and breaks the loop if this is the case. Otherwise, it increments the TTL and sends another ICMP package:

```
if (addr == Address.S_un.S_addr)
        bReachedHost = TRUE;
```

In conclusion, you should unload the icmp.dll and Winsock libraries:

```
if (hIcmp)
{
        FreeLibrary(hIcmp);
        hIcmp = NULL;
}
WSACleanup();
```

Run the TraceRoute program. Fig. 6.8 shows a window with the results.

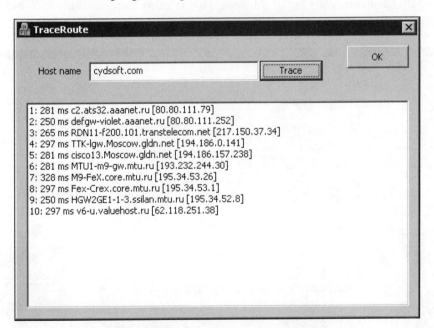

Fig. 6.8. Results of TraceRoute's work

I tried to make the example simple and its logic straightforward so that you can understand it easily. As a result, it has a minor flaw.

When an error occurs during execution, the program terminates and the icmp.dll and Winsock libraries remain in the memory. The simplest way to improve this is to load the libraries at the start and unload them at the finish, and if the libraries aren't loaded, the package-sending buttons should be inactive to prevent a user from clicking them.

There are header files for the icmp.dll library on the Internet that can simplify this example even further. However, I preferred not to use them to spare you from any confusion.

NOTE

The source code of this example is located in the \Demo\Chapter6\TraceRoute directory on the accompanying CD-ROM.

6.7. The ARP Protocol

I have already commented on the fact that you need the MAC address of a computer to access this computer via the local network. There is the ARP protocol that finds the MAC address from an IP address. This is done automatically and hidden from a common user. However, sometimes it is possible to control the ARP table manually.

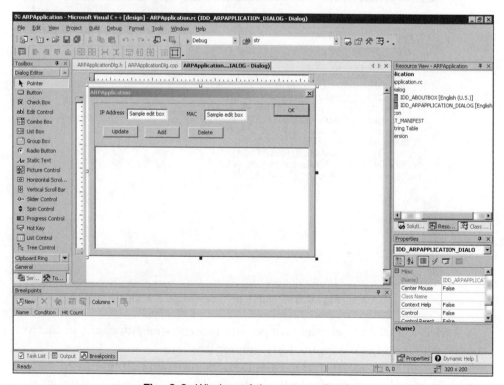

Fig. 6.9. Window of the new application

There is a utility named `arp` in Windows, but it is console, and it isn't convenient to use it. I'll demonstrate a simple graphical utility for you and use it as an example to explain how to work with this protocol.

Create a new dialog-based MFC application. Its main window should look like that shown in Fig. 6.9. Two lines are used for IP and MAC addresses. A click on the **Add** button adds a new ARP record, in which the MAC address will be computed from a specified IP address. A click on the **Update** button displays the ARP table in the **List Box**. The **Delete** button is used to delete a record from the table.

An event handler for the **Update** button is shown in Listing 6.10.

Listing 6.10. Updating the ARP table

```
void CARPApplicationDlg::OnBnClickedButton1()
{
        DWORD dwStatus;
        PMIB_IPNETTABLE pIpArpTab = NULL;

        DWORD dwActualSize = 0;
        GetIpNetTable(pIpArpTab, &dwActualSize, TRUE);

        pIpArpTab = (PMIB_IPNETTABLE) malloc(dwActualSize);
        if (GetIpNetTable(pIpArpTab, &dwActualSize, TRUE) != NO_ERROR)
        {
                if (pIpArpTab)
                        free (pIpArpTab);
                return;
        }

        DWORD i, dwCurrIndex;
        char sPhysAddr[256], sType[256], sAddr[256];
        PMIB_IPADDRTABLE pIpAddrTable = NULL;
        char Str[255];

        dwActualSize = 0;
        GetIpAddrTable(pIpAddrTable, &dwActualSize, TRUE);
        pIpAddrTable = (PMIB_IPADDRTABLE) malloc(dwActualSize);
        GetIpAddrTable(pIpAddrTable, &dwActualSize, TRUE);

        dwCurrIndex = -100;
```

```cpp
for (i = 0; i < pIpArpTab->dwNumEntries; ++i)
{
        if (pIpArpTab->table[i].dwIndex != dwCurrIndex)
        {
                dwCurrIndex = pIpArpTab->table[i].dwIndex;


                struct in_addr in_ad;
                sAddr[0] = '\n';
                for (int i = 0; i < pIpAddrTable->dwNumEntries; i++)
                {
                        if (dwCurrIndex !=
                            pIpAddrTable->table[i].dwIndex)
                                continue;

                        in_ad.s_addr = pIpAddrTable->table[i].dwAddr;
                        strcpy(sAddr, inet_ntoa(in_ad));
                }

                sprintf(Str, "Interface: %s on Interface 0x%X",
                        sAddr, dwCurrIndex);
                lbMessages.AddString(Str);
                lbMessages.AddString(" Internet Address | Physical
                                      Address | Type");
        }


        AddrToStr(pIpArpTab->table[i].bPhysAddr,
                  pIpArpTab->table[i].dwPhysAddrLen, sPhysAddr);

switch (pIpArpTab->table[i].dwType)
{
case 1:
    strcpy(sType, "Other");
    break;
case 2:
    strcpy(sType, "Invalidated");
    break;
case 3:
    strcpy(sType, "Dynamic");
```

```
        break;
    case 4:
        strcpy(sType, "Static");
        break;
    default:
        strcpy(sType, "");
    }


        struct in_addr in_ad;
        in_ad.s_addr = pIpArpTab->table[i].dwAddr;
        sprintf(Str, " %-16s | %-17s | %-11s", inet_ntoa(in_ad),
                     sPhysAddr, sType);
        lbMessages.AddString(Str);

    }


    free(pIpArpTab);
}
```

Look at the code closely. Note that the WinSock library isn't loaded. The winsock.h header file is included into the project because it declares data types used in the program. However, they are necessary only during compiling. Library functions necessary during execution aren't used.

If you add some code that contains at least one call to a function from the WinSock library (such as finding the host name from an IP address), you'll have to load the library.

First, a table of correspondence of IP addresses to physical MAC addresses is obtained. This is actually the ARP table. The function used to obtain it is the following:

```
DWORD GetIpNetTable(
    PMIB_IPNETTABLE pIpNetTable,
    PULONG pdwSize,
    BOOL bOrder
);
```

The ARP table is described with the following parameters:

❏ A pointer to a structure of the MIB_IPNETTABLE type that will contain the table.
❏ The size of the structure. If zero is specified, the function will return the amount of memory necessary for the table.
❏ A flag. If it is TRUE, the table will be sorted.

A `MIB_IPNETTABLE` structure specified as the second parameter looks as follows:

```
typedef struct _MIB_IPNETTABLE {
        DWORD dwNumEntries;
        MIB_IPNETROW table[ANY_SIZE];
} MIB_IPNETTABLE, *PMIB_IPNETTABLE;
```

Its first element specifies the number of entries in the table, and the second is a structure containing the table data:

```
typedef struct _MIB_IPNETROW {
        DWORD dwIndex;
        DWORD dwPhysAddrLen;
        BYTE bPhysAddr[MAXLEN_PHYSADDR];
        DWORD dwAddr;
        DWORD dwType;
} MIB_IPNETROW, *PMIB_IPNETROW;
```

The structure with the table data has the following elements:

❏ `dwIndex` — the index of an adapter
❏ `dwPhysAddrLen` — the length of a physical address
❏ `bPhysAddr` — the physical address
❏ `dwAddr` — the IP address
❏ `dwType` — an entry type that can take the following values:
- `4` — static. The entry was added manually using functions that will be discussed later.
- `3` — dynamic. The entry contains addresses obtained automatically with the ARP protocol (valid only during a certain period, after which the entry is automatically deleted).
- `2` — wrong. The record contains errors.
- `1` — other.

Basically, the ARP table is already created. If only one network card is installed in your computer, this will be enough because all entries in the table relate to it. If there are at least two network cards, some of the entries will belong to one interface, the others belonging to the other.

For the picture to be complete, you should display, which entries belong to each interface. There is the interface index in the `MIB_IPNETROW` structure, but it makes no sense for a common user. It would give more information when combined with the IP address of the adapter.

However, we haven't got the IP address of the adapter yet. To find it, you should obtain a table of correspondence of IP addresses to adapters. This can be done with the GetIpAddrTable function. It is similar to the GetIpNetTable function:

```
DWORD GetIpAddrTable(
  PMIB_IPADDRTABLE pIpAddrTable,
  PULONG pdwSize,
  BOOL bOrder
);
```

It also takes three parameters: a pointer to a structure of the MIB_IPADDRTABLE (pIpAddrTable) type, the size of the structure (pdwSize) and a sort flag (bOrder).

The first parameter is the following structure:

```
typedef struct _MIB_IPADDRTABLE {
        DWORD dwNumEntries;
        MIB_IPADDRROW table[ANY_SIZE];
} MIB_IPADDRTABLE, *PMIB_IPADDRTABLE;
```

The structure consists of two elements:

❐ dwNumEntries — the number of structures specified in the second parameter
❐ table — an array of structures of the MIB_IPADDRROW type

A MIB_IPADDRROW structure is:

```
typedef struct _MIB_IPADDRROW {
        DWORD dwAddr;
        DWORDIF_INDEX dwIndex;
        DWORD dwMask;
        DWORD dwBCastAddr;
        DWORD dwReasmSize;
        unsigned short unused1;
        unsigned short wType;
} MIB_IPADDRROW, *PMIB_IPADDRROW;
```

It consists of the following elements:

❐ dwAddr — an IP address.
❐ dwIndex — the index of the adapter related to the IP address.
❐ dwMask — a mask for the IP address.
❐ dwBCastAddr — a broadcast address. Most often, this is an IP address with a zero node number. For example, if you have an IP address 192.168.4.7, the broadcast address will be 192.168.4.0.

❑ dwReasmSize — the maximum size of received packages.

❑ ·unused1 — reserved.

❑ wType — an address type that can take the following values:

- MIB_IPADDR_PRIMARY — a primary IP address
- MIB_IPADDR_DYNAMIC — a dynamic address
- MIB_IPADDR_DISCONNECTED — an address on a disconnected interface; for example, a network cable is missing
- MIB_IPADDR_DELETED — the address is being deleted
- MIB_IPADDR_TRANSIENT — a transient address

When all the necessary data are obtained, a loop begins to scroll through all entries in the ARP table. However, before you display any information, you should find, to which interface it relates.

When obtaining the data, we chose the ordered mode, so we can hope that entries related to the first interface come first, and those for the other interface follow them. This is why the dwCurrIndex variable is assigned –100 before the loop. There will never be an interface with such an address. The first iteration of the loop will show that the entry on the ARP table doesn't relate to an interface No. –100. Therefore, the IP address of the network card, to which the entry relates, should be displayed. To do this, we use dwIndex parameter to look for an entry in the table of correspondence of IP addresses to the interface number. If the entry is found (which should be in our case), the table header is displayed. It should look similar to the following:

```
Interface: 192.168.1.100 on Interface 0x10000003
Internet Address | Physical Address | Type
```

Then the data from the ARP table are displayed until an entry related to another interface is encountered. Then another header is displayed, and so on.

In Fig. 6.10, you can see the results of the application's work displayed on my computer. Note that ARP entries may be missing from your computer because they exist only when working in a local area network. When working with the Internet via a modem, the ARP protocol isn't used.

You may have no idea of how this application can be used. I remember situations where it was most useful. Suppose you need to know the MAC address of a computer in your local area network, but the computer is located too far from you. Of course, you could walk to that computer and find its address with the ipconfig utility. However, you can carry out carry out the following procedure:

1. Start a ping program to check the connection to the computer. Echo packages will be sent that also need the MAC address, therefore, the ARP protocol will be used.

2. Start the program that displays the ARP table to find the MAC address of the computer you need.

Now let's look at how new entries can be added to the ARP table. Remember that all entries added programmatically become static and won't be deleted automatically by the operating system. When the **Add** button is clicked, the code from Listing 6.11 should be executed.

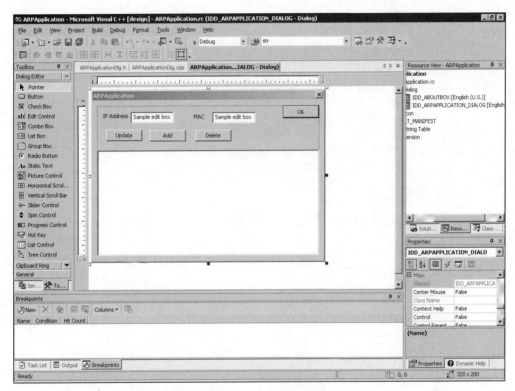

Fig. 6.10. Result of ARPApplication's work

Listing 6.11. Adding a new entry to the ARP table

```
void CARPApplicationDlg::OnBnClickedButton2()
{
        DWORD dwInetAddr = 0;
        char sPhysAddr[255];
```

```
char sInetAddr[255], sMacAddr[255], sInterface[255];
edIPAddress.GetWindowText(sInetAddr, 255);
edMacAddress.GetWindowText(sMacAddr, 255);
edInterface.GetWindowText(sInterface, 255);


if (sInetAddr == NULL || sMacAddr == NULL || sInterface == NULL)
{
        AfxMessageBox("Fill IP address, MAC address and
                       Interface");
        return;
}

dwInetAddr = inet_addr(sInetAddr);
if (dwInetAddr == INADDR_NONE)
{
        AfxMessageBox("Bad IP Address");
        return;
}

StrToMACAddr(sMacAddr, sPhysAddr);

MIB_IPNETROW arpRow;
sscanf(sInterface, "%X", &(arpRow.dwIndex));

arpRow.dwPhysAddrLen = 6;
memcpy(arpRow.bPhysAddr, sPhysAddr, 6);
arpRow.dwAddr = dwInetAddr;
arpRow.dwType = MIB_IPNET_TYPE_STATIC;

if (SetIpNetEntry(&arpRow) != NO_ERROR)
        AfxMessageBox("Couldn't add ARP record");
}
```

The most important component of this code is the `SetIpNetEntry` function that adds a new ARP entry and appears as follows:

```
DWORD SetIpNetEntry(
  PMIB_IPNETROW pArpEntry
);
```

Its one and only parameter is a structure of the MIB_IPNETROW type that was used when obtaining data from the ARP table. In this structure, you should fill four parameters: the interface (dwIndex), the MAC address (bPhysAddr), and the IP address (dwInetAddr) whose entry should be added, and the entry type (the MIB_IPNET_TYPE_STATIC value in the dwType field). The other elements of the structure aren't used, and you don't need to fill them.

Now let's look at the deleting function. When the **Delete** button is clicked, the code from Listing 6.12 should be executed.

Listing 6.12. Deleting an entry from the ARP table

```
void CARPApplicationDlg::OnBnClickedButton3()
{
        char sInetAddr[255],
                sInterface[255];

        edIPAddress.GetWindowText(sInetAddr, 255);
        edInterface.GetWindowText(sInterface, 255);

        if (sInetAddr == NULL || sInterface == NULL)
        {
                AfxMessageBox("Fill IP address and Interface");
                return;
        }

        DWORD dwInetAddr;
        dwInetAddr = inet_addr(sInetAddr);
        if (dwInetAddr == INADDR_NONE)
        {
                printf("IpArp: Bad Argument %s\n", sInetAddr);
                return;
        }

        MIB_IPNETROW arpEntry;

        sscanf(sInterface, "%X", &(arpEntry.dwIndex));
        arpEntry.dwAddr = dwInetAddr;
```

```
        if (DeleteIpNetEntry(&arpEntry) != NO_ERROR)
            AfxMessageBox("Couldn't delete ARP record");
}
```

To delete an entry, the `DeleteIpNetEntry` function is used:

```
DWORD DeleteIpNetEntry(
  PMIB_IPNETROW pArpEntry
);
```

It takes one parameter — a structure of the `PMIB_IPNETROW` type, in which you should fill only the interface and the IP address of the record you want to delete.

NOTE

The source code of this example is located in the \Demo\Chapter6\ARPApplication directory on the accompanying CD-ROM.

Conclusion

In this book, I showed you several examples, but I cannot say that they will allow you to understand all the methods that hackers use. This is an art, and you will have to study it for your whole life to fully understand. Information and computer technologies are developing so rapidly that it is impossible to keep up with everything.

Once for a whole year I was very busy with programming. As a result, I had to stop my self-study for this period. Finally, I looked around and found I was way behind others. I was still writing programs for MS-DOS while other programmers were studying Windows. I understood that it was time to alter my work because otherwise nobody would need my outdated knowledge. I quit and studied Windows for three months so that I could start writing commercial projects and find a job that would be in accordance with my new knowledge and allow me to learn more.

My readers often ask me what else they should read to become a real hacker or simply to acquire new knowledge. My answer is, "Everything!" I read all documents, help files, and articles that I come across. Specialized books are scarce, and you never know, which book contains new and interesting information that might allow you to create a perfect and original project.

However, even if you spend a lot of time on self-education, nobody can guarantee that you will become a real hacker. When I studied at university, I worked on a computer for 10 to 16 hours every day and had time to do everything I wanted. Now I'm married and have got two children. Although I try to work at least nine hours every day, it is impossible to do everything. I would like to do more and keep an eye on novelties in information technology, but it is unfeasible. There are too many areas that have no relation to each other.

In any case, I hope this book will help you find answers to some of your questions.

CD-ROM Contents

The CD-ROM accompanying this book contains the following programs:

Folders	Description
\Demo	The source code of simple programs for you to become familiar with actual applications. Though few in number, they are worth looking at.
\Demo\Chapter1	The source code for *Chapter 1*.
\Demo\Chapter2	The source code for *Chapter 2*.
\Demo\Chapter3	The source code for *Chapter 3*.
\Demo\Chapter4	The source code for *Chapter 4*.
\Demo\Chapter5	The source code for *Chapter 5*.
\Demo\Chapter6	The source code for *Chapter 6*.
\Soft	Demo programs from CyD Software Labs.
\Programs	ASPack is a useful program for compressing executable files.

H